The Copper Trade
Revised Edition

by Jay Stuart Wakefield

"Over and beyond mere living, the human Spirit adds and creates what is better than what was before" -R.Roefield

Cover photo by Richard Holt Wakefield, Yacht Valhalla in Bahamian waters, 1946

Other titles by Jay Stuart Wakefield

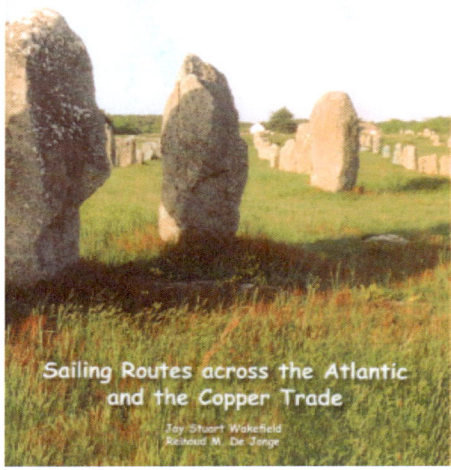

www.rocksandrows.com

Sites:

- Cairn of Barnenez
- Petroglyphs of Loughcrew
- Rings of Brodgar, Steness and Bookan
- Porcelano Cave
- Passage Grave of Karleby
- Fourknocks Passage Grave
- Boscawen-un Punt Circle
- Buriz Petroglyph
- Los Millares
- Petroglyph of Serrazes
- Rows and Petropots
- Rows of Kermario
- Rows of Kerlescan
- Rows of Leure
- Rows of Menec
- Monument of Lagatjar
- Disc of Nebra
- Rows of Tormsdale
- Poverty Point
- Monument of Ales Stenar

www.howthesungod.com

Sites:

- Tumulus of Kercado
- Tablet of Paredes
- Tumulus of Gavrinis
- Petroglyphs of Loughcrew
- Petroglyphs of Dissignac
- Stonehenge
- Petroglyphs of Kercado
- Petroglyphs of Chao Redondo
- America's Stonehenge
- Devil's Head Petroglyphs
- Three Rivers Petroglyph
- Embden Dragon, Kennebec
- Orient Tablet

Contents: The Copper Trade

	Page
Michigan Copper in the Mediterranean (Isle Royale and Keweenaw Peninsula, c. 2400 BC- 1200 BC)	5
Lugged Axeheads of Bronze Age Found on Isle Royale	11
Were the Copper Miners of Michigan Giants?	15
Poverty Point: Bronze Age Town & Gulf Ports on the Copper Trail; Open-fire Manufacturing of Copper Oxhides	17
Were Prehistoric Copper Oxhide Ingots Manufactured on the Mississippi Coast Near the Mouth of the Mississippi River?	27
New Finds Support Minoan Role in Transatlantic Copper Trade	33
The Sudurbardi Maze of Iceland: Some Evidence for Minoans along the Upper North Sailing Route to America	39
Megalithic Colony in Greenland	43
America's Stonehenge: A Map of the Atlantic Ocean in Stones	47
Ocean Pendants	51
Ocean Pendants of Ancient Travelers	61
Bronze Age Ocean Pendants	67
Crossing the Atlantic via the Azores	69
Bronze Age Colonies in the Azores and Canaries	75
The Sillustani Necropolis in Peru	83
The Colonization of North and South America by the Beaker People	89
The Use of Latitudes in Bronze Age Sailing	99
The Southern Crossing: New Evidence on Bronze-Age Axeheads	103
Sailing to America: Latitude Data for the Copper Trail to Isle Royale and Egypt Recorded on Bronze Age Axeheads	107
The SunGod Religion and Sailing Routes to Colonies in the Americas	113
A Date for the Arrival of Michigan Copper in Europe	121
A Culture Terminated by the Michigan Copper Trade: Understanding Bronze Age Malta	123
"Burrows Cave" Mapstones	129

Michigan Copper in the Mediterranean
(Isle Royale and Keweenaw Peninsula, c. 2400 BC-1200 BC)
by J.S. Wakefield, jayswakefield@yahoo.com

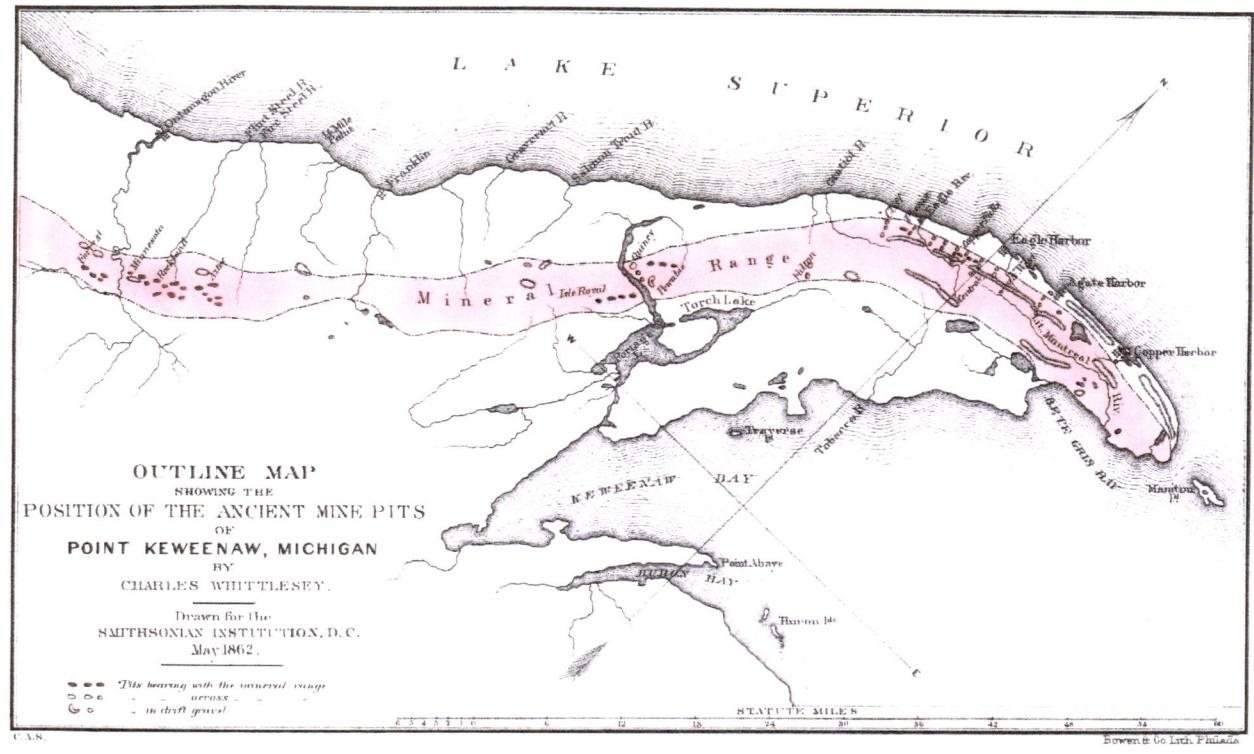

Fig. 1 The ancient mining region of the Keweenaw, from Whittlesey, 1862 (Rdf. 18) The technique of mining with firesetting, and stone hammers was used during the Bronze Age, both in Michigan and Europe. The highly recommended classic book by Drier and Du Temple has been recently reprinted, so is no longer a rare book (Ref. 1).

Summary

Recent scientific literature has come to the conclusion that the major source of the copper that swept through the European Bronze Age after 2500 BC is unknown. However, these studies claim that the 10 tons of copper oxhide ingots recovered from the late Bronze Age (1300 BC) Uluburun shipwreck off the coast of Turkey was "extraordinarily pure" (more than 99.5% pure), and that it was not the product of smelting from ore. The oxhydes are all brittle "blister copper" with voids, slag bits, and oxides, created when the oxhydes were made in multiple pourings outdoors over wood fires. Only Michigan Copper is of this purity, and it is known to have been mined in enormous quantities during the Bronze Age.

The Geology of Copper

Copper is said to be the most common metal on the face of the Earth with the exception of iron. However, most of it is in the form of low-grade ores that require a sequence of concentration mechanisms to upgrade it to exploitable ore through a series of proto-ores. Copper ores of the "oxidized type," including the oxide cuprite, and carbonates (malachite) are generally green or blue, and reducible to copper metal by simple heating with charcoal. Ores of the "reduced type" are sulfides or sulfosalts (chalcocite, chalcopyrite, tetrahedrite), and are not readily identified in outcrops as ores; they require roasting to convert them to oxides, then reduction of the oxides to produce metal. There are a number of places in the world where copper can be found in small deposits in the pure state, but it is usually embedded in a rock matrix, from which it must be freed by intensive labor or today, crushed in huge volumes, and treated to obtain the metal.

The Unique Geology of Michigan Copper

Early in Earth's history, there were huge volcanic outflows over the Great Lakes area. As new sediments overlaid these flows, copper solutions were crystallizing in the Precambrian flood basalts of the lava layers. The copper had been crystallized in nodules and irregular masses along fracture zones a few inches, to many feet wide. After a billion years, about a quarter of the age of the Earth, four major glaciations ground upon the edges of the old layered basalt lava beds, and exposed some of the embedded copper (Fig.2, top drawing). Isle Royale and the Keweenaw Peninsula remained high ridges of volcanic basalt. The scraping and digging by the glaciers, followed by surface exposure of the hardest material, the metal, was followed by sluicing of the land by glacial meltwaters. This left many mineral nodules of all sizes on the surface, in the huge pine forests. This was called "float copper" as it appeared that it had "floated" to the surface. Nodules of copper were discovered shining in the surf along the shores of Isle Royale.

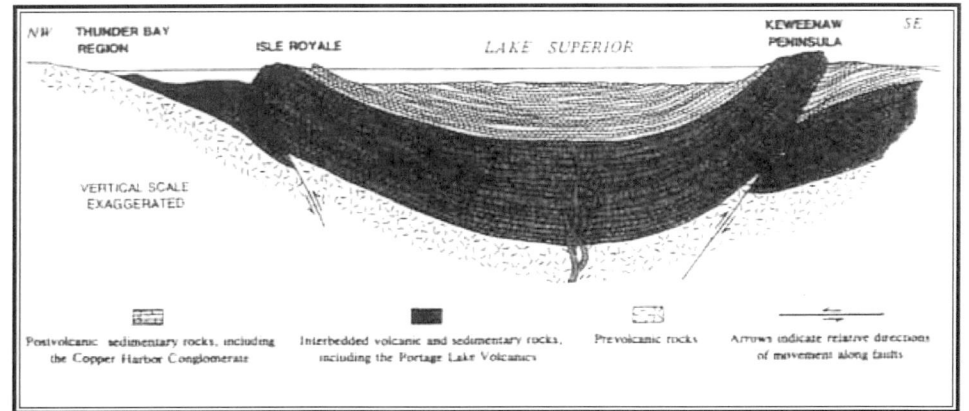

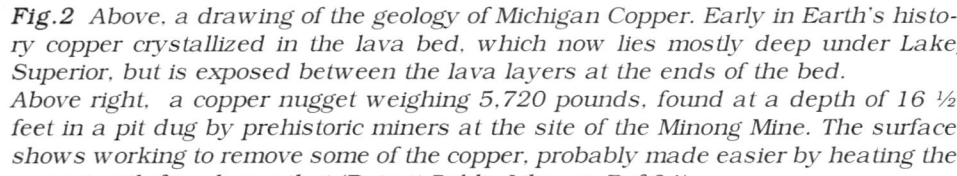
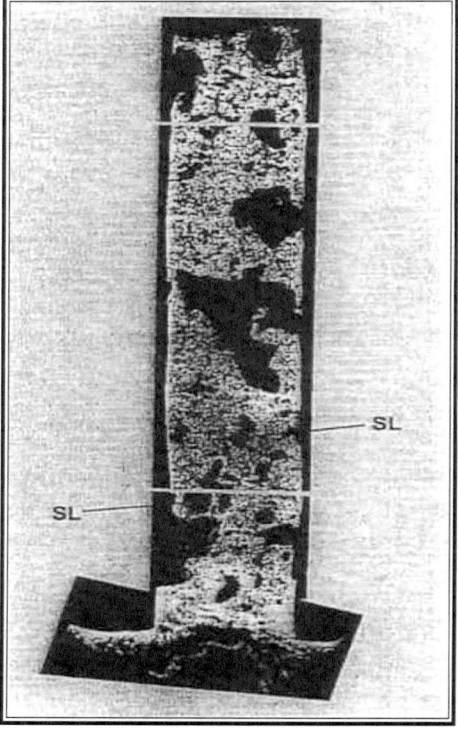

Fig.2 Above, a drawing of the geology of Michigan Copper. Early in Earth's history copper crystallized in the lava bed, which now lies mostly deep under Lake Superior, but is exposed between the lava layers at the ends of the bed.
Above right, a copper nugget weighing 5,720 pounds, found at a depth of 16 ½ feet in a pit dug by prehistoric miners at the site of the Minong Mine. The surface shows working to remove some of the copper, probably made easier by heating the nugget with fires beneath it (Detroit Public Library, Ref.24).
Far, right, a 4.2 cm core drilling showing the porosity and voids of "blister copper", found to be the typical structure of all the Uluburun Ingots studied by Hauptmann et al. There are a few slag inclusions, labeled SL (Ref.54).

The prolonged crystallization, followed by glacial exposure, was a unique sequence of events. When exploited, it took man from the stone age to an industrial world. The half billion pounds mined in prehistory were followed by six and a half billion pounds mined in the "industrial age" in America, starting in the late 1800s

Old World Copper

Most European copper was smelted out of copper ores starting about 4460 BC. These ores often had only a concentration of 15% copper in them, and had many trace element contaminants, such as lead (Ref.19). Buried hoards of bronze are usually composed of broken axeheads, miscellaneous broken pieces, and lumps, recycling the valuable metal. Henderson's book (Ref.19) reports a German study that did 12,000 [!] chemical analyses of copper-containing artifacts, with the aim of identifying "workshops." They were not able to do this, but noted that "hoards which often contain low impurity metal in South-Eastern England and Northern France may be linked to the occurrence of copper ingots, which also had low impurities." Barber (Ref.28) says that "ingot (or 'cake') fragments are a common feature of founder's hoards of the late Bronze Age, and often comprise pure, unalloyed copper." Barber (Ref.25) says only one mining site in the British Isles (Great Orme) shows evidence of activity after the early Bronze Age. Burgess (Ref.16) says of the British Isles Bronze Age, "the remarkable thing is that metallurgy seems to have started in the south-east, apparently as early as anywhere in Britain, [though] the south-east has no local ores."

The Miners of Michigan Copper

It is estimated that half a billion pounds (Ref.1) of copper were mined in tens of thousands of pits on Isle Royale and the Keweenaw Peninsula of Michigan by ancient miners over a period of a thousand years. Carbon dating of wood timbers in the pits has dated the mining to start about 2450 BC and end abruptly at 1200 BC. Officially, no one knows where the Michigan copper went. All the "ancient copper culture" tools that have been found could have been manufactured from just one of the large boulders. A placard in London's British Museum Bronze Age axe exhibit says: "from about 2500 BC, the use of copper, formerly limited to parts of Southern Europe, suddenly swept through the rest of the Continent." No one seems to know where the copper in Europe came from.

Indian legends tell the mining was done by fair-haired "marine men." Along with wooden tools, and stone hammers, a walrus-skin bag has been found (Ref.1). A huge copper boulder was found in the bottom of a deep pit raised up on solid oak timbers, still preserved in the anaerobic conditions for more than 3,000 years. Some habitation sites and garden beds have been found and studied (various ref.). It is thought that most of the miners retired to Aztalan (near Madison, Wisconsin) and other locations to the south at the onset of the hard winters on Lake Superior. The mining appears to have ended overnight, as though they had left for the day, and never came back. A petroglyph of one of their sailing ships has been found (Fig.7).

During this thousand-year period of mining, some of the miners must have explored the continent to the west, as evidenced by strangely large skeletons in a lot of places, such as the red-haired giants who came by boat to Lovelock Cave on Lake Lahontan (Nevada), that were found in 1924 with fishnets and duck decoys (Ref.77). There is "biological tracer" evi-

Fig. 3 This ancient ship's prow, made of 3 tons of copper, was photographed by the author in the French Maritime Museum, in Paris. We read that there were at least a thousand of these, one of the many military uses of copper.

dence for foot traffic back and forth across the continent, more that three thousand years before the Lewis and Clark Expedition. Huber (Ref.27) describes the "remarkable" presence of the shrub Devil's Club on Blake Point, the northern tip of Isle Royale, and on Passage Island, offshore, and also on small islands around Rock Harbor, on Isle Royale. Its usual habitat is the rainforest gullies of the conifer forests of the Pacific Northwest. Huber claims it appears nowhere else east of the Rocky Mountains. This plant has giant leaves, with spines underneath, and frightfully spiny woody stems. It has a history of traditional use as a medicine, to treat diabetes, tumors, and tuberculosis, with its effectiveness confirmed by modern studies. It appears likely it was carried in a medicine bag to this remote island in Lake Superior in ancient times, and the places where the Devil's Club are found are showing us where the miners were using medicines.

Silver in the Copper

Pieces of the "native" Michigan copper sometimes have crystals of silver inclusions, mechanically enclosed but not alloyed; this is called "halfbreed copper." In the commercial mines, the miners are said to have cut these silver nodules off with knives, and take them home. The presence of silver nodules in "Old Copper Culture" tools shows they were made by hammering, called "cold working." These hammered weapons and tools found in Hopewell mounds sometimes "show specks of silver, found only in copper of Lake Superior" (Ref. 69). Apparently, one instance of identification by silver inclusion has occurred overseas: In this letter of December 1st, 1995, Palden Jenkins, a historian from Glastonbury, writes, "I met the farmer who owns the land on which a megalithic stone circle is, called Merry Maidens, in far west Cornwall. While clearing hedges, he discovered an arrowhead, which was sent to the British Museum for identification. The answer returned: '5,000 years old; source, Michigan, USA'." (Ref.76).

Fig. 4 Above, the National Geographic sketch of the Uluburun ship, a trading vessel of 1300 BC, discovered wrecked off the Turkey coast. In its hold was found 10 tons of ox-hide-shaped copper ingots, The half a ton of tin ingots, and other trading goods. Below the ship, left, one of the ingots from the wreck (Ref.65); in the middle, an ingot in the British Museum (Ref.7), and to the right, some of the Uluburun ingots in the seabed. Bottom row, right, an ingot from Hagia Trihadha, Crete (Ref.14). Taylor adds that 3 were found near cagliari, Sardinia, inscribed with a trident, a double axe, and an angular P. The trident was the symbol for Poseidon, god of the Atlanteans, who Plato says ran the metal trade in the Ocean named for them. The 3 supervised men are carrying an oxhyde and baskets of bun ingots, on the tomb walls of Rekh-Mi-Re at Thebes (Ref.10). The bearded Phoenician-looking man is carrying an ingot on the wall of the Tomb of Huyat, also at Thebes (Ref.3). Left and right of this note, two ingots found in Egypt (Ref.3).

Trace Element Analysis

The temperature of a wood fire is 900° C, and with charcoal above 1000° C, but forced air fires are hotter, and met the need to obtain the 1084° C melting point of copper. The melting of crystallized copper, and pouring it into oxhide molds (the shape of the skin of a flayed ox) for shipping, wherever it was done, is the first step in its contamination. Re-melting, for pouring into tool molds, can involve the use of

Fig.5 Grave goods of a rich burial on exhibit at the hillside site of discovery, near the salt mines above Hallstatt, Austria. Twelve hundred rich graves were excavated, but are thought to be only half of the necropolis. The salt was valuable as a food preservative in prehistory. It could be traded to the copper merchants for copper cauldrons, copper and bronze tableware, tools, and even a Minoan red pot (white arrow). The authors believe you are looking at Michigan Copper, removed from the grave of a final customer. (Photo by Wakefield, 2008).

fluxes, fuel contamination, the addition of used/broken tools, and the addition of arsenic or tin.

Since metals always contain small portions of trace elements, it was thought we could follow the copper, by looking at trace elements in copper elsewhere, to see if it matched. The six early studies reported by Griffin (Ref.25), all report native copper at 99.92% copper. Rapp and others (Ref.8,53) report that using trace element "fingerprints," using mostly Lake Superior copper samples, probable geographic/geologic source identification can be done. The work of Hancock et al. (Ref.47) showed again that native copper, including Michigan copper, showed lower levels of tin, arsenic, gold, and especially cobalt, than "European copper" manufactured artifacts. The British Museum reported "generally low trace element content [in] our Egyptian artifacts" (Ref.2). Years ago, the author collected some European copper and bronze axes, thinking that he might do some sampling of them for some commercially-available trace element analysis. Unfortunately, sample testing is only useful for hammered copper tools, not melted/cast ones. Looking at artifacts, full of mixed contaminants in their manufacturing, has for the most part, not been helpful. We need to look at the least-disturbed samples, the ingot form in which copper was shipped.

The Uluburun Ingots

In the excellent 30-page 2002 study by Hauptmann et al., on the "Structure and Composition of Ingots from the 1300 BC Uluburun Wreck" (Ref.54) the authors say "the cargo represents the 'world market' of bulk metal in the Mediterranean. The wreck contained 354 oxhide-shaped ingots and 121 discoid, or bun ingots, altogether 10 tons of copper (see Fig.4). Additionally a ton of tin ingots were recovered, in 120 ingots and fragments, a ratio which roughly corresponds to the ratio of copper to tin in 'classical' bronzes." The cedar hull was badly damaged by a collision with the shore, but some of the wood was preserved by the corrosion products of the copper ingots. These ingots are all now in the Museum of Underwater Archaeology, in Bodrum, Turkey, with the ingots also found in the later date Cape Gelidonya shipwreck. These are more ingots than the total in all other museums and private collections put together. Some oxhide ingots have been excavated in the Minoan ruins of Hagia Triadha in Crete (dated to 1550-1500 BC), and others have been found in Sardinia, Cyprus, the Nile Delta, Turkey and Bulgaria. Researcher Zena Halpern, (Ref.71), reports "I saw heaps of copper ingots in the Maritime Museum in Haifa, Israel ... Metal bars in the oxhide shape dating from c.1700 BC have been found at Falmouth in Cornwall." England(Ref.78). Egyptian New Kingdom tomb paintings and temple reliefs depict a great number of copper ingots, but only one has been found in Egypt, as they were consumed there. (Ref.23).

For many years, the archaeological community has thought that lead isotope studies by an Oxford group, Gale et al. (Ref.23,35,44,56) have proved that the ingots all came from Cyprus. In 1998 the Gale group (Ref.56) reports performing "approximately one thousand [!] lead isotope analyses of ores and ingots, including

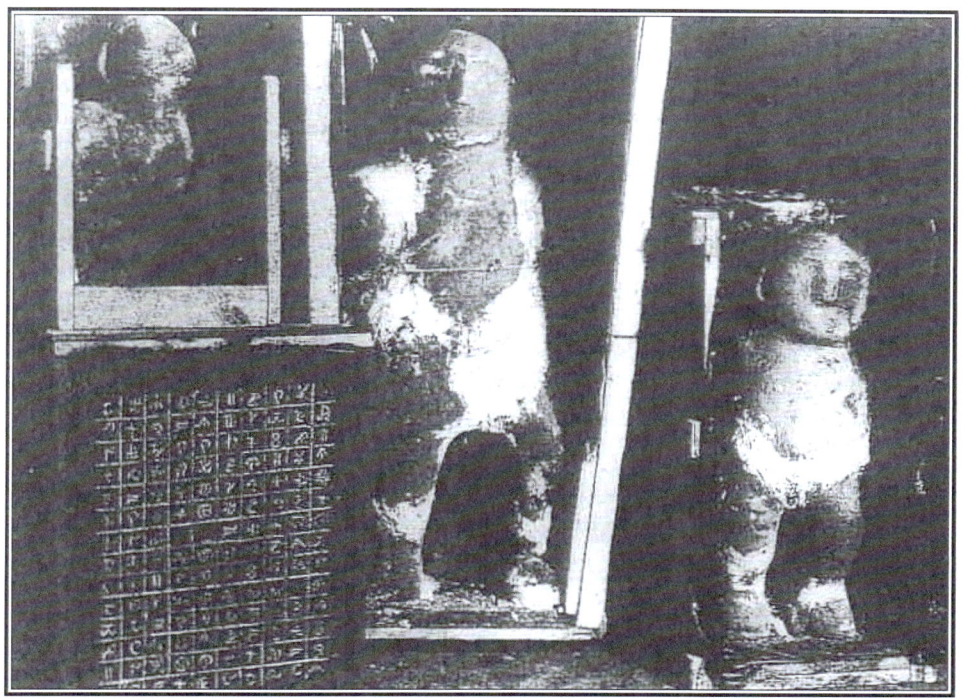

Fig.6 Above, the Newberry Tablet, and statues found with it in Newberry, Michigan was determined by Barry Fell in 1980 to be written in a "crolinized form of Minoan, having a vocabulary similiar to that of Hittite, but lacking in the formal declensions and conjugations of Hittite, a Cypro/Minoan script, comprising an omens text" (Ref.4).

about 60 Uluburun ingots." (They did not test a single sample of Michigan copper.) The study reports that the "Uluburun ingots are greater than 99.5% pure copper."

In the Hauptmann study, a steel chisel was used to cut pieces for surface sampling of 151 of the Uluburun ingots, and three oxhydes and one bun were drill cored all the way through. Their report states that he samples showed porous volume typical of "blister copper" that "exceeds by far our previous ideas on their inner structure, with void volume reaching 20% or higher, especially in the upper portions of the ingots. In general, cavities like these, called "spratzen," are caused by the effervescence of gases such as oxygen, carbon monoxide, and carbon dioxide, by water from burning charcoal. This is in contrast with copper from other periods and other localities... All the ingots contain angular-shaped inclusions of iron-silicate slags features compatible with natural rocks affected by the impact of high temperatures in the solid state. These can be removed by repeated melting, but,

Alex Fagotti shows me what remains of 3,000 year old miner's pits in the woods behind his rock shop, in the Keweenaw. Starting in the 1840s mines went down as far as 9,000 feet in some of these pits.

while these were regular steps ... at many metallurgical sites all over the middle and southern part of Africa, the Uluburun ingots were not processed in this way. The angular shape of the slag inclusions, the structure, and the existence of iscorite point to a pouring of copper into a mold when the slag was already solidified... Interfaces in the crystalline structure of the ingots points to different batches during casting. Almost all the samples contained cuprite (Cu_2O) distributed in changing amounts throughout the ingots, associated with large voids. The cuprite formed by corrosion in the sea does not penetrate for more than 5mm or so. An oxygen-rich atmosphere necessary to produce cuprite in an amount observed does not prevail during the smelting of (roasted) ores. We therefore can eliminate the conclusion that the ingots consist of as-smelted raw copper from a smelting furnace. Most of the ore available on Cyprusis of chalcopyritic composition, and relics of sulfides are quite difficult to completely remove, yet this mixed sulfide does not occur in the copper ingots."

The Hauptman study concludes that "from a chemical point of view, the purity of the ingots is extraordinary in comparison with other sorts of copper from Wadi Arabah (high lead), from the Caucasus (high arsenic), from Oman (high arsenic and nickel). The ingots are made of pure copper, and all the ingots show a homogeneous composition. From our metallographic investigations, we are able to exclude a conscious purification or even a refining process to produce the ingots. We see few indications that bronze scrap could have been added, due to the very low tin concentration, and would not include gas bubbles and slag inclusions. The ingots provide an explanation for the previously vexing question of how an ingot of a metal as ductile as copper could have been broken up into small pieces such as those excavated by the hundreds in Sardinia. Two characteristics of the Uluburun ingots stand out – the presence of a substantial degree of porosity, and a high concentration of copper oxide inclusions, which made it brittle. Simply dropping the ingots onto a hard surface would easily shatter the ingots."

A 32 page 1995 study by Budd et al. (Ref.55), reviewed all the work to date, and says "all the oxhide ingots are composed of essentially pure copper... No meaningful conclusions on provenance can currently be drawn from a consideration of trace element data for oxhide ingots, ores, and artifacts on Cyprus or Sardinia... It is no surprise that the only oxhide ingot mold ever found, at Ras Ibn Hani, Syria, in 1983 was surrounded by droplets bearing the same isotope signature as the vast majority of the oxhide ingots. The 1989 (Ref.35) Gale report concludes that the Aghia Triadha ingots on Crete "are certainly not made of Cypriot copper," and the copper source could not be identified. Dickinson, author of the Aegean Bronze Age (Ref.1) "From outside the Aegean came ...oxhide ingots. These have all, when tested, proved to be non-Aegean metal."

Where did the copper go?

Enormous orders for bronze weapons are recorded on excavated Bronze Age clay tablets, for swords in the tens of thousands. The Roman soldier is said to have worn up to 48 pounds of bronze in his uniform. Armies throughout the ancient world were equipped with bronze weapons. Statues and musical instruments, chariots, furniture and vases were made of copper and bronze. Even rooms were lined with copper and bronze. After the bronze Colossus of Rhodes was destroyed in an earthquake in 226 B.C., it was sold to a merchant, who used almost 1,000 camels to ship the pieces to Syria (Ref.13). "From only 5% of the Karum Kanesh tablets, we already know of 110 donkey loads carrying 15 tons of tin into Anatolia, enough to produce (at 5-7% tin content) 200 to 300 tons of bronze." (Ref.23).

Minoan Traders

A variety of cultural groups were involved in the mining, shipping, and trading of copper, among them the Egyptians, the Megalithic peoples of the western coast of Europe, the Atlanteans, and the Minoans. The Minoans have the reputation of controlling the copper trade in the Eastern Mediterranean. "It is in the New Palace period in Bronze Age Minoan Crete, that we find a large increase in population, particularly in settlements along the coasts, the growth of towns, which in some cases surround mini-palaces, luxurious separate town houses at palatial and other sites, and fine country villas... Villas and houses at Ayia Triadha and Tylissos contained not only weights and loom weights, but also copper oxhide ingots and Linear A tablets, and both are rich in luxury products and bronze objects. Minoan prowess in metal weapon production was not limited to the long sword, but included the short sword, the solid long dagger and the shoe-socketed and tube-socketed spearhead and arrowhead, all of which may have made their first Aegean appearance in Crete"... Neopalatial Crete is extremely rich in bronze, but very poor in sources of copper and of course totally lacking in sources of tin" (Ref.23). The Newberry Tablet of Newberry, Michigan (Fig.6) is in a Cypriot/Cretan sylabary. Cretan script may have been the basis of the Cree sylabary (Ref.7), and Mayan writing (Ref.3). The "Cavern of Glyphs" on the Ohio River had images of clothed figures that "singularly recall the dress of the Minoans, as seen on the frescoes at Knossos in Crete" (Ref.79). A Minoan pot has been unearthed in Louisiana. The Olmecs laid mosaic tiles at La Venta, (Mexico) upon asphalt, the same technique used in Crete (Ref.3). The excavation of the wealthy grave goods at Hallstatt (see Fig.5) show that traders brought Minoan pots as well as copper/bronze pots to trade for salt. It appears that the ruling elite of Hallstatt were among the end customers of Michigan copper, as well as the Egyptians. ■

References:

The Mystery Cave of Many Faces:
A History of Burrows Cave, Russell Burrows and Fred Rydholm, Superior Heartland Inc., 1991

The Lost Treasure of King Juba: The Evidence of Africans in America before Columbus, Frank Joseph, Bear & Co., 2003, ISBN 1-59143-006-2

Ancient Mariners in America, Beverly Moseley Jr., (CD), Midwest Epigraphic Society, 2006

Ancient Mediterranean Treasures in North America, Harry Hubbard, 1993-1995, Alexander Helios Inc., ISBN 0-9638190-0-3

Tomb Chronicles Part II: The Curse of Alexander's Tomb, 1995-1997, recorded by Harry Hubbard for Alexander Helios Inc., Lazeria Publishing Co., ISBN 0-9638190-2-x-13
Midwestern Epigraphic Journal, Vol.10, No.1, 1996
Ancient American, Vol.3, Issue 16

Lugged Axeheads of the Bronze Age Found on Isle Royale

by Jay S. Wakefield

Starting with a modest collection of American artifacts from my father, I have enlarged the collection by acquiring a world-wide collection of axeheads over the past 20 years. These illustrate the development of axes by mankind and are surrounded by archaeological books sorted by the same timeline. Some of the axehead designs are unusual and lead to the asking of interesting questions.

I first noticed "lug" type axes in the Petrie Museum at the University of London many years ago. There was a placard in a glass case near several stone axes that said that Mr. Petrie was puzzled by the adjacent lugged axes. One was Egyptian, the other from "Peru." (It looked like the one in my Photo 3.) Flinders Petrie was the first English archaeologist to dig in Egypt. They say he was permitted to remove all the "small" items he found. This crowded museum on part of a floor in an obscure brick building, now open Tuesday to Saturday from 2 p.m. to 5 p.m., is an amazing place and strongly recomended for a visit. Only 10% of the 80,000 objects housed at the Egyptian collection of the Museum are on display. However, they support an online photographic catalog of the entire collection. You can search under "axes" and find the prehistoric, pre-dynastic stone lugged axe I show as Photo 1. In this catalog I am unable to find the American artifacts he had collected and that he talks about in his book.

In his recently reprinted book *Tools and Weapons*, illustrated by the Egyptian collection in the University College, London, by Petrie (1917), his collections are discussed. Most Egyptian stone axe relics are of the simple cylindrical or ovoid "celt" type, while most of the 1,500 known copper and bronze axeheads are of the lugged type. Petrie notes (p. 1) that "stone implements no doubt are the parents of many of the metal forms."

Petrie says (p. 63) that "from Crete probably originated the double axe found in the early Minoan Age ... From Crete also probably started the adze with lugs... In Egypt, the adze long preceded the axe; metal was scarce, and to squander a pound of it for a single tool would

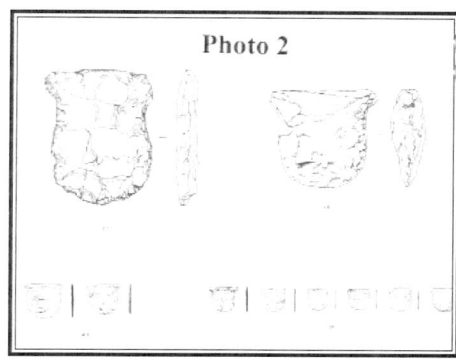

have been extravagant. It is only at the close of the prehistoric age [3000 BC], after the incoming of the dynastic people and within a generation of Mena and the 1st Dynasty, that copper began to be freely used. Now, simultaneously with this we find the adze greatly increased in size...

It seems these heavy adzes came from Cyprus, the copper land, and arrived in the same generation in which the heavy copper axes appear, at the epoch of final conquest by the dynastic people. The evidence so far is that the dynastic people

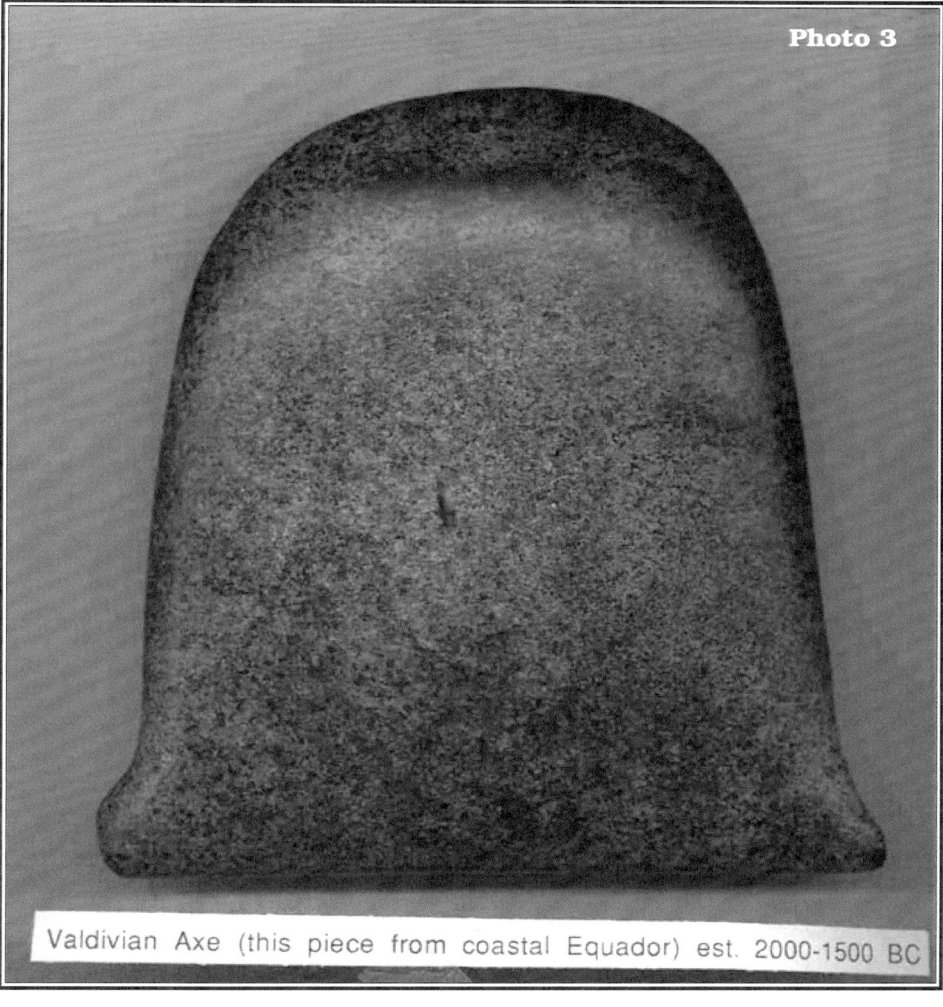

Valdivian Axe (this piece from coastal Equador) est. 2000-1500 BC

brought the free use of Cypriot copper into Egypt ... If it came from the mainland -- then Cyprus and Egypt in the 1st Dynasty both drew from that unknown source" (Petrie, pp. 5, 6).

Photo 1 (Petrie UC73192) shows a "prehistoric" lugged axe in the Petrie Museum's Egyptian collection. On page 8, Petrie says that a "type peculiar to Egypt was that with broad lugs by which to secure the blade to the handle ... Strange to say, this method of handling is totally absent from the rest of the Mediterranean lands, North Europe, and Asia. It seems almost incredible that a type characteristic of Egypt for thousands of years could never be established elsewhere. Yet this type recurs as the regular form in Peru and Central America. The entire absence of it in many intermediate lands must preclude our supposing a case of borrowing. It is one of the strong examples of independent invention." He goes on to say the European peoples "proceeded with the socket system ... The Egyptians, like the Peruvians, ... went on the natural lines of lengthening the blade along the handle to give a larger bearing and a means of firm lashing." Perhaps he might have been puzzled about the possible impact of a bunch of guys in a sailboat.

In the book considered the authority on Egyptian bronze axes, the *Catalogue of Egyptian Antiquities in the British Museum, Vol. VII, Tools and Weapons I, Axes* by W. V. Davies, many bronze examples of the "1,500 known" bronze axeheads are shown and annotated. Photo 2, items 27&28 from Plate 5, show two prehistoric lugged stone axes presented without comment.

Photo 3 shows a Bronze Age Valdivian stone axe (Ecuador) that looks similar to ones in the Museum in London that Petrie had collected. Paul Shao, author of *The Origin of Ancient American Cultures*, (Iowa State University Press, 1983) quotes James Ford: "The Valdiva ceramic complex, which suddenly appears about 3000 BC, in a limited region on the coast of Equador, is by no means primitive." Valdiva is on the north side of the Gulf of Guayaquil near the ancient natural harbors and river mouth used by Inca sailing rafts, the Japanese, and where Pizarro landed for his conquest of the Incas. Like nearby San Agustin up the Magdalena River in Columbia, the evidence shows these rivers provided easy access for explorers sailing the seas. Photo 4 shows another axe from Colombia and another from eastern Equador. Photo 5 shows an-

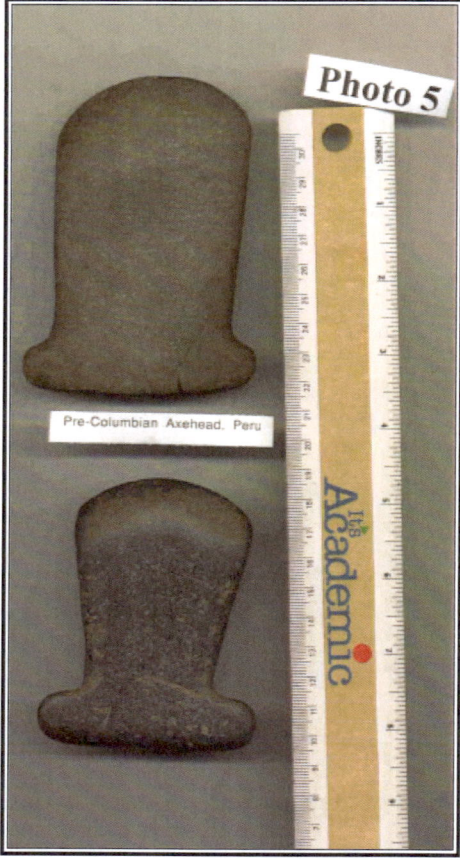

other two axes from Tiahuanaco on the Bolivian Antiplano around Lake Titicaca (pre-1500 BC). It appears these were probably modeled after the Egyptian lugged axes unless the Egyptian axes were South American exports or copies of them.

The fire-mining of pure copper in Michigan during the Bronze Age provided the oxhide ingots that were the world's first industrial metal product, which fueled a Bronze Age in Europe and perhaps worldwide (www.rocksandrows.com). The fire-mining common also in Europe in the Bronze Age consisted of heating the ground with huge wood fires followed by quenching the hot rockface with cold water and beating the metal out of the cracked rock with stone hammers. Thousands of "grooved" hammers were found on the Keweenaw Penninsula, while "ungrooved" hammers were found on Isle Royale. One farmer is said to have collected hammers in a wagon and built walls around his farm with them. Most are found broken, obviously shattered from use. Photo 7 is an example. It is interesting that the evidence found at Cedarland and Claiborne, where Michigan copper was melted into ingots, has revealed these two sites were staffed by people from two different cultures.

Photo 6 shows an unusual find-- a stone hammer with lugs--"found with two others" on Isle Royale by the seller's great-grandfather who worked in the mines there, long before the place was a National Park. Obviously these lugged hammers were considered unusual by the miner, or they would not have been collected. I can only conclude that this axehead provides yet another illustration of the diffusion of ideas through the replication of tool designs during the Bronze Age. This axe is another piece of concrete evidence of transoceanic involvement in the copper mining.

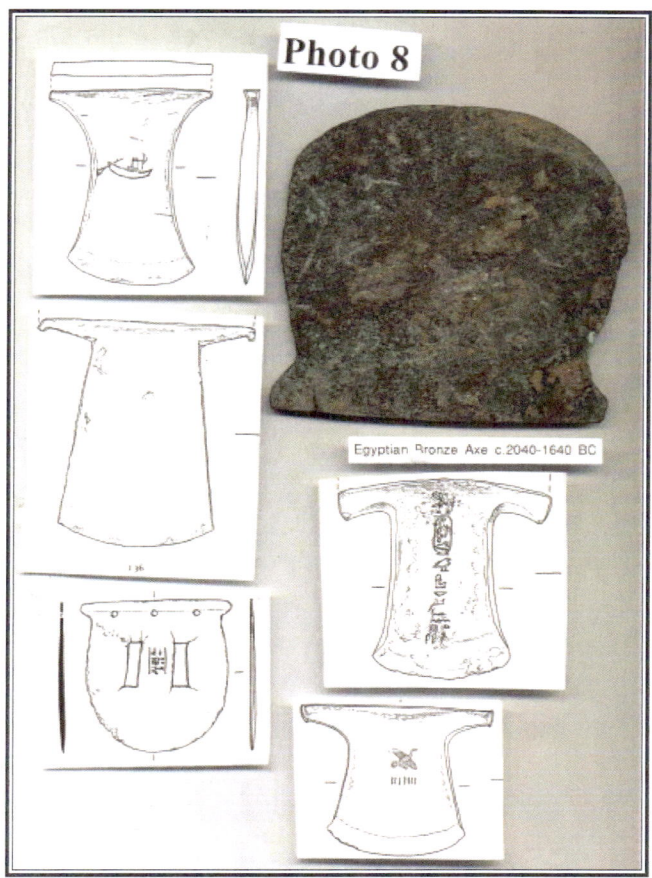

Later bronze axe designs were also often similar between Egypt and South America. Photo 8 shows Egyptian examples of bronze axes from the Davies book and an Egyptian lugged bronze axe, one of the 1,500 extant. Davies says: " By the beginning of the Second Intermediate Period, the 'round' forms of axe, which had predominated since the end of the Early Dynastic Period, were replaced both as a tool and weapon by a splayed type with straight or incurved sides. This new type has lugs at the rear."

Petrie gets more interesting when he discusses other Egyptian tools: "Double-edged knives start with the great expansion of copper tools at the rise of the dynastic people ... The later metal lugged axes were sharply square with the blade... As no trace of this type is found in Roman remains, it probably died out about 400 BC, killed by the advance of socketing" (p. 18). The predominance of socketing among American "copper culture" artifacts is evidence for the major involvement of European ("Bell Beaker Pottery") people in the prehistoric mining of Michigan copper. In his discussion of chisels, Petrie notes that "the socketed chisel was also developed in Peru (p. 21). When discussing "straight-backed knives," he notes "this form was nearly arrived at in the independent copper work of America...The halberd arose independently in America, as seen by two from Wisconsin, one curiously like the Coptic form." Do not forget that it is recorded in Egypt that King Sahura led an expedition to the distant land of Punt in 2497 BC, a voyage of three years, and crew members on other Egyptian voyages claimed to have been there too. (www.howthesungod.com)

Photo 9 shows four bronze axeheads from Bolivia. The bronze lugged axeheads are found among the Bronze Age artifacts of the Tiahuanaco culture of the Antiplano. This culture developed through a succession of phases over four thousand years, and the surrounding mountain river valleys probably were the origin of the tin that has not yet been sourced in antiquity. ∎

Were the Copper Miners of Michigan Giants?

by Jay S. Wakefield

The cover photo shows a petroglyph on a rock outcropping that I found last month (September 29, 2009). It was located six feet above what probably was a beach in Copper Harbor, when Lake Superior was higher, probably when ancient miners were working the area for copper (2400 BC to 1200 BC). My friend Tom Teel of Burt Lake, said "Wow, that is big"! So I took this photo with my hand in it. I am six feet tall, and my hand is 7 ½ inches long. My middle finger is 3 ½ inches long, so I calculate the glyph has fingers extending nearly two inches beyond mine. The depth of the glyph and the carving details need study.

The glyph appears to be evidence that among the ancient copper miners of Michigan, or their sailing crews, were "giants." In my new book *Rocks and Rows* I illustrate connections between the "Bell Beaker" pottery people of Europe, and their monuments which encode sailing routes to the Americas. The book *The Beaker Folk* is supportive of these people as giants: "For a long time it was confidently believed that there was a physically separate group of people who made and used Bell Beaker pottery (2400-1500 BC) and the [metal] artifacts found with it. (Ref.1). Early work suggested that the men in particular were more robust than usual, their skulls larger and rounder." The 1980 text goes on to say that now computers will enable better data recovery and analysis of this issue. Note the similarities of Figure 1, "a typical Beaker head" from this text, and Figure 2, a conception of an Adena head (Ref.3). Innumerable giant skeletons have been found in mounds in the Midwest as documented in many original sources, and summarized in others (Refs.3-5). Kimball tells a Tuscorora legend of the giants being annihilated around 1000 BC (Ref.4). The 57 red haired giant (seven foot) mummies found in Lovelock cave in Nevada excavated by University of California archaeologist Llewellyn Loud in 1924 are discussed by Childress over seven pages. Giants and giant skeletons have been found all over North and South America (Ref.4).

How do we explain these "giants"? I think we should consider

Typical copper pit as seen today covering the Keweenaw Peninsula of Upper Michigan. Photo by John Poppleton

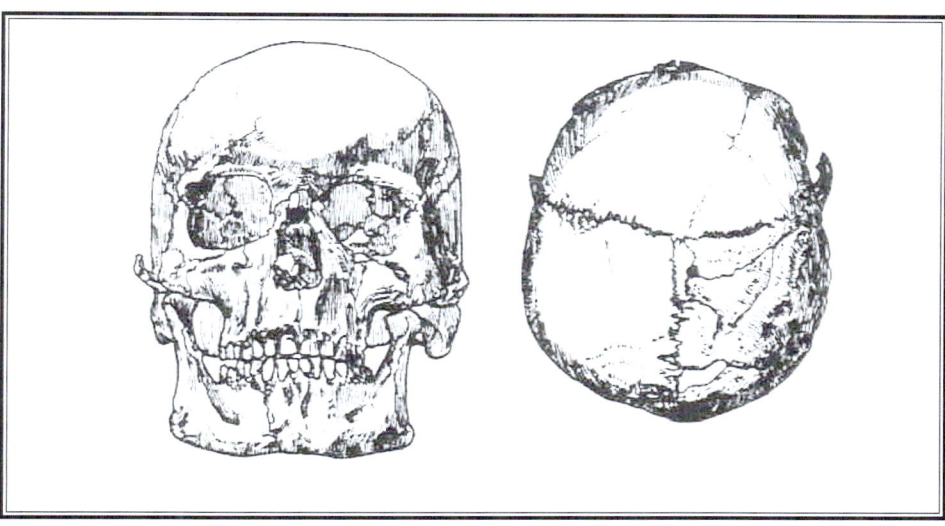

Figure 1. Round Beaker skull, notice the large square jaw, very similar to the Adena skull jaws of North America, (Ref. 1.).

the nutrition of the diet of these megalithic people living along the coasts of Europe (6500 BC to 1200 BC). The oceans had never been commercially fished, and not yet loaded with chemicals and plastic debris. Salmon ran in the rivers of Europe. Farming was expanding, but the people were probably not yet mineral-depleted. Two thousand years later, Vikings moved to Greenland, with its enormous marine resources. The new book (2009) *Vikings in America* says: "Viking Greenland was a prosperous nation for 5 centuries. ...Greenland to the Vikings was as California to the pioneers... Skeletal remains of early Viking settlers in Greenland show them growing around two inches taller than their ethnically identical contemporaries in Norway, while there is much evidence of robust health and longevity" (Ref.2).

References:
1. Harrison, R.J., The Beaker Folk, Copper Age archaeology in Western Europe, Thames & Hudson, New York, 1980 (ISBN 0-500-02098-1)
2. Davis, G., Vikings in America, MPG Books Ltd., Edinburgh, 2009 (ISBN 13:

Photo1: Giant Hand Petroglyph, near Copper Harbor, Michigan. (Photo by author, Sept 29, 2009).

So, I took these 3 photos with my hand in it. I am six feet tall, and my hand is 7 ½ inches long. My middle finger is 3 ½ inches long, so I calculate the glyph has fingers extending nearly two inches beyond mine.

Figure 2 "Conception of a mature North American Adena male", (Ref.3).

978 1 84158 701 1)
3. Hamilton, R., "Giants of the Ancient Ohio Valley", Ancient American, Vol.12, No.76
4. Kimball, 'G., "Giants", Ancient American, Vol.12, No. 74
5. Horton, B., "Two Prehistoric Indian Mounds Containing Giant Skeletons Discovered Near Morgansville, W. V.", Ancient American, Vol.13, No.82
6. Childress, D., Lost Cities of North and Central America, Adventures Unlimited Press, Kempton, Ill, 1992 (ISBN 0-932813-09-7)
7. Wakefield, J.S., de Jonge, R.M., Rocks and Rows, Sailing Routes across the Atlantic and the Copper Trade, MCS Inc., Kirkland, Wa. 2010 (ISBN 0-917054-20-2)

POVERTY POINT
Bronze Age Town & Gulf Ports on the Copper Trail
Open-fire manufacturing of Copper Oxhides
(Epps, NE Louisiana, c.2000-700 BC)

by J.S. Wakefield

Summary

The "Late Archaic" Poverty Point earthworks in Louisiana are the earliest and largest monuments in prehistoric North America. The site that remains covers a square mile, features six concentric segmented semi-circular walls, surrounded by six large mounds. The site is shown to be a prehistoric town, and a manufacturing and trading center which was a part of the worldwide megalithic culture. The site design reveals encoded latitudes of transatlantic sailing routes, and evidence of multicultural involvement in the manufacturing of copper oxhide ingots.

Introduction & Dating

The Poverty Point complex is a Louisiana State Commemorative Area, open to the public, and has been a National Historical Landmark since 1962. Collectors have been picking up artifacts since the 1870s, but it was not recognized as such a huge site until the ring pattern was recognized in a 1938 aerial photograph (Fig.2, right). The American Museum of Natural History dug at the site in 1942/3 and 1955, and showed "how large and unusual [the site] was" (Ref.1). Today, there is a road built through the rings, and 15,000 visitors a year pass through the site's museum. Some of the illustrations used in this article are from the book (The Ancient Mounds of Poverty Point, Place of the Rings) and website of John L. Gibson, previously employed as the site archaeologist, who devoted his career to the study of Poverty Point.

The site is located in the northeastern corner of Louisiana, northwest of Vicksburg, Mississippi at 33°N (Fig.1). Poverty Point is built on Maçon Ridge, a plateau 90 miles long, and five miles wide, in the swampy floodplains of the Mississippi River. Gibson reports 38 radiocarbon dates, all between 2278 BC (2470-2040) and 650 BC, with most between 1500 and 1300 BC. Gibson says that while the land and waters were biologically rich, the richest asset was the location. "This was one of the few places in the entire Mississippi valley where a departing pirogue could have been paddled without portages" (Refs.1,2).

The River and the Bayou

The huge ring complex is on a bluff above the west bank of Bayou Maçon. Other abandoned river channels and the route of the Bayou Macon indicate an active branch of the Mississippi flowed against the site in the past. Gibson's reconstruction drawing of the site (Fig.3) shows the steepness of the "precipitous bluff" on the east side of the site. The water of the bayou below is still, with fall maple leaves floating on the surface.
This is the Bayou Macon, which originates near another isolated oxbow bend of the Mississippi in Arkansas, now called Chicot Lake. This valley bottom of the Mississippi today contains many "bayous," which once were

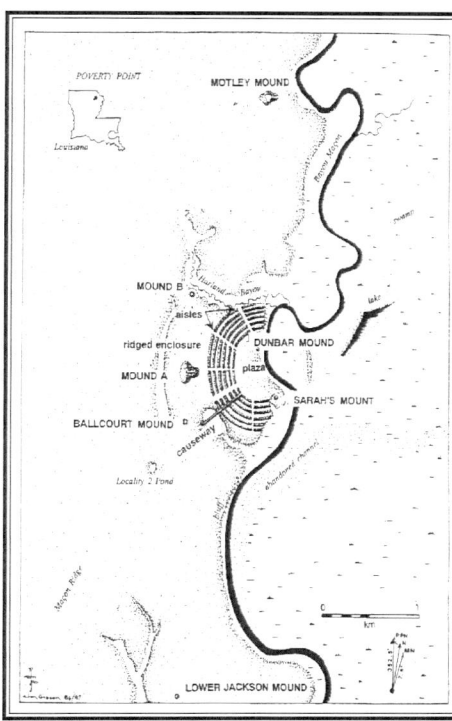

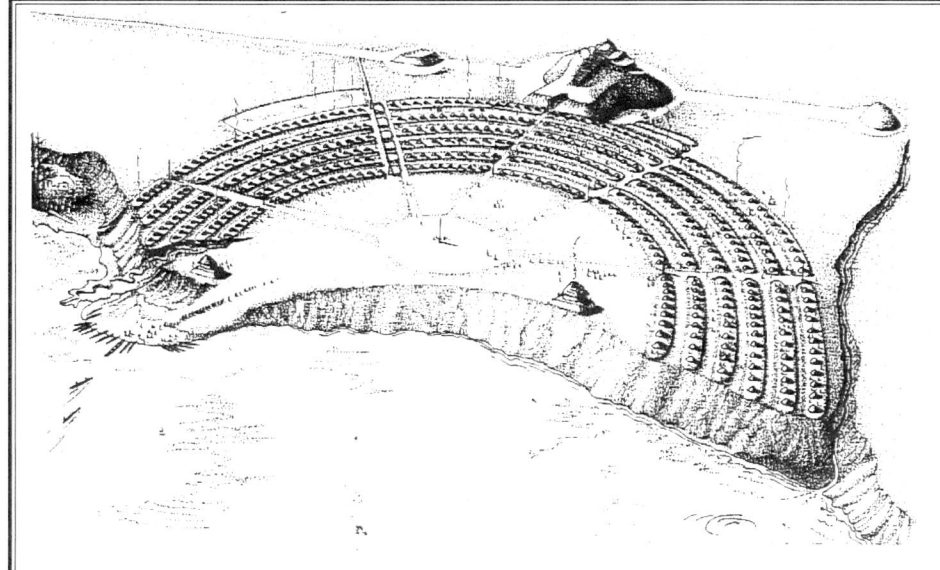

Fig.3 Above: Reconstruction drawing by Gibson, Poverty Point, c.1350 BC; Below: Groundplan of the earthworks of Poverty Point, as drawn by Gibson (Ref.1).

Figure 3 Top: Reconstruction drawing by Gibson, Poverty Point, c. 1350 B.C.. Below: Ground plan of the earthworks of Poverty Point, as drawn by Gibson (Ref. 1).

river channels, and vast swamps, with 29 Wildlife Refuges and Wildlife Management Areas. By air, the valley shows hundreds of old oxbows, and bayous. The Mississippi is a powerful river that spills a "half a million tons of sediment a day" into the Gulf of Mexico. The Chandeleur Islands in the Gulf (east of New Orleans, south of the State of Mississippi) "are remnants of a delta that vanished 1800 years ago (200 AD), when the river shifted its channel – something it has done six times in the last 9,000 years" (Ref.50).

"Precipitous bluffs" that are not rock are quickly eroded to a lesser slope unless they are being eroded at the bottom by active water. This "precipitous" bluff must have been made by a meandering branch of the Mississippi in relatively recent geologic times. Was Poverty Point built in a "C" shape as we see it in Gibson's Fig.3? Probably not. It was a trading center, where it was visited by people carrying heavy goods, including rock and metal, by water. These people would not have wanted to portage these goods in and out of bayous and swamps, and so would have chosen a site easily accessible by boat. Surely boats would have had direct access to the Poverty Point site. Four thousand years ago, prior to levees on the Mississippi, there was an annual flood season. The glacial meltwater from the Great Lakes and ice dam collapses at the southern end of Lake Superior brought major flooding events. These were times of fast flow. Then there were times of slow flow, when it is said a canoe could have been paddled up the Mississippi. When coming upriver from the Gulf, the Macon Ridge may have been the first high ground suitable for a settlement and trading site.

The site had been inhabited for more than a thousand years, but suffered a huge setback with the catastrophe of 1200 BC. Archaeologist Kidder says: "the elaborate trade and mound building abruptly ceased. Research has shown evidence for catastrophic flooding and global climate change c.1200-400 BC. The evidence comes from geological and soils mapping, archaeological and stratigraphic investigations, and an extensive program of coring. The greatly increased flood frequencies and magnitudes are associated with the demise of Poverty Point culture" (Ref.26).

That the site was originally circular is confirmed by the evidence

Fig.1 Top, State map of Poverty Point, located on the plateau of Maçon Ridge, about 10 miles west of the Mississippi, in the northeastern corner of Louisiana, at 33°N.
Below, regional map of Mississippi River floodplain, locating Poverty Point. (Ref.1).

Figure 1 Top: State map of Poverty Point, located on the plateau of Macon Ridge, about 10 miles west of the Mississippi, in the northeastern corner of Louisiana, at 33 degrees North.
Below: Regional map of Mississippi River floodplain, locating Poverty Point. (Ref.1).

reported by J.A. Ford and C.H. Webb following their excavations for the American Museum of Natural History in 1955 (Ref.49). They found the "distinguishing reddish brown clay soil [iron salts] of the Arkansas river" in the natural levees of the Bayou Macon and a layer of it in the trenches they dug across some of the rings. This layer "contrasted markedly with the gray soils deposited by the Mississippi". "The Braided Mississippi did much, but not all, of the final cutting into the eastern edge of Macon Ridge ... the meandering course of the Arkansas River ... carved the bluff and appears to have destroyed about half of the large geometrical earthworks" (Ref.49).

The original structure as a circular ring design is illustrated in Figure 6. Between 2500 BC and 1200 BC a thousand stone circles were built in the British Isles, showing a paradigm change in thinking when the other side of the world was discovered, and the world was confirmed to be round. This new conception of the world brought continued repetition of the representation of the Earth as a sphere. Many actual stone spheres are found. The most well known examples are in the Costa Rican Disquis Delta, but they are also found in Brittany and other places. The Bronze Age city of Atlantis was designed in circular shape. Stonehenge III was a circular site, also built at about 2,000 BC, the same time as Poverty Point.

The Earthworks: The Circular Rings

Poverty Point has "11.2 miles of artificial ridges," at one point about 7 feet high. A few of these were trenched by the American Museum in 1955, and were thought to support dwelling sites (Ref.49). These rings can

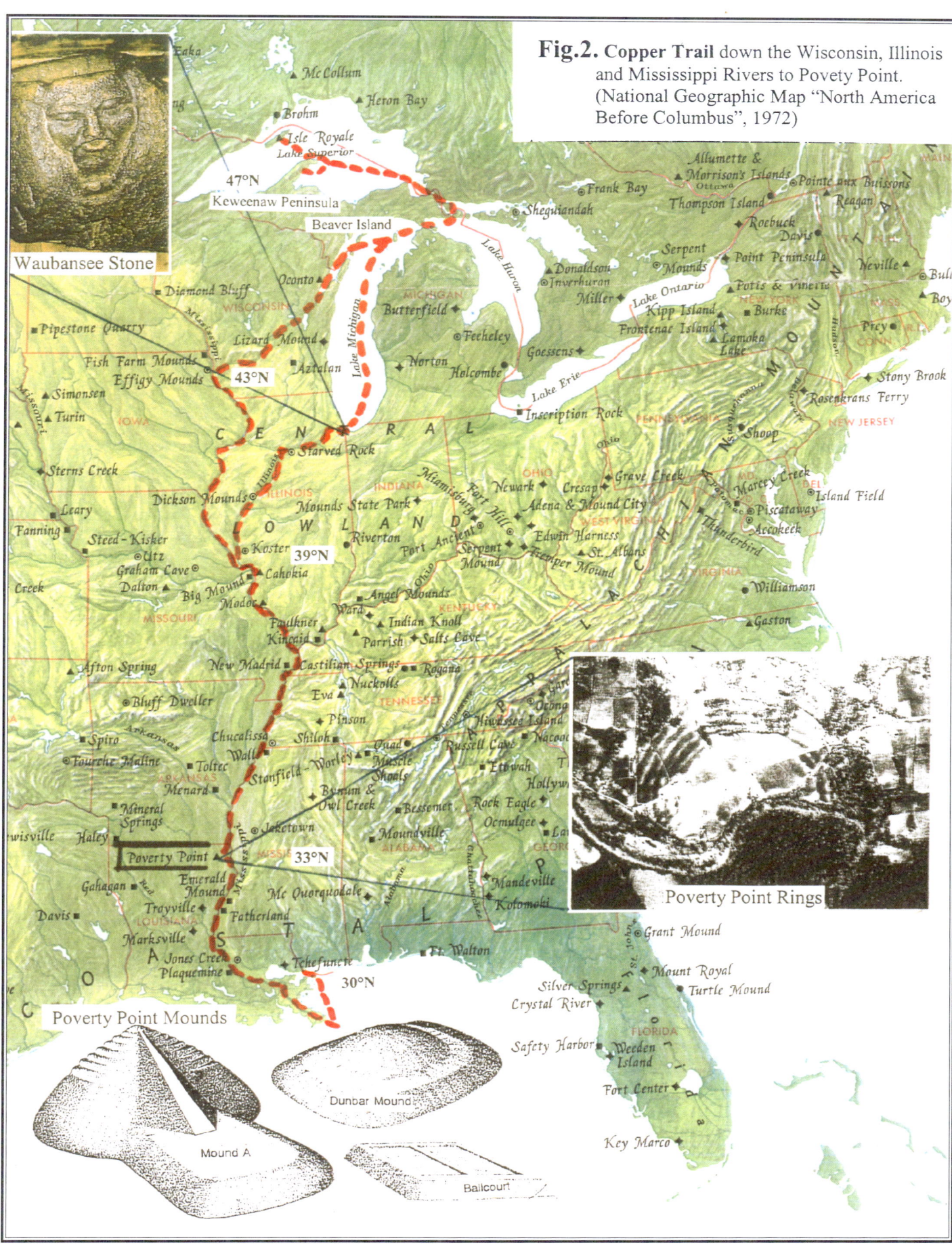

Fig.2. Copper Trail down the Wisconsin, Illinois and Mississippi Rivers to Povety Point. (National Geographic Map "North America Before Columbus", 1972)

be shown to have a geometric plan (Fig.6). From north to south, the mounds B, A, L, and J are situated on a straight line, called the western North-South axis. (The site axes are not true N-S lines, but point 8° NNW, called "Poverty Point North" ("PPN"). This is similar to Olmec La Venta, on the south side of the Gulf of Mexico, designed at about the same time, both oriented opposite their sites' (magnetic) deviation of 8° east.) The line through the mounds M and D, called the eastern North-South axis, runs parallel to it. The 90° right angle intersection of the east axis with line A-C from Mound A will be called point C, and the line A-C we call the horizontal axis. Apparently, this point C is considered the center of the plaza. The line connecting mound B and the center C makes angles of 45° with the horizontal and vertical lines. The line L-D, from Ballcourt Mound to Dunbar Mound, is at right angles, or near to right angles to B-C. These lines are the baselines of the complex.

There are 5 aisles which connect the central plaza with the area outside the rings. They divide the figure into segments of comparable size. The plaza was found to be "free of trash," but numerous filled-in holes up to 3 feet diameter were found "where posts had been set" on the western side. The SW segment possesses a special wall, parallel to the corridor beside it, which is called the Causeway. This Causeway continues to run beyond the rings in southwestern direction over a distance of 800 feet. No burials have yet been identified at Poverty Point.

The circular rings of Poverty Point model the planet Earth more accurately than you would expect. The rings are symbolic for the "Wheel of the Law," dedicated to Maat, the Egyptian goddess of law and order in the universe. The 6 walls in 10 segments of the full circle form 6 x 10= 60 units, showing the sailing route below Cape Farvel at 60°N. The 6 mounds X 6 rings = the latitude of Gibraltar at 36°N, and with 10 segments of the rings, may also show the size of the Earth, at 360°. Since a moira is the Egyptian distance unit for 1°, and our unit is the Nautical Mile (1°= 60 NM), they probably indicate the circumference of the Earth to be 360 moira, which would be 360 X 60= 21,600 NM, which is correct.

Gibson shows 38 radiocarbon date tests, with results running from

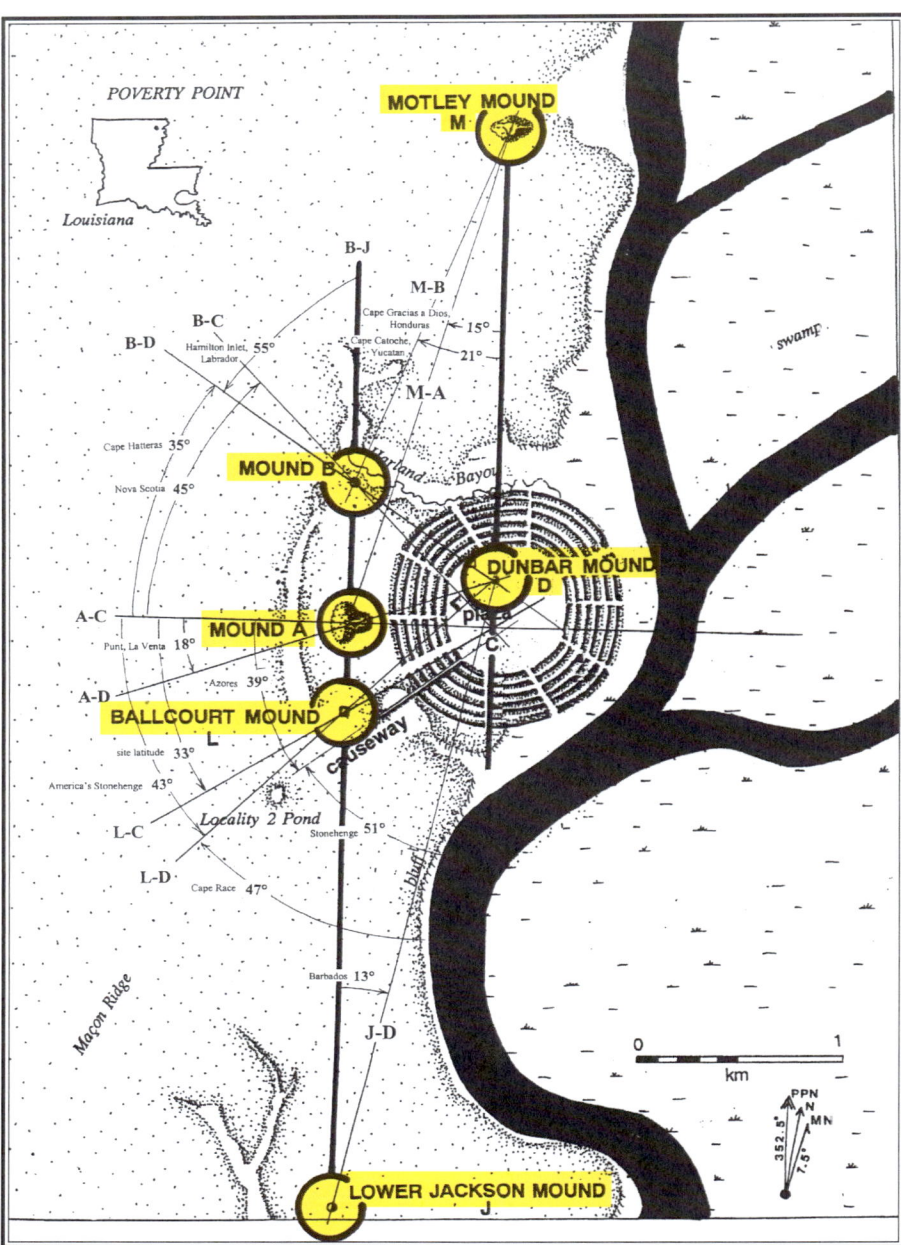

Figure 6. Baselines of the complex, with Rings, mounds, and waterways restored to probable original (c. 2000-1200 BC). Site angles added, with corresponding latitude locations noted.

2300 BC (possibly 2470), to 650 BC (possibly AD 70). These radiocarbon datings put the site in the Late Archaic period in North America. The massive earthworks and tons of "exchange rocks" were considered incompatible with the Archaic "hunter-gatherer" period. But no agriculture, and very little pottery could be found, which has been very troubling to archaeologists. When one finds corn agriculture, earthworks and pottery, the culture is called "Woodland," and these sites are one or two thousand years more recent than early Poverty Point. There are no large rocks at Poverty Point, so the site features earthworks, not huge stone monuments. The whole complex of mounds has a North-South length of 3.5 miles, and a width of nearly a mile. At the center of the site are the 6 concentric, semi-circular walls around a wide plaza. The 5-8 foot tall rings are now reduced to one foot by plowing. Following its 1950s work, the American Museum of Natural History in New York reported dark middens (old debris) on the fore and aft slopes of the rings, and postholes on the rings, suggesting occupied buildings on the rings. Their work consisted of test holes, not excavated areas, so no pat-

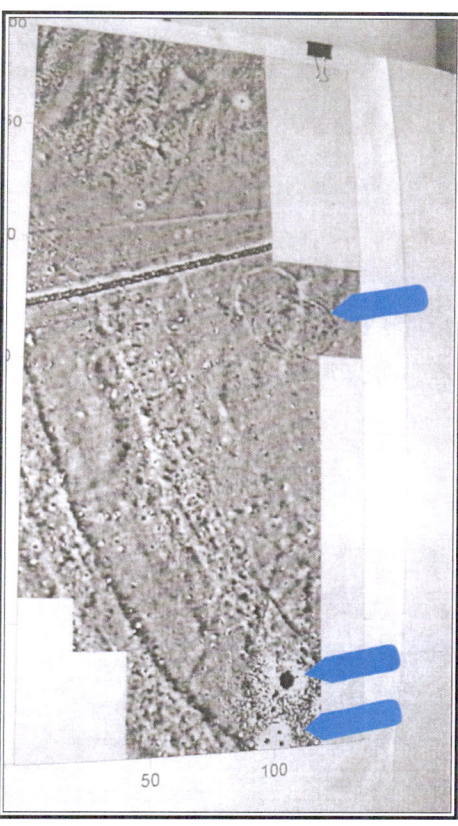

Figure 7. The first Magnetic Gradiometry Study, done by archaeologists Mike Hargrave and Burley Clay early in 2006. The State Archaeologist on site, Dianna Greenlee, explained that the dark spots are metal "hits." The large spots at the bottom are particularly interesting. She later reported some of these were "core tested," and showed dark "midden" material or hearths. Note the interesting overlapping circles mid-photo, which were explored by university students in June of 2009 (Photo by Wakefield, October, 2006).

terns of construction have been seen. Gibson reports that "less than 3/10 of 1% of the area of the rings has been excavated" (.3%).

The Site Design and encoded latitudes

We have found that the site latitude is usually encoded clearly in the site design at Bronze Age sites. The line LC points 33° from the horizontal axis. This is the latitude of Poverty Point, 33°N. The angles between the major axes of the site and the mounds, show many of the latitudes frequently found in megalithic sites on both sides of the Atlantic. The angle of the Causeway is 39°, the latitude of the West Azores (39°N), the focus of safe return trips to the Old World. The junction of the Illinois with the Mississippi on the Copper Trail, and the Serpent Mound of Ohio are also at 39°N. Its reciprocal, 51°, is the latitude where the Belle Isle Strait joins the Gulf of St. Lawrence, and is also the site latitude of Stonehenge, in England. Stonehenge had been enlarged by adding the large Sarcen Stones in its center at about 2000 BC, commemorating the discovery of the New World (Ref.3), its development probably slowed by the comet disaster of 2347 BC. This famous monument, also built in a circular design, was probably known to the builders of Poverty Point.

The angle between L-D and the axis, could be 45°, depending on just where the measurements were taken. This would add symmetry to the design, since B-C is at 45°. If not intentionally replicating this angle, it is likely that the intended angle is 43°, which shows the important Nautical Center of America's Stonehenge, at 43°N, north of Boston. This is the largest megalithic stone monument in North America, where sailors with shiploads of copper were taught how to sail back to Europe (Ref.3). This is also the latitude on the Copper Trail where the Wisconsin River joins the Mississippi. The reciprocal angle of line L-C is 47°, the latitude of Cape Race, the eastern Cape of North America. The latitude of the Keweenaw copper mines is also 47°N. Other angles important to sailing the Atlantic are indicated, 45°N (Nova Scotia), 35°N (Cape Hatteras), 55°N (Hamilton Inlet), 21°N (Yucatan), 15°N (Cape Gracias a Dios, Honduras), and 13°N (Barbados, and Mid Caribbean Islands).

Population / Food

Poverty Point was an unusual thing: a pre-historic, pre-agricultural manufacturing town, made possible by the immense biological richness of the area. Habitation areas have been identified around the site, especially on the north side, covering more than a square mile, though Gibson states "only a handful have received more than passing attention." Sixty encampments encircling the core complex are known. No descendants can be traced to any historic tribe or group, despite estimates that many thousands of people were living here, who did not depend upon agriculture, over a thousand year period. Fruits, acorns, pecans, and other nuts were important in the diet, but the superabundant food, available all year long, was fish. Gibson writes "in the 500 square mile swamp around the Poverty Point encampments, there were between 30,000 and 1,000,000 pounds of fish per square mile!" Gibson thinks it was a hunter-gatherer town, a place of residence, a trading center. This puts Poverty Point outside the classical "Late Archaic" archaeological model of hunter-gatherer life. Ford and Webb conclude that "the ruling class probably were invaders from the north, early Hopewellian people" (Ref.49).

Artifacts / Excavations

The old ground beneath the rings was "midden veneered," according to both Ford and Gibson, showing that people were already living or working on the ground before building started. Little pottery has been found, but numerous steatite stone bowls have been found. The steatite had to come from Michigan or the Piedmont Area. These stone bowls are ½"+ thick, and not practical to cook in over a fire, so cooking was done by dropping hot clay balls into the soup. Bi-conical cooking-ball fragments (called "Poverty Point Objects," or PPO's) "dominated the trash in the rings." Ford calculated that "associated with small fireplaces scattered throughout the soil, were a minimum of 2200 tons, or 24,000,000 PPOs" (Ref.49). Among the engraved ones, "bird representations were most prevalent," including the horned owl, hungry nestling, songbirds, and crow figures. Turtles, opossum, and panther also occurred, along with strange glyphs, and unique motifs. The trash also included whole and broken, and incomplete, resharpened, and recycled tools, manufacturing debris, fire-cracked rock, caches of projectile points, baked human figurines, plummets, copper beads, a copper bead-maker's kit (copper nuggets hammered into thin sheets, for winding around the copper wire), ornaments, both finished and unfinished, and most of all, exchange rock. In fact, Gibson estimates that "over 71 tons of foreign flint occurs on the site, an astonishing amount... Millions of items were left on the ground before the rings were built; they were left in the rings while under construction and during breaks in construction; and they were left atop the rings after construction was finished." The Ford report discusses 33 types of Archaic arrowheads over 20 pages, noting that there were thousands in various collections." Most of the plummets were hematite, 1/3 magnetite, one of copper. Ford says that "when the large number of plummets that have been gathered and sold to collectors over the last 50 years is considered, it is apparent that [hematite] was brought here by boat loads." Gibson says it is estimated that there remain 75-100 tons of exotic rock at the site, and there are hundreds of thousands of "perfectly good tools." He states: "expect the unusual, and it is likely to show up... If I had to sum up Poverty Point's gear and appliances in a single word, it would be abundant. If I could use two words, I would say abundant and rich."

Gibson reports that hundreds of post-molds and firepits were scattered across the rings. In excavating hearths and pits, some were found that "raised questions that can not be answered at present ... one burned area was 4' across ... seven superimposed hearths were dug on successive building layers, in the third upper western ring segment. Each was about 3' in diameter. ... An excavation on the first NW ring revealed an average of one pit for every compact-car sized area."(Ref.1). The rings had caches and deposits of objects. Perforators used to drill stone were concentrated in just the 3rd southwestern ring, and the fifth southern ring, yet the cores from which the perforators were made were primarily found on the other segments. Thus, the distribution of tools is very uneven, revealing divisions of labor, and manufacturing specialization. For example, Gibson writes "no tools described as 'women's culinary' were found in the western three ring groups, but were 10-20% of the finds nearer the Bayou. The west and Northwest ring sets were very low in all finds...over half of the little specialized drills were surface-collected from just two segments" (Ref.1).

Copper

Routes for the extraction of Michigan's copper have been traced downstream from Isle Royale and the Keweenaw Peninsula (Fig.2). These routes run past storage pits with corroded copper in them, past Beaver Island, with its ancient raised garden beds and huge 39-stone circle. In the Great Lakes, water levels fluctuated widely, as ice dams retreated, and the land rebounded from the glacial weight. At 2300 BC there was a high water stage, called the "Nipissing Stage" (Refs.19,21,39). Dr. Jim Schertz, Professor Emeritus with the Ancient Earthworks Society, says that when the water rose 40 feet above present levels, an outlet opened into the Illinois River, through the present chicago Ship Canal. On the south bank, where the river started, stood a 3,000 pound stone block, overlooking Lake Michigan. Known as the Waubansee Stone (top, Fig.2), now in the hall of the Chicago Historical Society. It is carved with the face of a man with a beard and holes connecting the bowl at the top to the mouth of the face. It appears to be the face of Moloch on a Phoenician Tophet, where

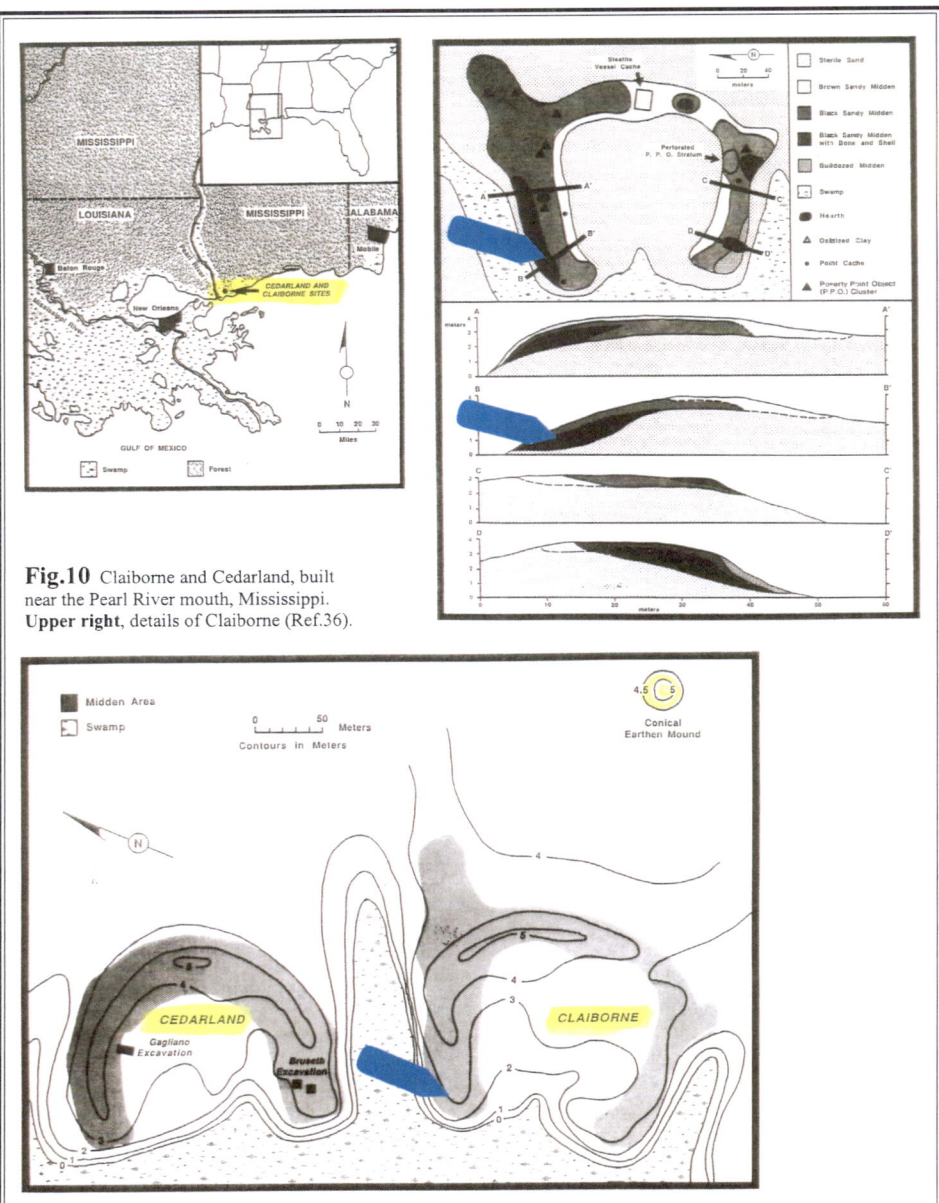

Figure 10. Claiborne and Cedarland, built near the Pearl River mouth, Mississippi. Upper Right: Details of Claiborne (Ref. 36).

sacrifices were made prior to the perilous voyage, loaded with copper, down the rivers to Poverty Point (Ref.40). Ships then entered the Chicago River, and then ran down the Illinois River, to the Mississippi, or from Green Bay, down the Wisconsin and the Mississippi to Poverty Point. Some copper went east, down the Ottawa River, and the Trent/Severn Waterway to the St. Lawrence River, and some went further south, and down the Chaudiere River from Quebec to Lake Megantic, then down the Kennebec river to the Maine coast (Ref.3). Nevertheless, most of the half billion tons of missing copper (Ref.10) must have gone down the Mississippi.

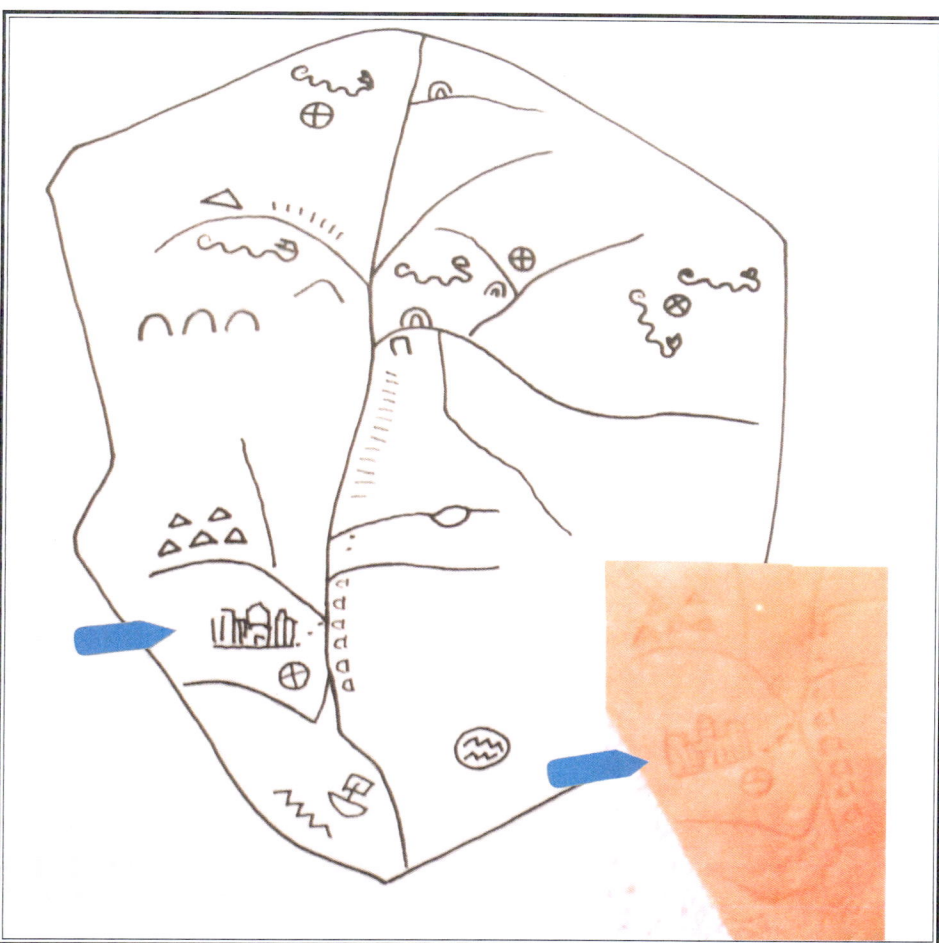

Figure 11. A drawing of a Burrows Cave mapstone, by graphic artist Beverly Mosely, Fellow of the Midwest Epigraphic Society. The stone is thought to have been created by refugees to America, early n the first century AD. The small image is a close-up photo of a corner of the stone, showing another view of the two or three story building, accessed by a trail from the junction of the Arkansas and Mississippi Rivers. Apparently, Poverty Point continued to be occupied and its wooden buildings maintained for a long time after the river shifted away from the site. Note the large villages upriver in the Spiro area. (Photo by Wakefield)

Jean Hunt, then President of the Louisiana Mounds Society, wrote in 1993 in Ancient American Magazine that "the Poverty Point archaeologist or curator talked about traces of large "spots" of copper on the surface, which he thought might have represented places where raw copper from the Michigan mines was placed while awaiting trans-shipment" (Ref.37). Metals would not be a normal surface finding. Daniel Wood also stated in Ancient American that "as many as 20 copper storage pits have been located at Poverty Point, measuring 15-20 feet in diameter (Ref.38). There was no visual evidence of these pits when I was there in 1996, but it appears they may show in the magnetic gradiometry (Fig.7). Wood describes a 20 x 50 foot Torch Lake (Keweenaw) pit that was found to contain 20 tons of carbonate of copper, that was dated c.1800 BC (also Ref.10), and other pits as far east as Sault Ste Marie, and others in southern Wisconsin.

The big unanswered question at this point is where the raw copper was heated on wood fires and poured into oxhide molds. No site has ever been identified. We know it was done with multiple pours, with enough moisture present to create voids in the oxhides, creating "blister copper" (see article on Michigan Copper in this book). Poverty Point is well forested land, and very humid, being on the Gulf Coast. The melting of the rough copper from the mines into standardized 60 pound one-Talent Oxhides would have required very hot fires. Multiple pourings into the clay moulds in the humidity of the Gulf Coast would have made the workers sweat profusely. Perhaps the sweat and humidity alone, or maybe wet "fresh" wood might have been enough to cause the ga voids that characterize the fragile "blister copper" oxhides. The carrying handles and flat shape of standardized oxhides would have been very helpful for shipping, carrying and selling the copper. With 99.7% of Poverty Point unexcavated, it may be this was the most important activity at Poverty Point, and clay or dirt molds should be watched for in future excavations.

Early in 2006, a magnetic gra diometry study done by Mike Hargrave and Burley Clay (Fig.7) shows large dark spots that were described as metal "hits," or "something in the dir that makes it magnetically different." The State Site Archeologist, Dianna Greenlee says that by the end of May 2009 they have surveyed the entire plaza and the first two rings. She reports that the dark spots were tested with "pulled cores," which showed dark midden material/hearths. They are especially interested in the circle patterns (see center of Fig.7). They have found many more of them, especially in the south Plaza, with larger circles in the east, smaller in the west. They are 50cm to 1 meter deep, in "good soil, so they are definitely prehistoric." A Joint Field School excavation was scheduled for June 3 to July 2, 2009, with 3 staff, and 23 students from the University of Louisiana, and Mississippi State University. The students dug 1 x 2 meter holes over four of the circle patterns. Greenlee reported that the circles were found to be circles of filled postholes, where the posts were supported by PPO's crammed next to them, producing the vertical stacks of PPO's found by the students. In Europe, where stone is available, posts were similarly surrounded by "setting stones", and these rings of stones reveal old post locations. Greenlee thought that more excavations will be helpful in determining whether the post circles were roofed, but thinks some were too large to roof. One radiocarbon date has come back at 1440-1280 BC. No copper objects or hearths were noticed by the students in these four locations in June/July 2009.

Gulf Ports

Figure 10 shows the Claiborne and Cedarland Rings, contemporary with Poverty Point, which Gibson calls the "oddest Poverty Point community of all." These mound-rings, in their tools and styles, resembled Poverty Point. They sat on the first high ground rising above the marsh at the Gulf entrance to the Mississippi River, along its Pearl River branch. He states that "since radiocarbon dates have shown these two rings were occupied at the same time, but the artifacts in them were so distinctly different, it was concluded that they were inhabited by two independent, ethnically separate groups, who lived side by side."

Cedarland

The paper of Bruseth, an archaeologist with the Texas Historical Commission, is most interesting: "Cedarland, located in 1957, mapped in 1970, has been extensively damaged by indiscriminate digging by relic seekers and by construction activities related to development of a port and harbor facility. The site was occupied for several centuries prior to 2000 BC, at the confluence of the Mississippi River and the Gulf of Mexico. During the 3rd millenium BC the Mississippi would have been in relatively close proximity, and it is probable that the site was the highest ground (5m) near the mouth of the river... The ring is a large oyster shell and earth midden overlooking the mouth of the Pearl River...This site seems to have formed by accretion, without planning or site layout... No burials have been found" (Ref.24).

Field inspections by Bruseth during bulldozing revealed debris consisting of bone, stone, and clay artifacts... He says "numerous clay-lined, basin-shaped hearths have been uncovered, but few have been carefully excavated ... Raw materials at the site include red jasper, black and white and grey chert, quartz crystal, various quartzites, and Great Lakes copper needles and sheet copper. The lithic materials are rare at Claiborne. Cedarland has 3 and 4 sided drills, while Claiborne possesses only bifacially-formed drills... [beautiful 3-sided points are a feature of the Danish neolithic at this time]. One to 2 meters of deposits indicate intensive utilization,... and re-use of hearths, but few have been carefully excavated (Ref.24).

Bruseth continues: "The hearths varied in diameter from 50 to 65 cm [20-26 inches, the size of oxhide ingots], were basin shaped, and occurred on a common horizontal plane. The walls consisted of oxidized orange soil. However, the tops were found at variable depths below the surface. This factor is interpreted to be the result of digging in and around the hearths after their initial use. As neither ash nor charcoal was observed within the features, they may instead have served as earth ovens rather than hearths. Under this interpretation, the oxidized soil of the features would represent prepared clay walls that became fired from heating in the oven. Numerous amorphous fired clay lumps surround the hearths and are commonly found throughout much of the midden. The author has examined several examples for evidence of deliberate shape, but in all instances they were found to be amorphous and unintentionally formed. It was initially thought that these might be baked clay objects used in conjunction with the clay-lined hearths. However, it is probable, based on their small size and lack of clear form, that they are fragments from other clay-lined hearths. Extensive digging and reuse of the hearths evidently scattered burned clay wall fragments throughout the midden" (Ref.24).

Claiborne

Radiocarbon dates for Claiborne, discovered in 1967, range from 2040 BC to 1150 BC. Bruseth says "Claiborne appears to have been a well-structured village throughout much of its history. A conical mound is directly east of the site [as shown in the lower illustration of Fig.10]. No clay-lined hearths have been found, but a huge hearth 25m x 3-5m wide was opened by successive bulldozer cuts, a feature which apparently moved upslope by accumulation from use. Smaller hearths of 4m, and 2m x 1.5m were also found. Claiborne plummets are made of magnetite and hematite, while plummets at Cedarland are only made of other materials. Bruseth describes other materials revealed that the "inhabitants of both rings were involved in long-distance exchange, but did so differently, despite being side-by-side. Of special note are the effigy forms, such as locusts, owls, and bivalves, which are not found at Cedarland. There are ceramics... fiber tempered pottery, but none at Cedarland. The two sites are distinctive in layout, feature type, and artifact content, and present a perplexing problem. ...Other sites are known, which most likely represent support camps, to these 'specialized activity areas'. These sites flourished well before the earthwork construction at Poverty Point.... Perhaps the monumental earthworks [at Poverty Point] have caused us to underestimate the importance of pre-earthwork occupation." Bruseth concludes the report of his excavation by writing that "the two sites were inhabited by two independent groups who lived side by side" (Ref.24).

Sailors will understand that small sailboats of 30-50 feet, now circling the globe by the multitude, or small ships in prehistory of 70-200 feet, would be heading for a "port." They would not be likely to attempt to sail directly up the huge, muddy, and treacherous Mississippi when in its fast flood stage, but would seek a nearby landing spot, where they could drink fresh water, bathe, and secure and repair their vessels for awhile. Along the shallow beaches of the Gulf Coast, the Pearl River mouth provided the needed deep water entrance. Two separate ports developed. We know there were several different cultures involved in the copper trade. Gibson states that "like any busy place, especially where traders and visitors from strange lands congregated, Poverty Point was exposed to many foreign influences ... many of Poverty Point's basic raw materials came from lands inhabited by strangers." We know the Egyptians and Minoans were involved in copper trading, because paintings of them are on Egyptian tomb walls, carrying copper oxhide ingots. Bruseth says Barry Fell has reported that the language of the Atakapas, the Tunicas, and the Chitimacha tribes of Louisiana had striking similarities with Nile Valley languages involving words one would associate with Egyptian trading communities. Quoting the archaeologist Bruseth again: "Extensive surveys of sites along the Pearl River with similar projectile point types, appear occupied by different groups. We know that trade was crossing ethnic boundaries and probably crossing language boundaries. These are certainly groups of people that operate mostly unto themselves most of the time. There are strangers involved" (Ref.24).

Claiborne, with its conical mound, like those in the Canaries, may well have been an outstation of the Atlantean culture. Early written history, Plato principally, tells about the Atlantean culture, which grew rich on trading in "orichalcum," a pure copper, across the Atlantic Ocean, which is named for them. Their principal city of

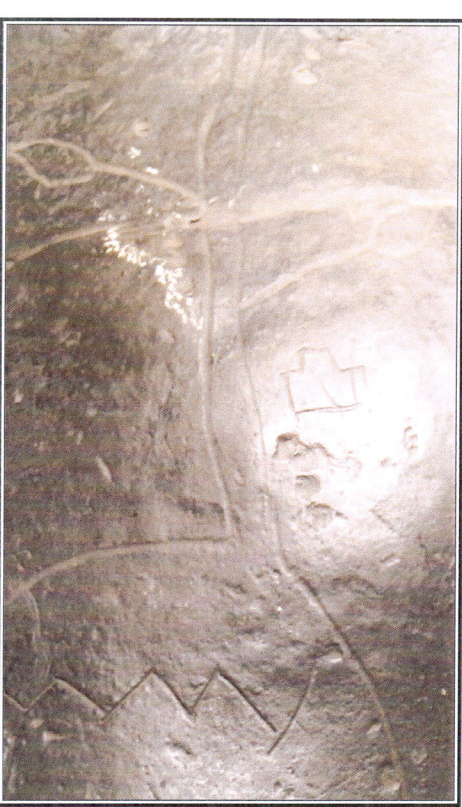

Figure 12. Closeup of another Burrows Cave Mapstone of the Mississippi River, showing what appears to the a two-story building on the east side of the Mississippi River. It appears that since the Mississippi had changed its course to the East by the time of these mapstones. This mapmaker apparently had only heard about the place, and put it on the wrong side of the river. (Photo by Wakefield)

Atlantis was designed with circular rings. The population of Poverty Point is thought to have increased greatly after 1200 BC, a date when a comet impact caused all the cities in the Mediterranean to be destroyed in earthquakes and fire, and submerged the Atlantean city, after the eruption of Mt. Atlas (Ref.14). Despite the flood of refugees to the west, the comet disaster ended the Michigan mining, the Atlantic trade, the mound building at Poverty Point, and the European Bronze Age, all at the same time.

Climatologists call the following cold (2° fall) and wet period (1250-1000 BC) the "Plenard Period." So many sites are now underwater, we have lost grasp of how big the trade in copper was in prehistory. The underwater breakwater of Bimini in the Bahamas is well known. (Bimini = Ba [soul] min [Egyptian god of travelers] nini [homage]= "homage to the soul of Min"(Ref.44). Less well known are the enormous walls of 8m x 6m blocks at a depth of 14m that run for several miles on the coast of Morocco, and the old megalithic coastal cities of Lixus and Mogador (Ref.37).

Archaeologist Bruseth's midden cross-sections of the Claiborne site appear to provide evidence for copper oxhide manufacture. Fig.10, upper right, shows a hearth as long as a football field: 6' deep, 300' long, in a midden twice as long. "Numerous amorphous fired clay lumps surround the hearths, and are commonly found ...A typical cluster of 86 clay objects... The author has examined several examples for evidence of deliberate shape, but in all instances they were found to be amorphous and unintentionally formed ...A radiocarbon date of 1425 +/- 140 BC ... the stratum seems to represent an activity area where perforated varieties of baked clay objects were being fired. This interpretation is based on the nearly total absence of complete baked objects, and the abundance of charcoal concentrations... Artifact types in the stratum are almost exclusively fragmented baked clay objects... The broken clay objects are interpreted to represent specimens that fragmented during the firing process" (Ref.24). The clay fragments were probably hammered off the copper oxhides when they cooled. Bruseth notes that "the predominant artifact categories included lithic debris and cobbles with battered ends" (Ref.24). So it appears stone hammers were used to break off the molds.

Burrows Cave Maps

Several mapstones (Figs.11,12) from Burrow's Cave (Ref.41) show two story buildings that seem to be at the Poverty Point site. No other site is known that may have had two-story buildings. These mudstones are believed to have been carved in the first century AD, so more than 1200 years after the comet disaster and the end of the copper mining, and even 700 years after the end of the life of the site, according to the archaeologists. Apparently there was a long continued use of the site, since two-story wooden buildings require a lot of maintenance. We see no remains today, other than unexplained postholes, because the buildings were not built of stone. Note that the site could no longer be seen from the river (which had moved), as it is accessed by a trail from the junction of the Arkansas River in Figure 11. Note a 2-story building placed on the wrong side of the river, and without a trail, in Figure 12. Mistakes happen when you sail by, and only hear of a place, without seeing it.

Conclusions

Although big stones are totally lacking, the Poverty Point site should be considered as part of the worldwide Megalithic Culture in the Bronze Age because of its circular design, conical pyramids, latitude ecodings, multiculturalism, and the pottery found at the site. It has "ports" on the Gulf (contemporary with Olmec cities and most of the dynasties of Egypt), where middens show it is likely that the copper oxhides were made, which fueled the Bronze Age in Europe. ■

Were Prehistoric Copper Oxhide Ingots Manufactured on the Mississippi Coast Near the Mouth of the Mississippi River?

by Jay S. Wakefield

Copper: According to American Indian oral tradition, Michigan copper was mined in antiquity by "red haired white-skinned 'marine men' who came from across the sea." Tens of thousands of pits up to 30' deep were mined using fire setting and stone hammers, with an estimated half a billion tons of pure crystallized copper removed from the glacier-exposed lava beds. From wood timbers anaerobically preserved under water in the ancient mine pits, this mining has been radiocarbon dated to between 2400 BC and 1200 BC, a period of more than a thousand years. During this same period, Europe experienced the Bronze Age, though historians and archaeologists now say they have no idea where the copper came from. One of the more interesting finds in digging out one of these old mine holes (Drier and Du Temple, *Prehistoric Copper Mining in the Lake Superior Region*) was a walrus skin bag, indicating the miners had traveled overseas in the north. If people came from overseas to mine copper in Michigan during the Bronze Age, there can be little doubt they transported it back overseas for use in the manufacture of bronze.

Ancient routes for the transport of Michigan's copper have been traced downstream from the mines on Isle Royale and the Keweenaw Peninsula, past storage pits with corroded copper in them, and beyond Beaver Island with its ancient raised garden beds and huge 39-stone circle. In the Great Lakes, water levels fluctuated widely, as ice dams retreated and the land rebounded from the glacial weight. Around 2300 BC, there was a high water stage called the "Nipissing Stage." Dr. Jim Schertz, Professor Emeritus with the Ancient Earthworks Society (*Old Water Levels and Waterways during the Ancient Copper Mining Era*) says that when the water rose 40-50 feet above present levels, an outlet opened into the Illinois River through the present Chicago Ship Canal. On the south bank, where the river started, stood a 3,000 pound stone block, overlooking Lake Michigan. Known as the Waubansee Stone, it was carved with the face of a man with a beard and holes connecting the bowl at the top to the mouth of the face. Another stone is said to have been on the north bank. At these stones, sacrifices may have been made prior to the perilous voyages loaded with copper down the rivers to Poverty Point, Louisiana.

Archaeologist Marco Giardino PhD, on the Claiborne site, pointing to areas saved under concrete slabs for future excavation. Behind him are the waterways of the Bayou, which have served both the ancient ports and the modern port. Hurricane Katrina blew 23 feet of water over the site where Marco is standing.

Poverty Point: Six huge earth mounds and six enormous concentric earth rings characterize the enigmatic Archaic period town of Poverty Point, formerly accessible only by boat from the Mississippi. The site is carbon dated to 2400 BC, with the big mounds made around 1500 BC. It is one of the largest and oldest centers of civilization on Earth.

Jean Hunt, then President of the Louisiana Mounds Society, wrote in 1993 in *Ancient American Magazine* that "the Poverty Point archaeologist or curator talked about traces of large 'spots' of copper on the surface, which he thought might have represented places where raw copper from the Michigan mines was placed while awaiting trans-shipment." Dexter and Martin (*America's Ancient Stone Relics*) report that Mitchell Hillman, Assistant Curator for the Louisiana Office

On the left is the west edge of the site of Claiborne, seen adjacent to barges docked in the newly dredged Port. (Port Benville Industrial Park, Mississippi, May 2010)

of State Parks, has found spots of copper on the surface both north and south of Poverty Point for a distance of five to fifteen miles on both sides of the river. Researcher Daniel Wood, in another *Ancient American Magazine* article, "Bronze Age Michigan," describes a 20'x 50' Torch Lake (Keweenaw) pit found to contain 20 tons of carbonate of copper, dated c.1800 BC. Other pits were discovered as far east as Sault Ste Marie and others in southern Wisconsin. Early in 2006, a magnetic gradiometry study done at Poverty Point by Mike Hargrave and Burley Clay shows large dark spots that were described as metal "hits." (See *Rocks & Rows*.)

Oxhides: Bronze Age raw copper was exchanged in 60-lb (one Talent) oxhide ingots shaped like a flat square, with the four corners extended like the legs of a hide taken from a real ox. These extensions made the ingots easier to carry, as illustrated by paintings upon Egyptian tomb walls. Copper oxhide ingot cargo found on ancient shipwrecks is "extraordinarily pure" but full of slag bits, "spratzen" voids, and copper oxide inclusions, which made the oxhides brittle. This brittle copper is called "blister copper." Researchers have reported their conclusions that the oxhides must have been manufactured by multiple pourings of melted copper into clay molds in open air over wood fires. The big unanswered question at this point is where this was done. No site has been identified. Only one mould, in Syria, has ever been found, but that one, when tested, was found to have tiny bits of copper in it.

Gulf Sites: While it is likely that copper exchange and the manufacture of copper oxhide ingots occurred at Poverty Point, other sites have come to my attention while studying the matter. Archaeologist James E. Bruseth, with the Texas Historical Commission, in his chapter in the book *The Poverty Point Culture* reports on two Late Archaic sites located on high ground fifteen feet above the marshes at the mouth of the Pearl River of Mississippi. In Archaic times, the Mississippi River had a fast-flowing flood season, alternating with periods when a canoe could be paddled upstream. It emptied into the Gulf of Mexico to the east of where it does now, close to the Pearl River mouth. This first high ground rising above the marshes, now called "Cedarland" and "Claiborne," would have been attractive to ancient mariners who needed moorage, rest, and fresh water.

The site originally consisted of two large (500' diameter) semicircular middens of ash up to six feet deep, overlooking a bayou of the Pearl River mouth. Cedarland is known to have been occupied around 2200 BC, more than four thousand years ago, and was "participating in the Poverty Point trade network"

Google Map, satellite photo, showing overall location of sites (printed from Google Earth). The Space Center and the Industrial Park are boxed in red.

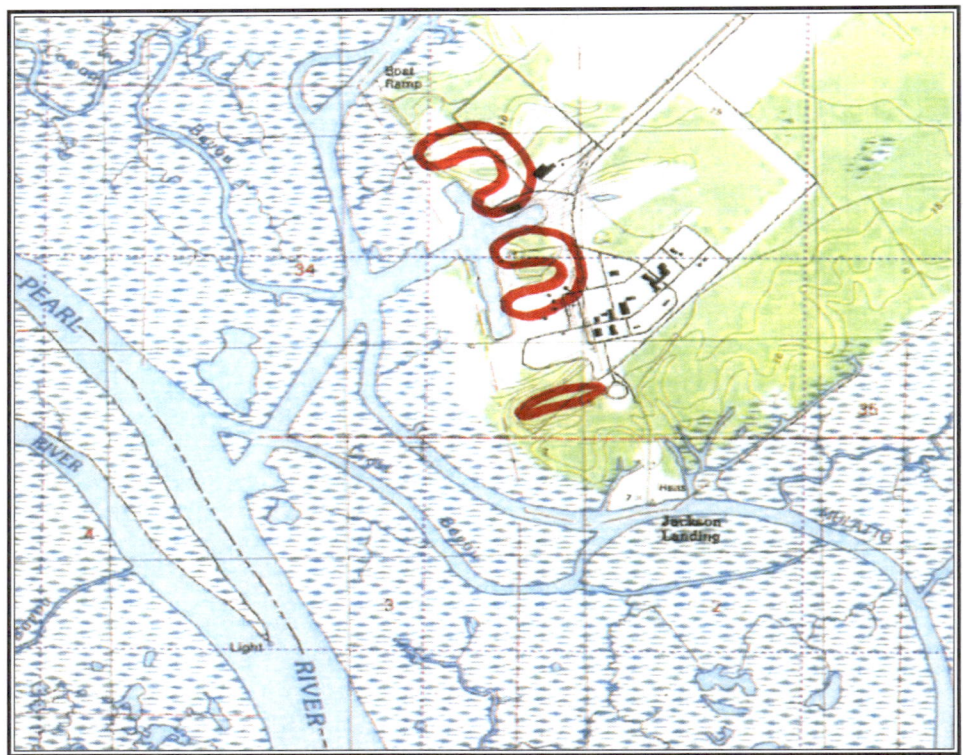

USGS map printed at REI from National Geographic TOPO on CD-ROM, scale 1:30,750. Approximate locations of Claiborne and Cedarland Archaeological sites, now within Port Benville Industrial Park. Mulatto Bayou Earthwork (12-18' x 1200') also indicated.

(Bruseth). Bruseth states that "radiocarbon dates have shown these two rings were occupied at the same time, but the artifacts in them were so distinctly different, it was concluded that they were inhabited by two independent, ethnically separate groups, who lived side by side." He calls them "specialized activity areas," inhabited by two different groups with ethnic and language differences. The groups were strangers from each other and different from the native sites up-

Above, the National Geographic sketch of the Uluburun ship, a trading vessel of 1300 BC, discovered wrecked off the Turkey coast. In its hold was found 10 tons of oxhide-shaped copper ingots, with half a ton of tin ingots, and other trading goods. Below the ship, left, one of the ingots from the wreck held by two ladies; in the middle, an ingot in the British Museum; to the right, some of the Uluburun ingots in the seabed. Below, an ingot found at Hagia Trihadha, Crete. Three found near Cagliari, Sardinia, were inscribed with a trident, a double axe, and an angular P. The trident was symbol for Poseidon, god of the Alanteans, who Plato says ran the metal trade in the Ocean named for them. The 3 supervised men ("Keftiu"- Minoans or Atlanteans) are carrying an oxhide and baskets of bun ingots, on the tomb wall of Rekh-Mi-Re at Thebes. The bearded Phoenician-looking man is carrying an ingot on the wall of the tomb of Huyat, also at Thebes. The two lowest ingots were found in Egypt.

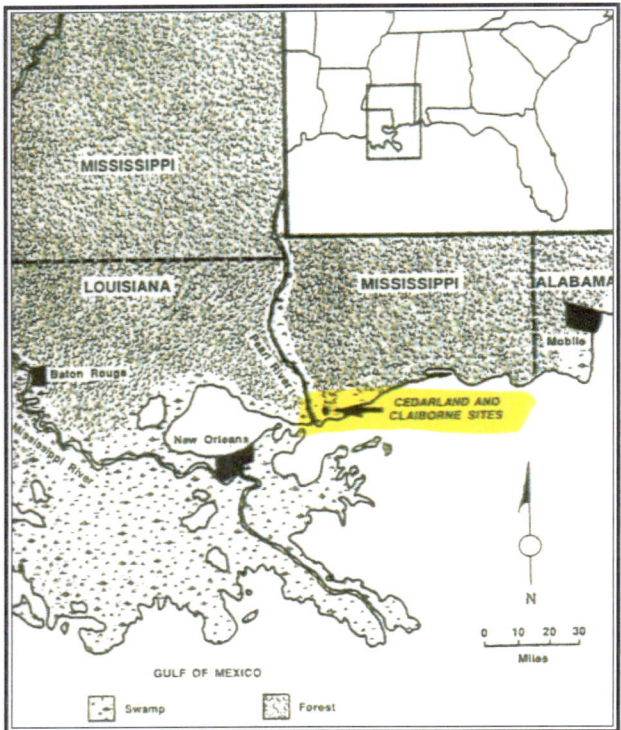

Claiborne and Cedarland built near the Pearl River mouth, Mississippi. Upper right, details of Claiborne.

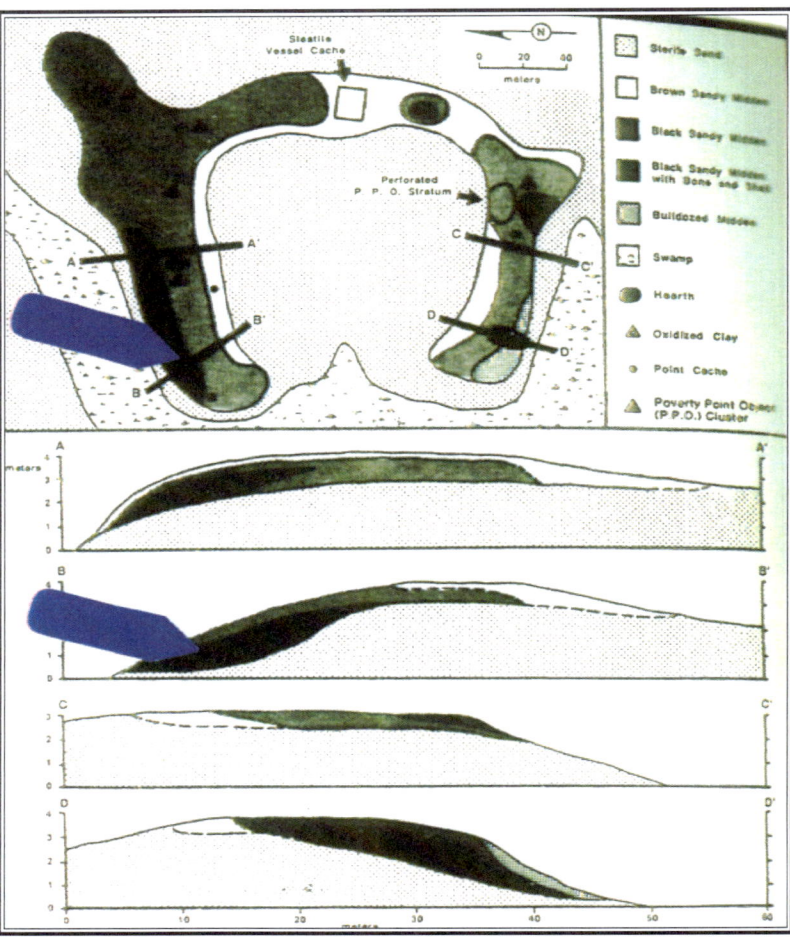

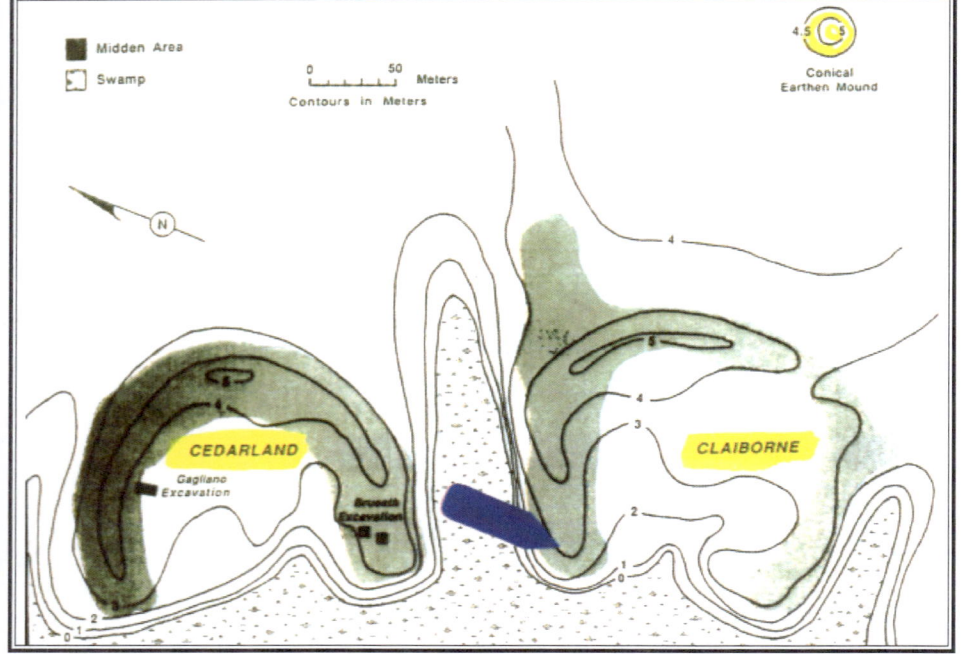

river. A corroborating report by Dr. Greg Little (*Atlantis Rising*, Sept/Oct, 2010) illustrates new evidence for three separate anchoring, docking, and breakwater formations underwater off the west side of Bimini. "All three have stone anchors and show evidence of being used by a maritime culture." We cannot identify these groups yet, despite Egyptian language remnants in some Louisiana tribes and Egyptian and Minoan artifacts found in the Mississippi basin.

The Cedarland and Claiborne sites have suffered indiscriminate digging by relic seekers since the 1950s, with large collections held locally. Today the sites have been substantially destroyed and damaged by the construction of a new industrial port on top of the ancient industrial port sites. Entry through the Port Benville Industrial Park is now controlled by a gatehouse and industrial fencing.

Today, huge barges carrying Saturn rockets, enormous tanks of hydrogen and other fuels, are towed past the ancient site for static testing at the NASA Stennis Space Center further up the bayou. It is ironic that the same now remote waterway where much of the copper of the Bronze Age was shipped to Europe is the same waterway where all the U.S. rocket engines are tested before going to space.

Cedarland: Field inspections by the archaeologist Bruseth during bulldozing for the new port revealed debris consisting of bone, stone, and clay artifacts. His book states: "Numerous clay-lined, basin-shaped hearths have been uncovered, but few have been carefully excavated. Raw materials at the site include red jasper, black and white and grey chert, quartz crystal, various quartzites, and Great Lakes copper needles and sheet copper. The lithic materials are rare at Claiborne. Cedarland has 3- and 4-sided drills, while Claiborne possesses only bifacially-formed drills... [Beautiful 3-sided points are a unique feature of the Danish neolithic at this time.] One to 2 meters of deposits indicate intensive utilization...and re-use of hearths, but few have been carefully excavated."

Bruseth continues: "The hearths varied in diameter from 50 to 65 cm [20-26 inches, the size of oxhide ingots], were basin shaped and occurred on a common horizontal plane. The walls consisted of oxidized orange soil. However, the tops were found at variable depths below the surface. This factor is interpreted to be the result of digging in and around the hearths after their initial use. As neither ash nor charcoal was observed within the features, they may instead have served as earth ovens rather than hearths. Under this interpretation, the oxidized soil of the features would represent prepared clay walls that became fired from heating in the oven. Numerous amorphous fired clay lumps surround the hearths and are commonly found throughout much of the midden. The author has examined several examples for evidence of deliberate shape, but in all instances they were found to be amorphous and unintentionally formed. It was initially thought that these might be baked clay objects used in conjunction with the clay-lined hearths. However, it is probable, based on their small size and lack of clear form, that they are fragments from other clay-lined hearths. Extensive digging and reuse of the hearths evidently scattered burned clay wall fragments throughout the midden."

Claiborne: Radiocarbon dates for Claiborne range from 2040 BC to 1150 BC. Bruseth says, "Claiborne appears to have been a well-structured village throughout much of its history. A conical mound is directly east of the site. No clay-lined hearths have been found, but a huge hearth 25m x 3-5m wide was opened by successive bulldozer cuts, a feature which apparently moved upslope by accumulation from use. Smaller hearths of 4m and 2m x 1.5m were also found. Claiborne plummets are made of magnetite and hematite, while plummets at Cedarland are only made of other materials."

Bruseth describes other materials revealed that the "inhabitants of both rings were involved in long-distance exchange, but did so differently, despite being side-by-side. Of special note are the effigy forms, such as locusts, owls, and bivalves, which are not found at Cedarland. There are ceramics...fiber tempered pottery, but none at Cedarland. The two sites are distinctive in layout, feature type, and artifact content, and present a perplexing problem. ...Other sites are known, which most likely represent support camps to these 'specialized activity areas.' These sites flourished well before the earthwork construction at Poverty Point. ...Perhaps the monumental earthworks [at Poverty Point] have caused us to underestimate the importance of pre-earthwork occupation."

Bruseth concludes the report of his excavation by writing that "the two sites were inhabited by two independent groups who lived side by side. Extensive surveys of sites along the Pearl River with similar projectile-point types appear occupied by different groups. We know that trade was crossing ethnic boundaries and probably crossing language boundaries. These are certainly groups of people that operate mostly unto themselves most of the time. There are strangers involved."

Archaeologist Bruseth's midden cross-sections of the Claiborne site show a hearth as long as a football field, 6' deep and 300' long, in a midden twice as long. "Numerous amorphous fired clay lumps surround the hearths and are commonly found...a typical cluster of 86 clay objects. ...The author has examined several examples for evidence of deliberate shape, but in all instances they were found to be amorphous and unintentionally formed. ...A radiocarbon date of 1425 +/- 140 BC...the stratum seems to represent an activity area where perforated varieties of baked clay objects were being fired. This interpretation is based on the nearly total absence of complete baked objects and the abundance of charcoal concentrations. ...Artifact types in the stratum are almost exclusively fragmented baked clay objects. ...The broken clay objects are interpreted to represent specimens that fragmented during the firing process" (Ref.24). The clay fragments were probably hammered off the copper oxhides when they cooled. Bruseth notes that "the predominant artifact categories included lithic debris and cobbles with battered ends." It appears these stone hammers were used to break the clay moulds off

The melting of rough copper (1084°) from the mine pits into standardized 60-pound, one-Talent oxhides would have required a charcoal fire (1000°) and added forced air because a simple wood fire is only 900°C. Multiple pourings into clay moulds in the humidity of the Gulf Coast would have made the workers sweat profusely. Perhaps the sweat and humidity, combined with green firewood floated down the Pearl River to the site, might have been enough to cause the gas voids that characterize the fragile "blister copper" oxhides. Hopefully future excavations on the remaining portion of the Claiborne site and the study of basement collections of clay fragments will confirm the use of clay moulds for the casting of copper ingots.

Timeline Context: Time is a hard concept to comprehend, given the United States has been a nation for only 230 years and our lives are so short. We forget that the United States was a colony for 156 years before that (1620 to 1776). Between the founding of Poverty Point (2400 BC) and Columbus (1492 AD) is a period of almost 4000 years, and Poverty Point at its height (1500 BC) was 3000 years earlier than Columbus at 1492 AD. Our lack of experience with such long time spans and what might have been accomplished in them is one of the major stumbling blocks to our understanding of human accomplishments in prehistory.

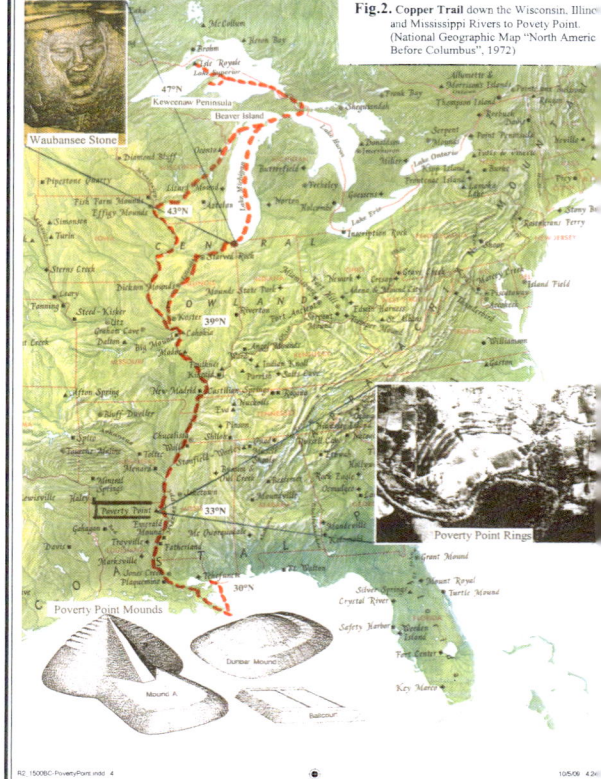

Fig.2. **Copper Trail** down the Wisconsin, Illinois and Mississippi Rivers to Povety Point. (National Geographic Map "North America Before Columbus", 1972)

References:

1. Wakefield, J.S., and R.M. De Jonge, Rocks & Rows, Sailing Routes across the Atlantic and the Copper Trade, 2010, (ISBN 978-0-917054-20-4.) See www.rocksandrows.com

2. Gibson, J.L., The Ancient Mounds of Poverty Point, Place of the Rings, University Press of Florida, 2001 (ISBN 0-8130-2551-6), pgs 3, 82

3. De Jonge, R.M., and Wakefield, J.S, How the Sungod Reached America c.2500 BC, A Guide to Megalithic Sites, 2002 (ISBN 0-917054-19-9). See www.howthesungod.com

4. Kennedy, R.G., Hidden Cities: The Discovery and Loss of Ancient North American Civilization, Penguin Bks, NY 1994 (ISBN 0-14-02.5527-3)

5. Wood, D.J., "Bronze Age Michigan", Ancient American, Vol. 8, Number 51.

6. Drier, R.W., Du Temple, O.J., Prehistoric Copper Mining in the Lake Superior Region, A Collection of Reference Articles, published privately, 1961, and reprinted in 2005

7. Drews, R., The End of the Bronze Age, Changes in Warfare and the Catastrophe c.1200 BC, Princeton University Press, Princeton, N.J., 1993. (ISBN 0-691-04811-8)

8. May, W., and Joseph, F., "Egyptian Mortuary Statuette Found in N. Illinois", Ancient American, Vol.10, No.64

9. Schertz, J., Old Water Levels and Waterways during the Ancient Copper Mining Era, Dept. Of Civil & Environmental Engineering, Madison, Wis, 1999

10. Jewell, R., Ancient Mines of Kitchi-Gummi, Cypriot/Minoan Traders in North America, Jewell Histories, Pa 2004 (ISBN 0-9678413-3-X)

11. Byrd, K., The Poverty Point Culture, Local Manifestations, Subsistence Practices, and Trade Networks, incl: Bruseth, J., "Poverty Point Development as Seen at the Cedarland and Claiborne Sites, Southern Mississippi", Geoscience Publications, Louisiana State University, Baton Rouge, La. 1990 (ISBN 0-938909-50-9)

12. Rydholm, F., Michigan Copper, The Untold Story, A History of Discovery, Winter Cabin Books, Marquette, Mich., 2006 (ISBN 0-9744679-2-8)

13. Byers, D., & Joseph, F., "A Minoan Pendant found in Ohio", Ancient American, Vol 13, #83, July, 2009, p.6.

14. Ford, J.A., and Webb, C.H., "Poverty Point, a late Archaic Site in Louisiana" Vol.46: part 1, Anthropological Papers of the American Museum of Natural History, New York, 1956

15. Williams, M., Archaeological Excavations at the Jackson Landing/Mulatto Bayou, Archaeological Report No. 19, Mississippi Department of Archives and History, Jackson, 1987

New Finds Support Minoan Role in Transatlantic Copper Trade:
Stone Circles, PetroPots, Petroglyphs, and Ship Carvings
by Jay S. Wakefield

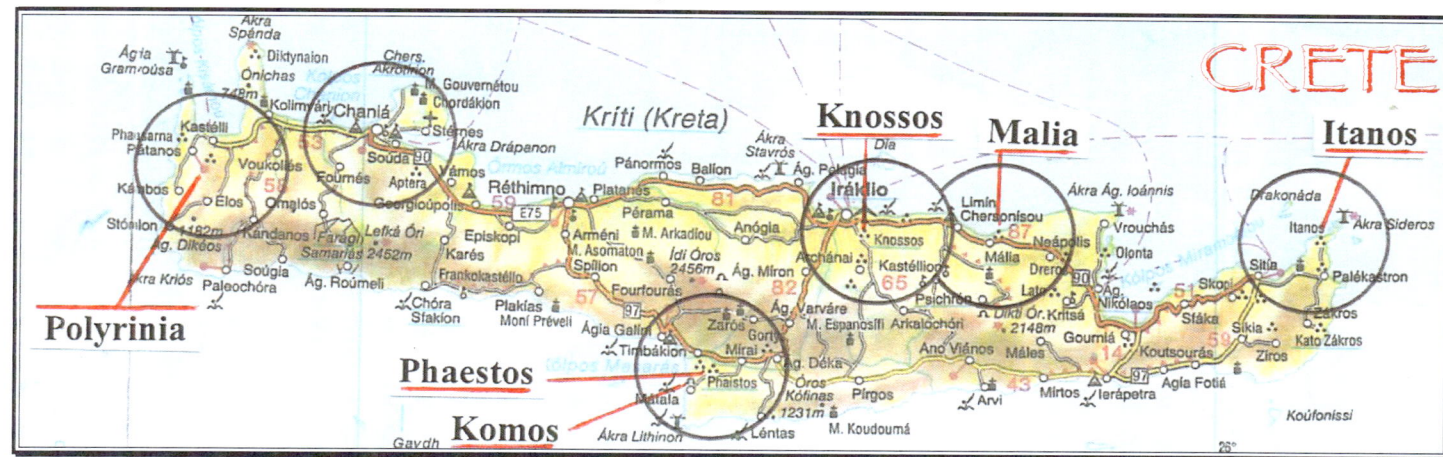

Map locating Minoan sites in the text

Abstract

In this article the reader will find that Minoans were connected to the Western European Bronze Age culture. Also discovered was a ship glyph on a copper ingot and a similar glyph in a foundation stone in the Minoan port city of Malia. A petroglyph similar to one at the Minoan city of Phaestos has been found carved in a stone on Beaver Island in Lake Michigan and on the Newberry Stone of Michigan.

In May 2012, a two-week trip to Crete with my friend Reinoud de Jonge revealed some surprising archaeological artifacts. My first trip to Greece was in 1964, with magical music and dancing on the roof of the interisland ferry and the stoning of a woman in black in Patras, just like in the Zorba movie. This time the magical music and violence were gone. There were new highways, huge hinged solar panel arrays, and wind farms, so the modernization of infrastructure brought by membership in the European Union was very visible. Numerous unfinished concrete buildings were the only sign of the economic troubles we have been hearing about. The people were friendly and helpful. Tourism was light, the tourist season just starting up. The waterfront restaurant tables were filled with locals, their girlfriends dressed in tight black skirts. Waterfront hotels were reasonable and available. The huge flowers planted along the roads were in bloom in pink. It was a good time to travel there.

Stone Circles and Circle Art on Pottery

The second photo (#2) shows a stone circle we were surprised to find at Polyrinia on a hilltop in Western Crete. Nearby was another stone circle. Both circles overlook nearby lands and the Bay of Kissamou to the north. An old Christian church (not in the photo) is near the upper ring. I took the trail to the Acropolis

Photo #2: One of the three stone circles at Polyrinia

Photo #3: One of two petropots at Minoan Aptera

and found a disturbed smaller ring beside the trail near the top. There are many ruins and walls of various ages up there and Roman water cavern reservoirs in several places. In the museum in Kania, formerly a beautiful old church, there are some pots decorated with red concentric circle art, also seen on the Beaker pottery of megalithic Western Europe and the pottery of predynastic Lower Egypt. Various artifacts in the museums of Crete are decorated with linked spiral designs similar to the patterns seen in the ruins on Malta. It was clear that the Neolithic people of Crete were not isolated from the cultures of Western Europe and other Mediterranean cultures.

Petropots

The next photo (#3) shows Reinoud walking inside a disturbed stone circle, most of it obscured by the bushes in the photo. This is an obscure place we found while bushwhacking to find Minoan Aptera behind a roadside sign. Up close in the photo in a stone wall overlooking the circle, you will see one of the two petropots cut into this wall. We found petropots to be a surprising feature of sites in Iberia (Spain and Portugal), as shown in a chapter on them in our book *Rocks & Rows* (Ref. 11).

Photo #4: Lightbox of Tholos Tomb

Lightbox

On the other side of the hill, we found the overgrown tholos tomb, with its forty-foot-long descending stone entranceway. Behind the large stone portal was a very high corbelled chamber with a lightbox (Photo #4) above the entrance like Newgrange in Ireland. (Famous other examples of these tombs are seen in Antequerra, Spain, and Mycenae, Greece.) The signpost called the site "Azoires Stylos." We know that the Bronze Age sailing routes across the Atlantic utilized the Azores Islands on the return route (*How the SunGod Reached America*, Ref. 12). In any case, the Minoans, thought by Cyrus Gordon to have originated from the Delta of Egypt (Refs. 7, 8), were now connected to Western Europe Bronze Age culture by stone circles, petropots, and a lightbox!

Photo #5: Trident petroglyph, Knossos

Tridents: Religious Symbols?

Photo #5 shows one of the 18 Poseidon's trident glyphs at the palace of Knossos on the central north coast of Crete. I photographed 13 tridents at Phaistos (central southern Crete) and others at Malia (north coast of Crete). The tall east wall of the top plaza of Knossos appears to have been reconstructed. My guess is that during the rebuilding in 1900, they noticed trident glyphs on many of the loose stones and faced them all outward, most now too high to reach. As petroglyphs go, many of these are lightly inscribed like the one in the photo. They remind me of contemporary Christian fish graffiti as though they were all carved closely in time during a religious fervor for Poseidon, later Greek god of the sea, during the growth of Minoan Atlantic culture.

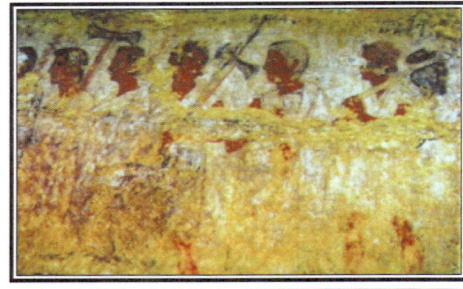

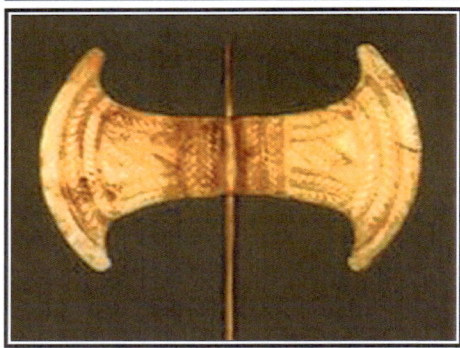

*Photo #6: Top; Etruscan fresco, Stockholm, Sweden
Bottom; Minoan AXE*

Double Axe: Cultural Symbol of Minoa?

The other most frequent petroglyph is the double axe. I found 11 of these glyphs at Knossos and 13 at Phaistos. Some bronze double axes have been found in areas near the Michigan copper mines. Many were found on Crete in clefts and caves, the cleft or womb of the Earth Mother (Ref. 24). So the axes are a union of the male power of the metal axe and the Earth, or a union between Heaven and Earth, male and female, like the Asian circular yin and yang symbol. Photo #6 shows big double axes in a funeral procession in an Etruscan tomb fresco, shown in Stockholm's Mendelhavsmuseet. This is evidence that the Etruscans were probably descendants or refugees from the destroyed Minoan Atlantic Empire (Ref. 25).

Photo #7: Oxhide ingot with Circle Cross

Other Petroglyphs of Crete Including Circle Crosses

Petroglyphs of large stars are frequent, with 14 at Phaistos. Also appearing repetitively are "trees" (five at Knossos, seven at Phaistos), "circle crosses," and the three-branched "birdfoot" of the Earthmother. All of these are characters in Linear A. There are six enigmatic "faces" at Phaistos (Ref. 14). Circle Crosses, such as this one on a copper oxhide ingot from the Ulu Burun shipwreck (Photo #7), are seen at Phaistos (Photo #8). Circle Crosses are widely seen in ancient pictographic writing and appear on Burrows Cave mapstones (Inset, Photo #8), this example associated with the Kaweenaw Peninsula copper mine locations in Michigan.

Photo #8: Circle Cross, Phaistos, inset: Burrows Cave stone

Academicians Write about Copper Voyages and Ingot Finds

Academics are starting to provide some support for the source of the copper ingots being overseas. Professor Minas Tsikritsis of Iraklion, Crete, has computer analyzed a text by Plutarch, which he says is a description of a copper sailing journey from Canada to Carthage. His extensive computer analysis of the Phaistos Disc has led him to think it is about a trip to America (Ref. 21).

Michael Jones' master's thesis (2007) on the oxhide ingots of the Ulu Burun shipwreck (Ref. 23) says "it is extremely significant that the earliest ingots came from Crete, and the earliest securely dated ingot came from an unknown source ... probably outside the eastern Mediterranean. The oxhide shape clearly became an international standard ... they seem to have been transported by sea ... it is implied that scrutiny of the ingot's quality was not considered necessary. They had a well-known standard of purity ... One advantage of working with pure metal is the dramatic reduction in the amount of heat required to melt it: 180 Kcal/Kilogram versus 1400 Kcal/Kgm when starting with a high-grade oxide. The use of oxhide ingots seems closely connected with the Minoan palaces; they're found in the metallurgical installations and storerooms in Crete at Hagia Triadha, Zakros, Tylissos, Gournia, Palaikastro, Mochlos, and Poros-Katsambas, as well as Phaestos and Knossos. A total of 150 ingots have been discovered in terrestrial sites, most frequently on or near the sea. Thirty complete ingots and 39 fragments are known from Minoan Crete. Damaged Linear B tablets from Knossos before 1400 BC show 60 ingots (ingot-shaped ideograms). A Mycenean Linear B tablet from the Palace of Pylos dating to 1200 BC indicates 300-400 copper workers employed by the palace issued 1.5 to 12 kg of metal each. There is a complete absence of information on the organization of mining and smelting activities" (Ref. 23). All this implies massive shipments of copper ingots from somewhere else.

Ingot Molds of Clay

Famed George Bass, American founder of the Underwater Museum in Bodrum, Turkey, "believes that some physical features of the ingots, such as the ridge along the edges, may be due to casting in clay molds. Templates of wood may have been used to form the molds, which would explain their rough surfaces and the lack of mold siblings. Analysis of ingot fragments show a dendritic structure (large grain sizes) in the copper, indicating they cooled slowly in well-insulated molds. Copper oxide structures, which form only in an oxidizing atmosphere, show they were poured in an open mold exposed to air." All these findings support the manufacturing of the ingots over open wood fires at Poverty Point, Cedarland, and Claiborne, as proposed in *Rocks & Rows* (Ref. 11).

Photo #9: Double axe petroglyph at Malia

Photo #10: 3 shrine pots at Malia ship glyph

Ship Carving in Palace of Malia

In the foreground of Photo #9 is a petroglyph of a Minoan double axe on a cracked stone. Two other double axes are carved on nearby stones. In the background is a stone wall showing the foundation stones that remain of the ancient palace of Malia, a northern shore seaport city. The corner shown is near the NW corner of the palace facing the nearby harbor and the sea to the northwest, where the fleet was located and the direction sailed to exit the Mediterranean toward the western copper country. The next photo is a close-up (Photo #10) which shows the wall corner with its three carved libation bowls and a petroglyph on the triangular stone behind the wall. Close-up Photo #11 shows the petroglyph, which is a sailing ship in the harbor with its sail down. It appears that this was a shrine with three offering bowls, or oil lamps, related to obtaining a safe and productive voyage for copper in use prior to the destruction of Malia by the tsunamis and pyroclastic flows of the Thera volcano at Santorini in 1600 BC.

Ship Carving on Ulu Barun Copper Ingot

Photo #12 is a close-up of one end of a copper oxhide ingot found on the Ulu Barun shipwreck off the Lycian coast of Turkey. The photo sent to me by Don Frey, who made hundreds of dives on the wreck, shows a remarkable image of a sailing ship, also with its sail down. The ingot is on display in the Museum of Underwater Archaeology at Bodrum, Turkey, in the castle made from the stones and columns of the Colossus of Halicarhassus. The wreck has been carbon dated to 1300 BC, so the ingot was probably carved with the ship glyph in Crete and held in a palace treasury for hundreds of years. There are no "primary marks" made in the mold on any of the 350 Ulu Burun ingots. When the ingots were made by the melting of Michigan float copper around the time of the great mound building at Poverty Point (1500 BC), marks were not

Photo #11: Ship petroglyph at Malia

Photo #12: Ship carving on Ulu Burun ingot

Photo #13: Cymbal in Iraklion Museum

Photo #14: Corn Cob closeup on Cymbal

left on them by the molds. All of the 187 Ulu Burun ingots with markings (52 types) on them are "secondary marks" made with a chisel.

There are several reasons why it is thought that these markings were carved into the ingots following their arrival by ship. First, there are several examples of the same marks on both tin and copper ingots, which "surely came from different places." Also, broken ingots have the same symbol on both pieces of the original ingot. Many of the incised marks have fishhooks, tridents, a fish, possible quarter rudders, and ships. Half an oxhide with the "rudder" image was recently found in a hoard at Mochlos which was dated to 1500 BC, so the markings were in use at least 200 years before the Ulu Barun shipwreck (Ref. 23). The Ulu Burun ingot with the ship carving is identical to the Malia petroglyph ship, so it appears that the port of entry for this ingot was Malia, where the ingot was carved and perhaps stored prior to sale or re-shipment. For the first time, a copper ingot has been tied to a Minoan port.

Worldwide Corn and Latitude 36

Photos #13 and #14 show a bronze "cymbal" found in the Idean cave where Zeus is reported to have been raised. In the center, Zeus stands on a bull and "tears a lion apart with his hands." Beside him, "kourtes," shown as winged Assyrian demons, clash four cymbals (Ref. 2). It is mounted on the wall of the Archaeological Museum in Iraklion. The close-up shows three of the 36 corn cobs. This is a nice illustration of how corn has spread around the Earth of 360 degrees or 36 Big Moira units of ten degrees each (*How the Sun God*, Ref. 12). This is dated to the "Archaic Period," or "Proto-Geometric Period," (1000-800 BC) after the Minoan Bronze Age but 1500 years before Columbus. The number might also refer to latitude. Crete lies between 35 and 36 degrees north, as does Carthage, Gibraltar, the East Azores, the Grand Canyon, and most of the sites studied in Oklahoma by Gloria Farley. Her friend Alan Gillespie remembers this as the "sacred latitude" for finding sites (Ref. 9).

There is a huge and beautifully finished Minoan "offering stone" at Malia with 34 outside bowls, so 35 or 36 including the center. At Knossos there are 18 ancient wide-entry stairs to the palace, rising from the road leading to the port and the sea. Knossos has 18 huge "West Storage Magazines," which were found with many huge ceramic storage jars still in them. Eighteen is half of 36, half the circumference of the earth. The Holy Latitude of Punt in the west, the home of the Olmec in the Gulf of Campeche and symbolic for the afterlife and the Realm of the Dead, is 18 degrees north. Latitudes were clearly important in the navigation technology of the Minoans and regarded with reverence.

Minoan Phonetic Syllabaries around the World

Cyrus Gordon provides a helpful explanation of Minoan language and writing (Refs. 8, 13). "We know that Crete was polyglot and a system of writing was used on Crete for more than one language." He describes an "international complex of peoples" on the Levant (the eastern shore of the Mediterranean), who had their original origins on the Egyptian delta, including the Hittite, Akkadian, Hurrian, Sumerian, and Hebrew. Minoans developed a NW Semitic dialect "akin to Ugaritic" of the Levantine coast. The Phaistos Disc was a pictographic form of the language called "Cretan Hieroglyphs" (Ref. 8). But what was developed next was a stylized version, a syllabary now called "Linear A" where each sign was a syllable (phonetic). Each sign had the phonetic value of the beginning of the word depicted. There are "logograms" for numerals and commodity pictographs.

There have been only 150 fired (accidentally burned) clay tablets discovered, mostly in southern Crete, many at Phaistos and Komos, its port. They are records of commercial transactions. Most of the writing was probably on papyrus imported from Egypt. Gordon says a number of dialects may have been able to use the Linear A "Aegean Syllabary." The very different languages Minoan and Mycenaean were both able to use the modified Linear B syllabary. Most of the signs and phonetic values are the same in both (Ref. 8).

Mayan "culture bringer" legends say that their white god Kukulcan taught the script he brought with him. Many Mayan symbols are similar to Linear A, and in some cases the phonetic values are known to be similar (Ref. 19). It was also brought to North America, as seen in the Algonquin syllabary (Ref. 18). The Basques, with their language "unrelated to any modern European languages," are also said to be able to read Minoan (Ref. 20). These language remnants show that

Photo #15: Tsunami debris, Itanos 2012

the Minoans were sailing over much of the world for more than a thousand years and suggest answers to long-standing mysteries, such as the origin of Kukulcan (Minoan) and the Basque people (Minoan Atlantic).

Disaster: End of the Minoans

The Thera volcano erupted with a massive explosion in 1600 BC, which caused four successive 90-meter tsunami waves which devastated the Minoan Civilization (PBS Home Video, Ref. 3). The fleets were destroyed, and most of the coastal cities were washed away. This initial volcanic explosion was followed by a collapse of the caldera under the sea, so the sea rushed in and this generated an estimated 48,000 cubic kilometers of superheated dry steam, which slid across the sea at high velocity as seen at Krakatoa. This pyroclastic flow crossed Crete to the southern city of Phaistos in one and a

Photo #16: Phaistos petroglyph (Wakefield)

Photo #17: Beaver Island petroglyph (Bussey)

half minutes, incinerating the city at 600-700 degrees C. The great oak and cedar forests were all ignited at once. All the cities burned, along with perhaps a million people. The second tsunami from the steam explosion was larger, perhaps 100 m tall, and extinguished all shore-side fires, washed all the bodies of people and animals into the sea, and reduced cities, like the city of Malia with its three- and four-story buildings, to its foundation stones (Ref. 22). Today, one can still see mixed pottery, pots, and debris washing into the sea in several places, especially at Itanos (Photo 15).

Those folks remaining were violently conquered by the Mycenaean Greeks from the north. Knossos was one of the few sites rebuilt. Four thousand Linear B tablets have nearly all been found at Knossos and Pylos and Mycenae in Greece. The Greeks used the Minoan B syllabary from 1500 BC to the end of the Bronze Age at 1200 BC. The Greeks later learned to use the Phoenician alphabet as written language further developed. To trace Minoan exploration and shipping routes, we should learn to recognize Linear A or B if we see it.

Scandinavia: Minoan Ships and Mining

Johan Jarnes has found Linear A and wire silver mines near his home in Konsberg near Oslo, Norway. He has obtained help from linguist Kjell Aartun. He has read five Linear A symbols as "pure and soft" along with other symbols including a wine bag and a ship glyph (Ref. 10). Two Scandinavian professors, in their new book *The Rise of Bronze Age Society: Travels, Transmissions, and Transformations* (Ref. 1), claim the Bohuslan ship carvings on the west coast of Sweden are recordings of visits by Mediterranean Bronze Age ships.

Beaver Island: Minoan Petroglyphs at Copper Miner Site

By looking for Minoans, we are starting to find more evidence of them. Compare Photo #16 which I took of a strange petroglyph at Phaistos with Photo #17 of a petroglyph taken by Marie Busey this summer (2013) on Beaver Island, Michigan, where she has found stone circles. The symbol also appears marked near the center on the Minoan Newberry Tablet found in Michigan (Photo #18). We expect further fruitful research on the accomplishments of the Minoans. ∎

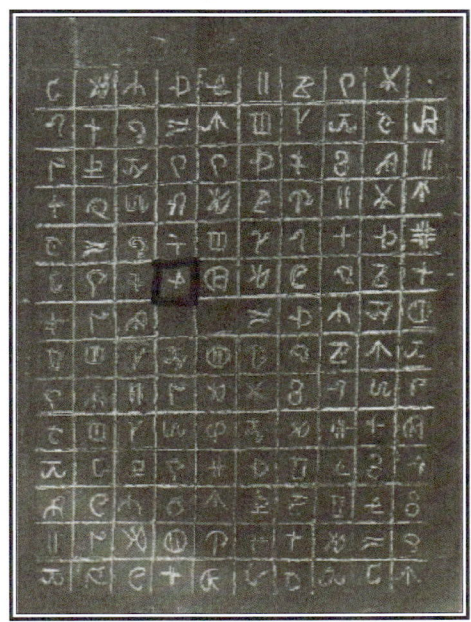

Photo #18: Newberry Tablet, marked around glyph

References:

1. Kristiansen, K. and Larsson, T.B. The Rise of Bronze Age Society: Travels, Transmissions and Transformations, Cambridge University Press, 2005, 4th printing, 2001, ISBN 978-0-521-60466-6.

2. Vasilakis, A. Herakleion Archaeological Museum, Adam Editions, Pergamos S.A., ISBN 960-500-261-2.

3. The Sinking of Atlantis, PBS Home Video, DVD, www.pbs.org, ISBN 0-7936-9450-7.

4. Galanopoulos, A.G., and Bacon, E. Atlantis: The Truth Behind the Legend, Bobbs-Merrill Co., 1969.

5. Muhly, J.D., Copper and Tin. The Distribution of Mineral Resources and the Nature of the Metals Trade in the Bronze Age, Archon Books, 1973, ISBN 0-208-01217-6.

6. Betancourt, P.P. and Ferrence, S.C. Metallurgy: Understanding How, Learning Why. Studies in Honor of James D. Muhly, INSTAP Academic Press, 2011.

7. Gordon, C.H. Riddles in History, Crown Publishers, 1974.

8. Gordon, C.H. Forgotten Scripts, Dorset Press, 1987, ISBN 0-88029-170-2.

9. Farley, G. In Plain Sight, ISAC Press, 1994, ISBN -880820-08-0.

10. Jarnaes, J. For Kongsberg, Kronos Media, 1999, ISBN 82-995158-0-7, http://jarnaes.worldpres.com, araenil@yahoo.com.

11. Wakefield, J.S. and de Jonge, R.M. Rocks & Rows: Sailing Routes across the Atlantic and the Copper Trade, MCS Inc., 2010, ISBN 0-917054-20-2.

12. Wakefield, J.S. and De Jonge, R.M., How the SunGod Reached America, c.2500 BC: A Guide to Megalithic Sites, MCS Inc., 2002. ISBN 0-917054-19-9.

13. Gordon, C.H. The Common Background of Greek and Hebrew Civilizations, Norton Library, 1965, ISBN 0-393000293

14. Wakefield, J.S. The Petroglyphs of Minoan Crete, Shutterfly, 3/10/13.

15. Booysen, R. Thera and the Exodus, O-Books, 2013, ISBN 978-78099-449-9.

16. Forbes, R.J. "Ancient Geology, Quarrying, and Mining." Studies in Ancient Technology, Vol.VII, E.J. Brill, Leiden, 1963.

17. Forbes, R.J. "Copper, Tin, Bronze, Antimony, Arsenic, and Iron." Studies in Ancient Technology, Vol. IX, E.J. Brill, Leiden, 1972.

18. Jewell, R.L. Ancient Mines of Kitchi-Gummi, Jewell Histories, Pa. 2011, ISBN 978-0-9678413-2-8.

19. Honore, P. In Quest of the White God, G.P. Putnam's Sons, New York,1964.

20. Turbach, Dr. Fritz, personal communication, 2012.

21. Tsikritsis, Dr. Minas, personal communication, 2012; http://Canada.greekreporter.com/2012 /04/21; Plutarch: On the Apparent Face on the Orb of the Moon, para: 941-A &942; Disc of Phaistos: A Guide to its Decipherment.

22. Baird, W.S. www.minoatlantis.com.

23. Jones, M.R. "Oxhide Ingots, Copper Production, and the Mediterranean Trade in Copper, and other Metals in the Bronze Age," Master's Thesis, Texas A&M University, 2007, ht tp://nautar ch. tamu. edu/pdf - files/JonesM-MA2007.pdf.

24. Eliade, M. The Forge and the Crucible, the Origins and Structures of Alchemy, U of Chicago Press, Chicago, 1956, ISBN 0-226-20390-5.

25. Bean, G.E. Turkey beyond the Menander, Bath Press,

The Sudurbardi Maze of Iceland
Some Evidence for Minoans along the Upper North Sailing Route to America

by Jay S Wakefield and Valdimar Samuelsson

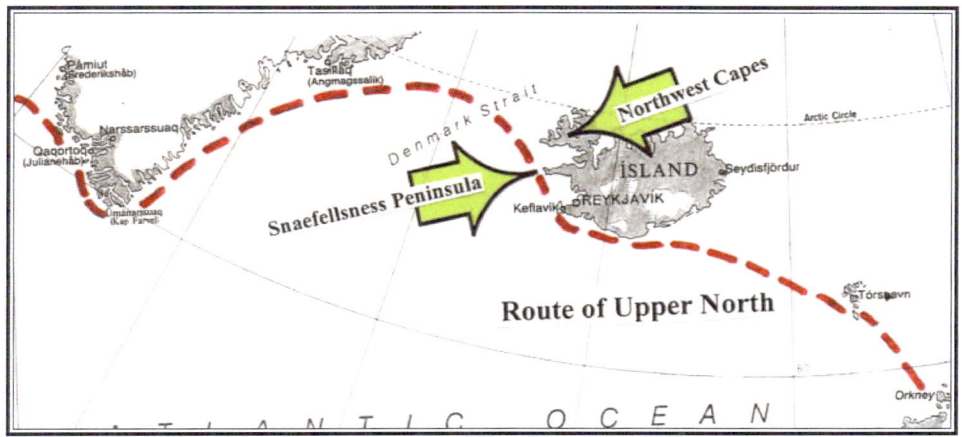

MAP ONE: Route of the Upper North

MAP TWO: Snaefellsness Peninsula, south of Northwest Capes

PHOTO ONE: Southern side of southermost Northwest Cape

PHOTO TWO: Snaefellsjokull volcano

It is widely agreed that the sailing Route of the Upper North passed around southern Iceland, then by the Northwest Capes, and across the sea to Greenland. This sailing route (map 1) is believed to have been used in the Bronze Age shipment of Michigan Copper to Europe (2400 BC to 1200 BC). In How the SunGod Reached America, and Rocks & Rows, we have shown that early megalithic explorers thought the best route west would be at the Arctic Circle at 67°. This is the reciprocal to 23°, the most important number in celestial navigation, and a holy number in the Sunreligion of the Megalithic Culture. The Arctic Circle runs above Iceland, so implies a sailing route from the Northwest Capes of Iceland to Cape Holm, north of Tasilaq, Greenland.

During a cruise my wife and took around Iceland in July, 2011, we saw that the Northwest Capes of Iceland have huge and dramatic sea cliffs. The highest cliffs (photo 1) are along the south side of the southernmost cape. The Capes are mostly bare rock and talus slopes. The vegetation is so low, that they say that if you get lost in Iceland, all you need to do is stand up. Using binoculars from our ship, no megalithic ruins could be seen, such as standing stones or stone

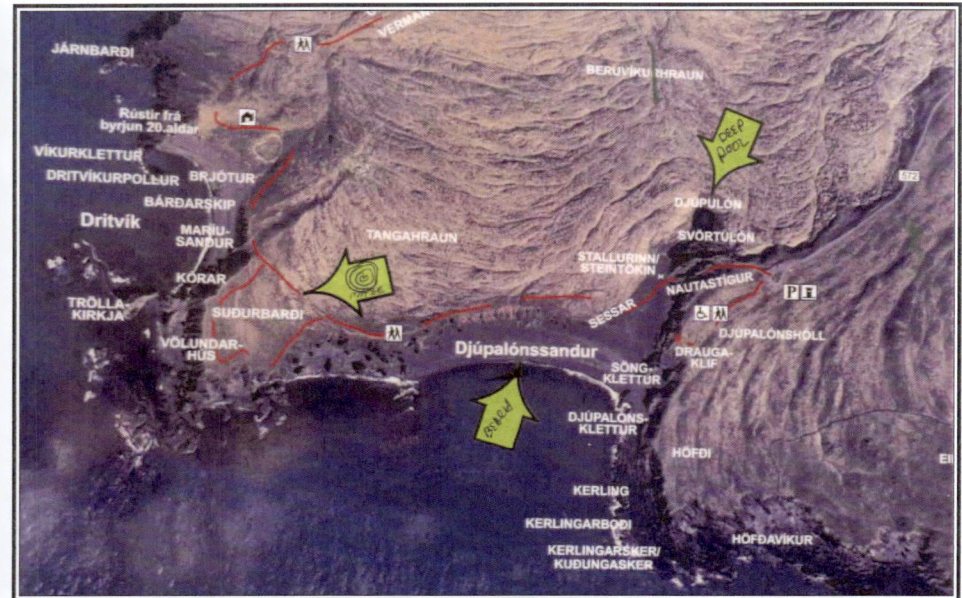

PHOTO THREE: Aerial photos of Djupalonssandur (deep pool sandy beach)

circles. The museum director at Isafjordur, the largest town in the Capes, had never heard of any standing stones, dolmen, or stone circles in the Northwest Capes. Deep in the fjords there are some small towns, but they are off the ringroad around Iceland, so are very isolated.

Maps 1 and 2 shows the tip of the Snaefellsness Peninsula, south of the Northwest Capes. Crowning the end of the peninsula is the icecapped Snaefellsjokull volcano (photo 2). This mountain, at 4700 feet, was once considered the highest volcano in Iceland, and it is the largest one that stands alone. It is covered by one of the most beautiful glaciers in Iceland. Although there are no reports of eruptions during the human history of Iceland, it is not yet considered extinct. The first ascent was made in 1754, but it is best known for Jules Verne's novel Journey to the Center of the Earth, in which the characters descend through the glacier to the bowels of the earth. It is clearly a big ice cream cone mountain, when seen from Reykjavik, 40 NM away. It is said this mountain can be seen from 60 or 70 miles away at sea.

On Map 2 you will note a beach with wind protection from the northwest, which is in a circle (arrow) I have drawn on the map. Photo 3 is an aerial photo of the beach area. The black sand beach, called Djupalonssandur ("deep pool sandy beach") is shown in photo 4, with the spring fed deep ponds "djupulon" behind the beach seen in photo 5. This place could have provided invaluable water and shelter to mariners during the summer sailing season. The path to the fishing bay "Dritvik", crosses a rocky promontory called "Sudurbardi", "where remains of a maze called the "Sudurbardi Maze" can be seen (photo 6, from signboard for visitors).

Photo 7 shows the maze, Valdimar, and the volcano Snaefellsjokull in late summer. The photo was taken by Valdimar's wife, Gudrun Bjornsdottir.

Valdimar says that "in 1900 a man named Pall Melsted said that the ring was "hardly see-able". A photo of it in that condition was published in 1985. Now it has been cleared of overgrowth. The age of the structure is unknown. Valdimar notes that the word for "maze" in Icelandic (close to Viking) "volundarhus", was not found in the Icelandic written language until the 14th century. The area near the maze has ruined old stone walls, dug-out flat areas, and mysterious structures poking through the turf 150m from the maze (photo 8). This place appears to have been used as a campsite over a long period of time. It would have been a good observation post for weather or boats to the west.

When Arthur Evans unearthed the palace complex of Knossos in 1900, he named the previously unknown civilization "Minoans", after its mythical king Minos. (The Bronze Age people of Crete are called "keftiu" (kftiw) in Egyptian documents.) They are understood to have controlled the Mediterranean trade in copper ingots. It is now known that the enormous explosion of Thera volcano in 1600 BC caused four 30m tsunamis in succession that destroyed the Minoan fleets and northern and eastern coastal cities. During the subsequent 400 years of the Bronze Age (before the cosmic impacts of 1200 BC), what was left of the Minoans were conquered, and is known as the Mycenean Greek period in Crete, then writing with "Linear B".

Mazes are a well-known cultural characteristic of the Minoan civilization during the Bronze Age (3000 BC to 1200 BC). Some are round, some square, some

have different numbers of "rings". The Sudurbardi ring has nine. Photo 9, called the Cretan Maze, is the oldest known maze design. It is a "unicursal maze", a single path without choices or branches, also called the "7-circuit maze". You can google color photos of a similar one at Ulmekarr, Grabbestad, on the Bohuslan coast of Sweden, where so many petroglyphs of ships are found, thought to have been visiting from the Mediterranean (Ref.17). Others are found in coastal areas, up to the Cola Peninsula, on the arctic Sea. This maze is reported to mirror the motion of the planet mercury over a long period of time. It is thought that the labyrinths were connected with funeral rites in antiquity, representing the soul's return to Mother Earth, wandering through the realm of the dead. This maze symbol was found on a clay tablet in the ruins of Pylos, where a palace fire baked the tablet, preserving it. This maze has also turned up on an Etruscan wine jug in Italy, a petroglyph in Spain (google labyrinth, Meis, Galicia), petroglyphs by the tin mines near Tintagel, Cornwall (google "Rock Valley carvings"), as graffiti in an Egyptian quarry, and on a roof tile of the Parthenon. It appears on one side of a silver coin of Knossos of Crete of the Greek period (photo 9).

Another unusual feature of this coast that could have helped direct mariners to this beach below Snaefellsjokull, are volcanic pillars, called the "Londrangar". These remnants of an old cinder cone stand 75 meters and 61 meters above the beach, to the east (see other circle on Map 1). These are the hardened "plugs" that once were the core of a volcanic sidecone. The huge standing stones erected along the coast of Brittany during the Bronze Age are not this large. The photo 2 shows these "Londrangar" in a telephoto, at 1AM on July 14, in the midnight sun from the ship, with an inset taken by telephoto. Clearly, these would also have been important landmarks for mariners in sailing boats, especially when the mountain was shrouded in clouds. Ancient sailing directions might have said: "round the south shores of the Island, make your last camp at the foot of the white mountain, near the two standing stones".

Valdimar showed us the "Hvalseyri Stone" on the end of a small peninsula near Reykjavik, today on a private golfcourse (photo 10). The stone is considered covered with Viking runes. However, the Poseidon Trident (closeup, photo 11), is not a rune, but looks like a Minoan religious glyph. I photographed dozens of these petroglyphs in Crete in May (2012), and show one here (from Knossos) for comparison, also a common Minoan coin with the glyph (photo 12). A small tail crook and midcross can be seen on the trident, which are not present on the Minoan glyphs. This may mean the glyph is a "signature mark"- an "I was here" graffiti. Scholars in Denmark had sent an order in 1818 to all pastors/priests in Iceland to record all ancient findings. Photo 13 shows a page of glyphs recorded (ref. 14) from a cave 8 km east and 1 km inland from the maze. Since a friend of Valdimar's knows of the

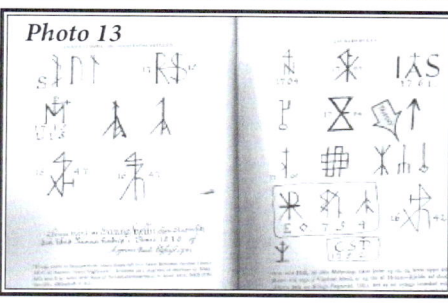

cave, but not the marks, they may not be able to be seen today. Many are dated. Note the uncrossed trident in one of them. There is no mention in his notes of the overgrown maze in his district by the priest. So it appears there has been a tradition of inscribing "Signature Marks", which are mostly non-runic symbols. The trident glyphs may have been new creations, but probably are symbols passed down from earlier cultures.

A line drawing map of the North Atlantic Ocean, drawn by an Icelandic bishop in 1606 (Map 3, Ref.15) shows Snaefellsjokull Volcano prominently labeled "A", and the sailing route from there to Greenland is indicated with a dotted line. This map is confirmation that the encampment site at Djupalonssandur beach was on the sailing Route of the Upper North. Other evidence of Minoan sailing in northern European waters has been reported. In 1995, Hans Peter Duerr, a Director of the Max Planck Institute, described in a German magazine GEO, finding shards of 13-14th C Minoan tripod cooking pots in a peat layer dated to 1200 BC beneath the medieval coastal city of Rungholt. This town had sunk below the waves in a North Sea storm tide

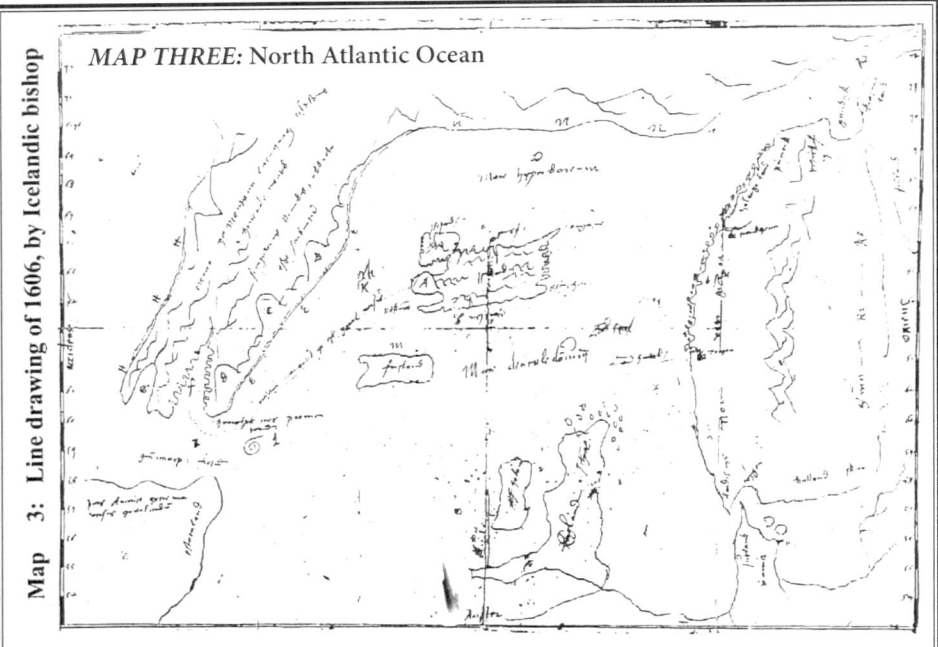

MAP THREE: North Atlantic Ocean

Map 3: Line drawing of 1606, by Icelandic bishop

In 1606, Gudbrandur Thorláksson, an Icelandic bishop, made this line drawing of the North Atlantic in which Greenland is represented in the shape of a dragon with a fierce, toothy mouth. Modern maps show that this is not at all the shape of Greenland, but it is exactly what it looks like from the southern fjords, which cut jagged gashes miles deep into the high mountains. (Royal Library, Copenhagen)

in 1362. He also reported a seal with a Linear A inscription on it. Duerr thinks they were obtaining tin from Cornwall. Gavin Menzies thinks they were also behind the ancient amber trade (Ref. 16). Johan Jarnaes of Kongsberg, (near Oslo) Norway, has documented the mining of wire silver near his home, and has found associated petroglyphs of a ship, a wine bag, and Linear A, the symbols used to record the Minoan spoken language prior to 1600 BC (Ref..18).

The Lonely Planet Guidebook to Iceland says that when the first Norse people arrived at Litla Dimun island in the Faroe islands, they discovered a strain of dark brown Soay Sheep from St.Kilda, west of the Hebrides. While these may have been brought by earlier Irish monks, the Guide notes that when St.Brendan passed through, he described a place he called the "Island of Sheep". So these sheep marked the passage of even earlier people. A number of books report that when the Vikings reached the Southwest Capes of Greenland, they found stone ruins. Kayakers have reported seeing megalithic constructions, but when asked, they preferred to keep them secret. So Bronze Age use of the Upper North Route may be recorded for the Faroes, but is not yet documented in Greenland.

In the bigger picture, other evidence comes to bear on the issue. From nine handaxe sites in southwest Crete, archaeologists now believe that early paleolithic hominids crossed the Mediterranean Sea to Crete at least 130,000 years ago. American finds include the Michigan Newberry Tablet, the Minoan "Prince of Lillies" pendant recently found by Dan Byers in mud dredged from the Ohio River, The Minoan "Snake Goddess" bronze found in Maine by Michael Rose, and the California Maze described by Frank Joseph. Recently American tobacco beetles have been found beneath lava in the house of a merchant in the Minoan town of Akrotiri. Archaeologists should no longer claim that it was impossible for Minoans to have been sailing Iceland waters and camping on Iceland shores four thousand years ago. The Snaefellsjokull Volcano would have been a clear landmark on Minoan voyages to obtain the copper that enriched their civilization. ∎

References:

1. Landscapes of the West Fjords, CD, Multimedia Interactive CD-ROM,

2. "http://www.momogumi.info"

3. "http://www.amazingart.com"
4. "http://www.gwydir.demon.co.uk/jo/maze/cretan/index.com"

5. Iceland, Greenland, & the Faroe Islands, Lonely Planet Publications, 2001, ISBN 0- 86442 686 0

6. Traeger, Burkhard, Das Krettsche Labyrinth (German)

7. Labyrinthos, Caerdroia ¬Journal of Mazes and Labyrinths, "http://www.labyrinthos.net" www.labyrinthos.net

8. Joseph, F., & May, W. "Minoans in America", Ancient American, Vol.7, Issue 43

9. Joseph, F., "California's Maze Stone", Ancient American Vol. 3, Issue 24

10. Wakefield, J.S., Rocks&Rows, Sailing Routes across the Atlantic and the Copper Trade, "http://www.rocksandrows.com" (ISBN 0-917054-20-2)

11. Jewell, R., Ancient Mines of Kitchi-Gummi, Cypriot/Minoan Traders in North America, Jewell Histories, Pa 2004 (ISBN 0-9678413-3-X)

12. Rydholm, C.F., Michigan Copper, The Untold Story, a History of Rediscovery, Winter Cabin Books, Marquette, 2006 (ISBN 9744679-2-8)

13. Sinking Atlantis, PBS Home Video (the Thera tsunamis that drowned the Minoans 1600 BC)

14. Frasogur um Fornaldar leifar 1817-1823, published by Stofnun Arna Magnussonar, 1983, Reykjavik, Iceland (Icelandic)

15. Kurlansky, M., Cod, Penguin Books, 1997, ISBN 0-14-02.7501-0, pg.23

16. Menzies, G., The Lost Empire of Atlantis, Harper Collins, 2011, ISBN 0-06-204949-6, pg. 97.

17. Kristiansen, K., Larsson, T., The Rise of Bronze Age Society, Cambridge Press, 2005, ISBN 978-0-521-60466-6

18. Johan Jarnaes, "http://www.history" www.history-forum.org/threads/172-Prehistoric-connections-Crete-Norway

Megalithic Colony in Greenland

Jay Stuart Wakefield

That Megalithic structures which were probably three thousand years old were found there by the Vikings when they arrived is supported by early research work. The deep hospitable fjords west of Cape Farvel, southern Greenland, were on the "Route of the Upper North", the stepping-stone route to America from Orkney to the Faroes, Iceland, Greenland, and Baffin Island. This route was recorded in many Bronze Age petroglyphs and monuments, especially Stonehenge (www.HowtheSungod).

Photo 1

The classic 1946 book The Ruins of Great Ireland in New England was written by William B. Goodwin. When he wrote the book, he was owner of American Stonehenge, in Salem, New Hampshire. The book contains some interesting photos and discussion about the Gardar (also "Garda") site in Greenland. **Photo 1**, from this book, shows some of the Gardar ruins.

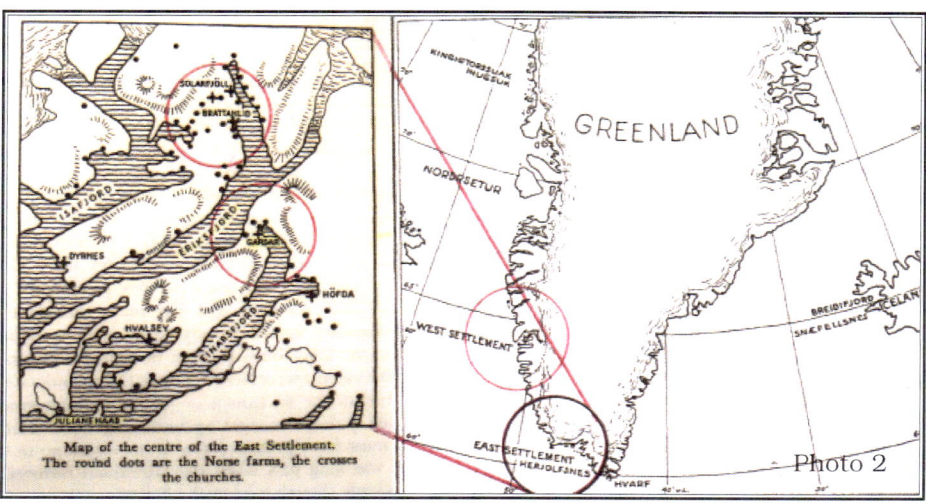

Photo 2 shows the location of Gardar on an isthmus between the fjords of Erik and Einar in the "Eastern Settlement" in southern Greenland. Eric the Red, founder of the Viking colonies in Greenland, made his farm at nearby Brattahlid (about 900 AD), now located just across Ericsfjord from the Narsarsuaq airport. (This big airport was where PBY Flying Boats were based, assigned to escort allied convoys in WWII.) From reading Viking Eddas and Sagas, Goodwin says that Eric gave Garda to his daughter Freydis in a marriage settlement. The name given to her homestead was Garda, which means "stronghold" or "enclosures" in Old Norse. She lived there 28 years until she went to Vineland in 1013, and returned to her homestead the following year. "She was as rough and headstrong as her father ... for her lack of humanity and the totally uncalled-for murders during the voyage, her posterity is not mentioned in the Sagas, being under the ban of Lief's curse". At Garda was held the first Law Moot, the Greenland Thing, or governing council. In 1125 was Garda became the seat of the first Christian Bishopric of Greenland, and the stone ruins became part of the Bishop of Garda's personal farmstead.

I have found that **Photo 1** was reproduced from an important 1936 scientific book entitled Viking Settlers in Greenland, by Poul Norlund, Ph.D, Keeper of Medieval Antiquities at the Danish National Museum, and member of the Commission for Scientific Research in Greenland. The Norlund **Photo 3** (the same picture), has below it a line drawing of the large stone structures, and a scale. On the Internet I found two views of these stones as they appear today, **Photo 4** from the front, and **Photo 5**, the rear view. From the archaeology work in the foreground of **Photo 5**, and the general rock litter, one can see that many stones have been used, re-used, and "cleaned up", over the years. This can be seen at another stone construction, Photo 6, from the Norlund book, and a current Internet photo of the same stones, **Photo 7**.

Norlund reports that when they arrived, the Viking colonists found "traces of earlier habitations" – "men's dwellings, and the remains of boats and stone implements" (pg.27). He reports that Scraelings (Eskimos) were not seen for over 100 years, except far up the Greenland coast. They apparently ocasionally fought the strong and aggressive Vikings, and with the climate deterioration of the 14th Century (300 years later) they eradicated the starving Vikings in the Western Settlement (in 1360), and burned the last Norsemen in their church (in 1500). In any case, the Eskimos are not known for ever building with megalithic stones.

The south side of an outhouse, perhaps the tithe barn, at Gardar bishop's farm, built of gigantic blocks. (P. 37, No. 5.)

Photo 4

Norlund says that "the Greenland fjord-chiefs with Erik at their head had scarcely set up their temples when Christianity swept over them. One who resisted most was Erik the Red ... he viewed the missionary with displeasure ... his wife, caught up with the stream of the new teachings, declined to share his bed as long as he remained heathen, at which he was most indignant" (pg.30). There were 280 large farms, with

Photo 5

twelve parish churches in the Eastern (southern) Settlement, and four in the Western (northern) Settlement, an estimated 4,000 inhabitants. "The Episcopal Seat was fixed upon Gardar. ... Very imposing colossal blocks of stone had been employed in the walls, both of the churches, and some of the outhouses (outbuildings), stones weighing anything from four to five and even up to ten tons. ... This building method can scarcely have been learned by Norsemen in Iceland, and it is not likely that they had (learned) it from Norway, where cyclopean masonry was not in use. On the other hand, it is typical of the Scottish Isles ... maybe there was cultural influence from that quarter".

The author notes that Norlund was partially correct - the megalithic ruins did come from lands inhabited by people who built cyclopean monuments. Norlund did not grasp that the cyclopean buillders did not influence the Vikings, but were thousands of years earlier. Nevertheless, the observations of these early researchers are helpful today. ∎

Inner door to the large cow byre of the bishop's farm, converted by the Eskimos into a storehouse. It is built of enormous blocks of stone. The lintel stone weighs about 5 tons.

America's Stonehenge: A Map of the Atlantic Ocean in Stones
by J. S. Wakefield and R. M. de Jonge

America's Stonehenge, formerly called "Mystery Hill," is the most important megalithic complex in North America, with radiocarbon dating of c.2200 BC. It is situated near a tributary of the Merrimack River in North Salem, New Hampshire, at 43°N. During the time of use of the site, there was a salt water harbor around the site. At the center of the complex, called the "Main Site", there are about 15 stone chambers, some connected to each other. Stones weighing up to 50 tons were used in the structures. As shown in the attached site groundplans, the "Main Site" is surrounded by a complex layout of stone walls, with many large standing stones, called "menhirs," incorporated in the walls. These features are typical of the megalithic culture, well known along the west coast of Europe, dating from 6000 to 1500 BC. It is not surprising to find megalithic remains at the latitude of America's Stonehenge, which is similar to the latitude and climate of the homelands in Europe.

The complex has been studied by the University of Pennsylvania for its astronomical alignments, and their results are shown on the "Astronomical Alignment Map." We found that the site is also geographic. The angles of the menhirs and walls encode latitudes that were important in the sailing technology of the time. These angles enable us to reconstruct the geographic design of the site. It is shown to be a map, in stones, of the North Atlantic Ocean, with the important lands and islands identified by correct latitudes. So we think this site was used to teach oceanic geography and sailing routes, a place to get accurate predictions for the safe timing of sailing voyages, and a place to make the sacrifices that would ensure safe passages.

The walls just below (south) of the Main Site represent the southern part of the North Atlantic Ocean. The lower south wall is the equator, the outer west wall is the stylized coast of Central America. The outer east wall is labeled the Cape Verde Islands, off the African coast. The central north-south wall divides the ocean into the well-known eastern half and the less-known western half. This wall coincides with the Mid-Atlantic Ridge of today, which was suspected in that time because of islands which had been discovered in mid-ocean, and is drawn in many megalithic inscriptions.

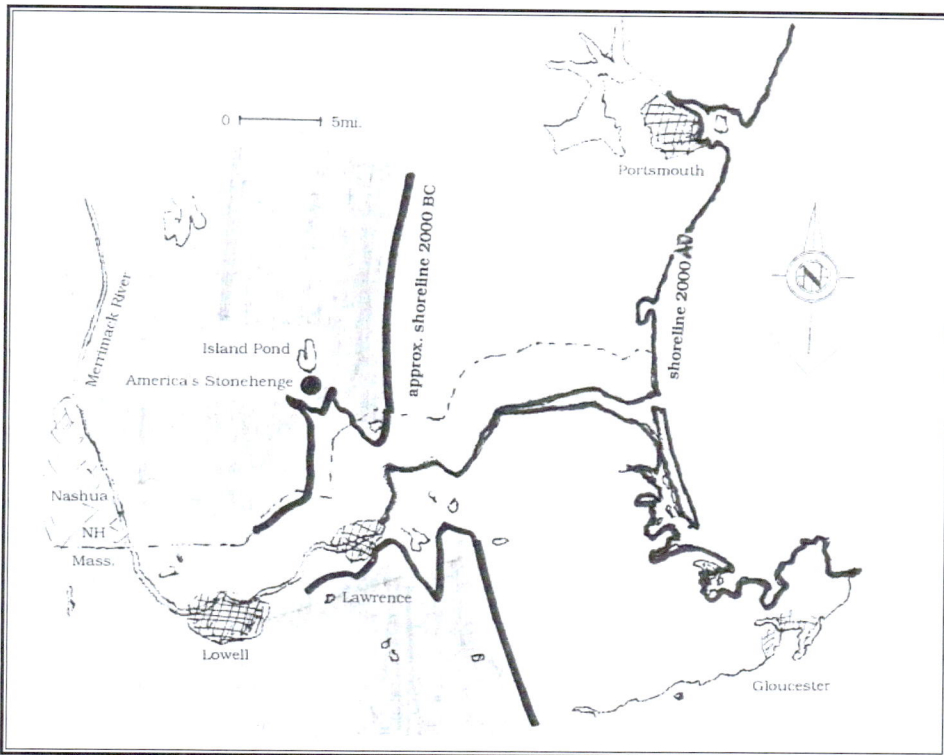

America's Stonehenge (Mystery Hill) is 20 miles from the Ocean today and six miles from the Merrimack River. The finding of beaches far inland in Maine has shown that this coast has risen (100m since 10,500 BC) because the weight of the mile-high ice sheet has melted off (Ref.27). Careful estimates by Paine show that at 2000 BC the sea level was 40m higher than today (Ref.3), so there were salt water harbors around Mystery Hill. A partial reason for the eventual decline of America's Stonehenge as time went by may have been its increasing distance from the seashore.

Due north of the Main Site is a single wall, angling off to the upper right. This represents the east coast of Greenland (shaded area). The Loughcrew petroglyphs, the latitudes encoded in Stonehenge, England, and the huge circle monuments in the Orkneys show that this coast had been discovered by c.3300 BC, a thousand years before the construction of this wall in New Hampshire. The east point of this wall is Cape Brewster at 70°N, and the lower end of the wall is Cape Farvel, the south point of Greenland, at 60°N (formerly represented by two stone towers, now destroyed). So the Main Site is a walk-in model of the Atlantic Ocean from the Equator to Greenland in the north.

Due east of the Main Site is a single wall, representing the Mediterranean Sea. Close to the end there is a short branch to the south, which is the river Nile, then the center of the greatest civilization on Earth. Not shown on these maps is a large stone that you will find at the south end of this wall, representing the capital city of Egypt, the center of the Sun religion. The Mediterranean wall is in two parts, because in early times this sea was considered to have two parts, east and west of Sicily, both portions too big to see shores when sailing in the middle of them. Outside the Mediterranean, they would sail westward to Madeira, then to the Canary Islands, and then to the Cape Verde Islands. This is the start of the "Southern Crossing" (marked in black dots) with the tradewinds to the NE coast of South America, through the opening in the southern inner wall, where the well is located.

It had taken thousands of years for the megalithic people of Europe to learn the tradewind sailing routes across the Atlantic so that roundtrip voyages could be accomplished. The Southern Crossing runs via the Canaries and the Cape Verde Islands to South America. Because of the tradewind and its current, it is impossible to sail this route in the reverse direction. For that reason, like the Spanish Galleons later, they had to sail north, following the Gulfstream along the east coast of North America, the western walls of the Main Site. Note the route starts in wall openings on either side of Cuba, and then between Florida and Bimini. To the north, there is an enlarged representation of important Cape Hatteras. Similarly, Cape Cod shows a large stone representing the Peaked Hill Bars, dangerous to sailors rounding the Cape. Nova Scotia is shown prominently, and Newfoundland, the easternmost point on the continent, has a stone chamber.

From these features we can see what is going on at America's Stonehenge. The Main Site was built to help people who wanted to return easterly across the North Atlantic. Note the topographic lines: the site terrain slopes downward from the center of the Main Site toward the east. From high on the site, people could survey the layout of the walls to see how this could be accomplished.

The oldest way back was via the Upper North Crossing, along the east coast of Greenland. Many megalighic petroglyphs show this route. However, this is a long and difficult route in cold latitudes. For that reason, Iceland, though important in that route and common in petroglyphs, is only indicated in this site by a small group of stones, if at all. The eastern part of the Main Site deals only with the return route via the Azores, the archipelago discovered in the middle of the ocean in c.3600 BC, and celebrated in the Tumulus of Gavrinis in Brittany, now on the coast of France. The Azores had been considered the western home of the Sun god for a thousand years and had been depicted in a great many megalithic inscriptions and monuments. At the right, below the Ceremonial Center, is the "Pattee Area" where cover stones have been removed. Two chambers here correspond with Madeira, and others corresponded with the Canary Islands. These islands were familiar to sailors and, sited at comfortable latitudes, provided rest stops on the return voyages as well as the outgoing voyages.

The Ceremonial Center is by far the most important feature of the the Main Site. It consists of 3 chambers, the West Chamber, the Oracle Chamber, and the Cavern, corresponding with the three island groups of the Azores. In the middle is the Processional Walkway, symbolizing the north-

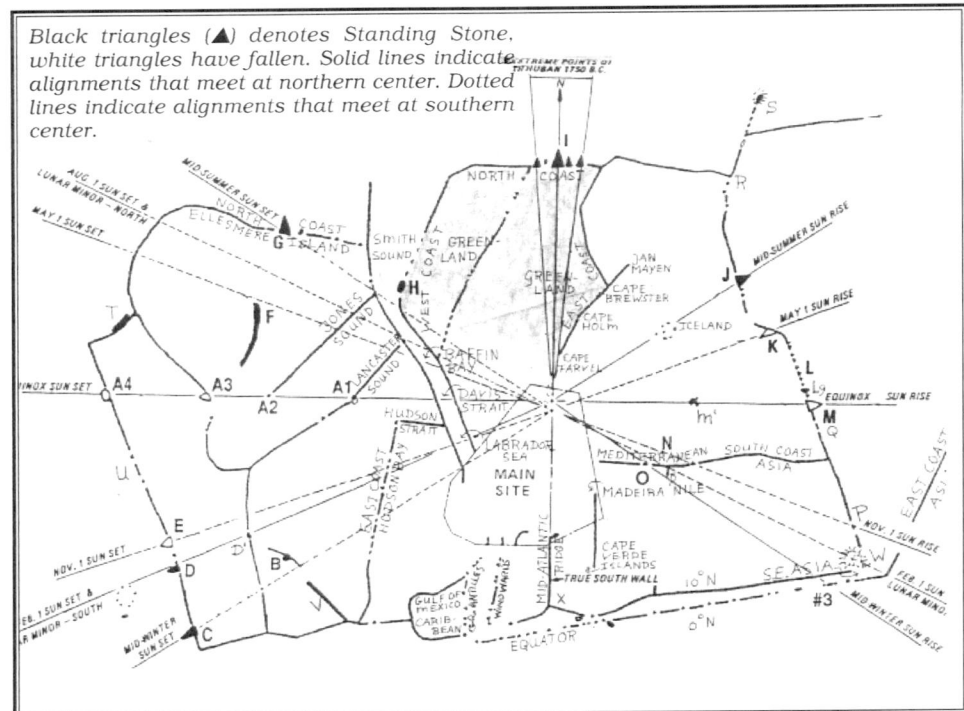

Black triangles (▲) denotes Standing Stone, white triangles have fallen. Solid lines indicate alignments that meet at northern center. Dotted lines indicate alignments that meet at southern center.

Ground plan of America's Stonehenge, showing menhirs and stone walls (ref. 1) with geograpic meanings. The straight lines are astronomical alignments. All alignments are positioned around 2200 BC.

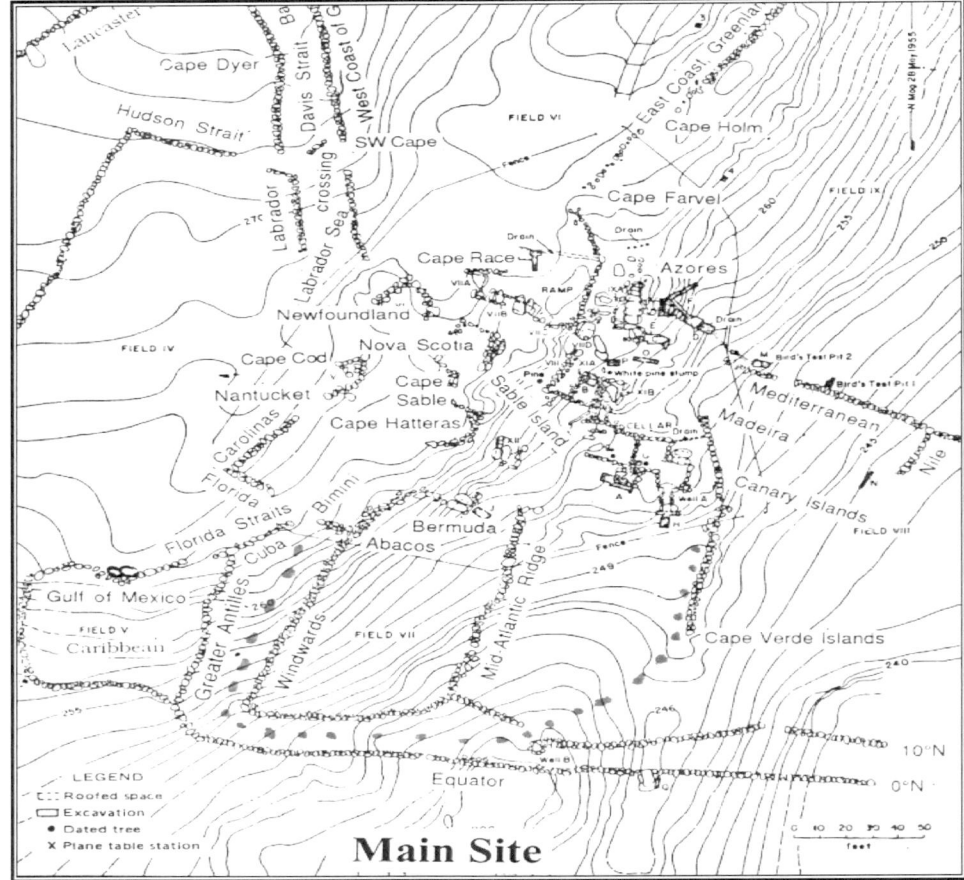

Topographic Map of Mystery Hill, North Salem, New Hampshire: (After North Salem, N.H., Site Excavations Report, 1955, by G.S. Vescelius.) Walls and chambers of the Main Site with geographic meanings added by authors. The route of the Southern Crossing is the "black dotted line."

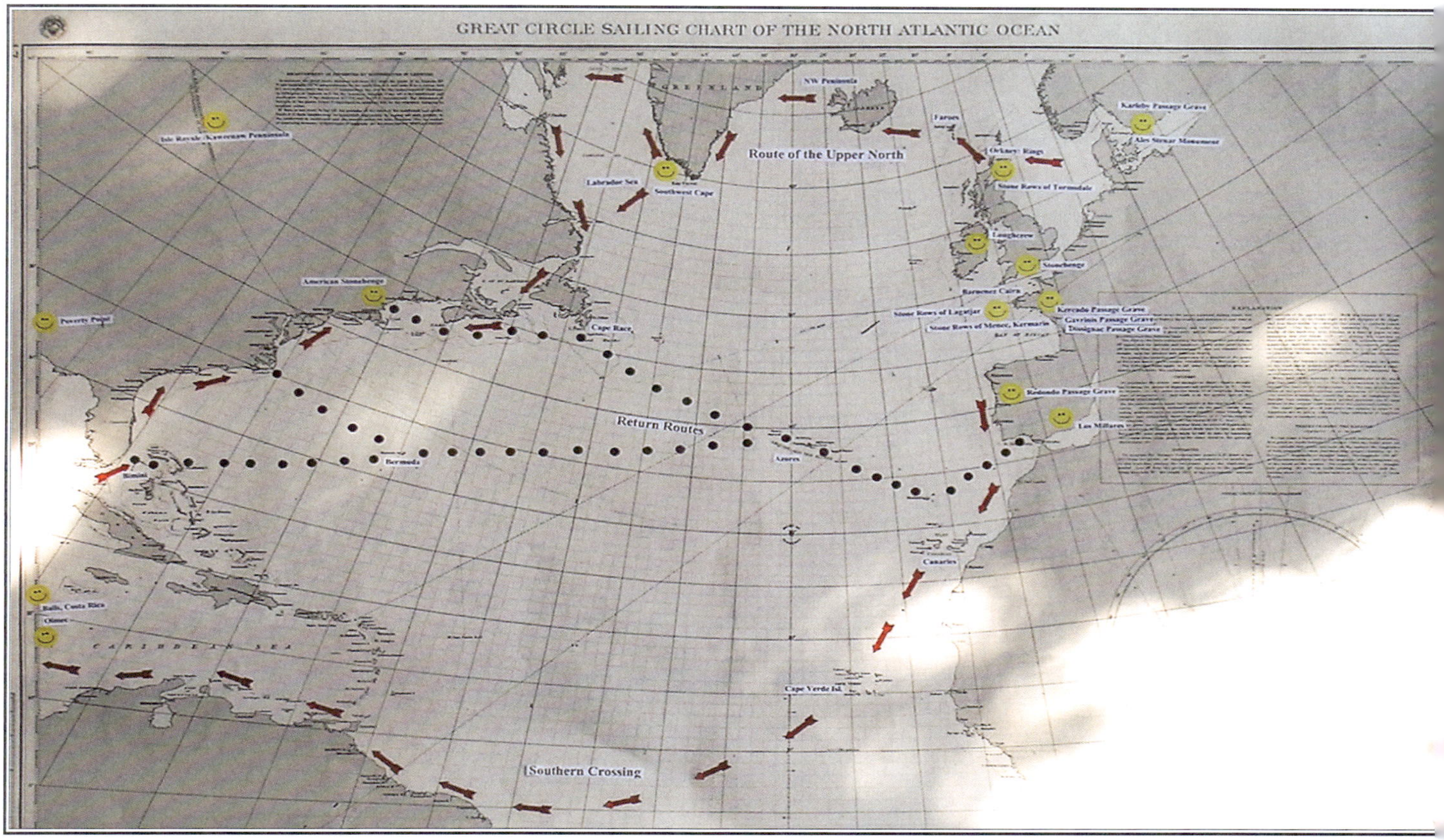

Chart of megalithic sailing routes on the Atlantic Ocean, with the "Southern Crossing" (arrows pointing from east to west), the "Route of the Upper North" (arrows pointing from west to east), and the Return Route (black dots) via the Azores, and the later routes via Bermuda.

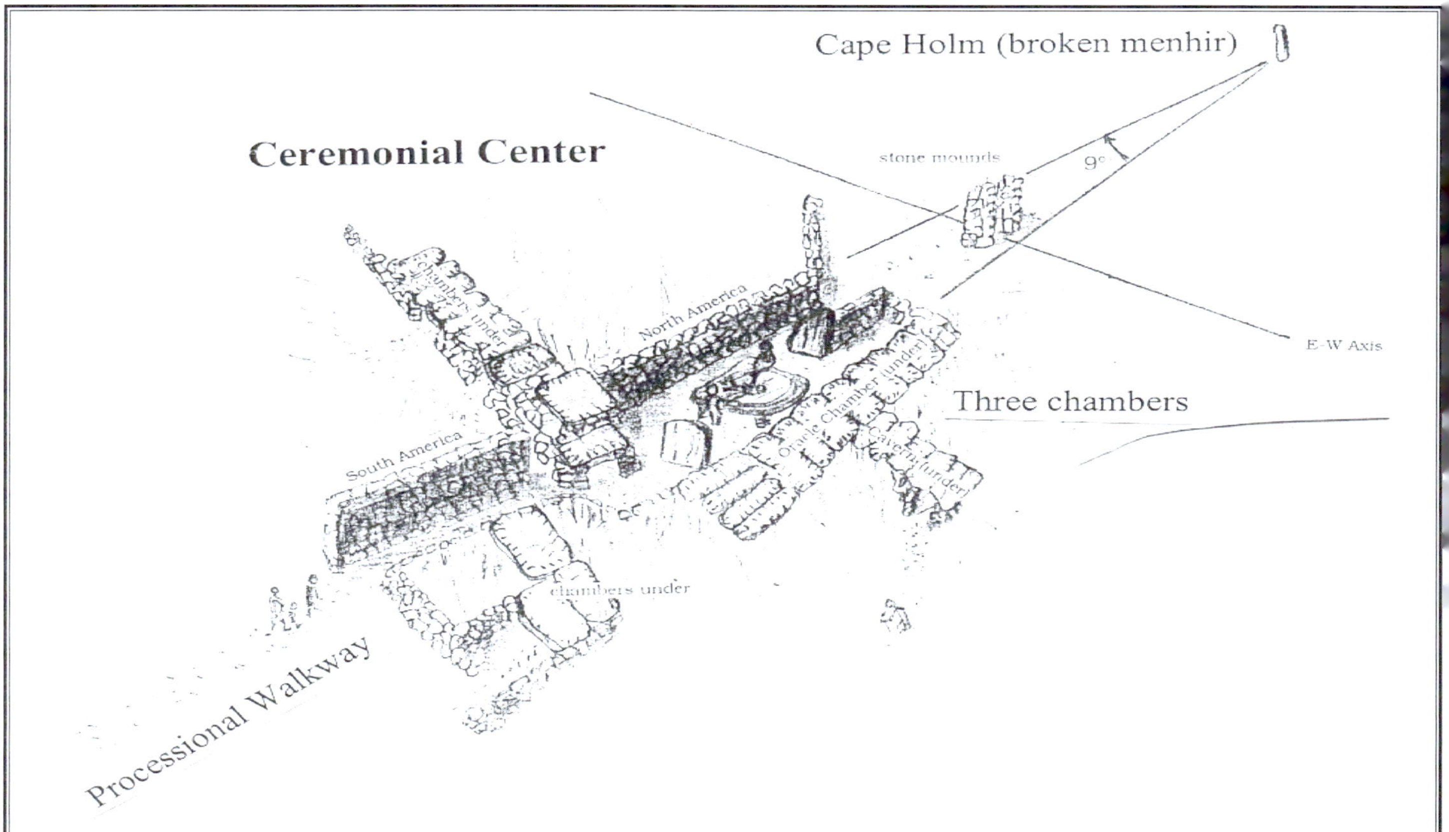

View of the Ceremonial Center from the southeast, with chamber plans and geographic meanings. The side walls focus on the now fallen menhir at the uper right (also in photo 12), representing Cape Holm.Greenland (at 67degrees North). Some of the cover stones, lower on the sketch, have been removed by quarrying.

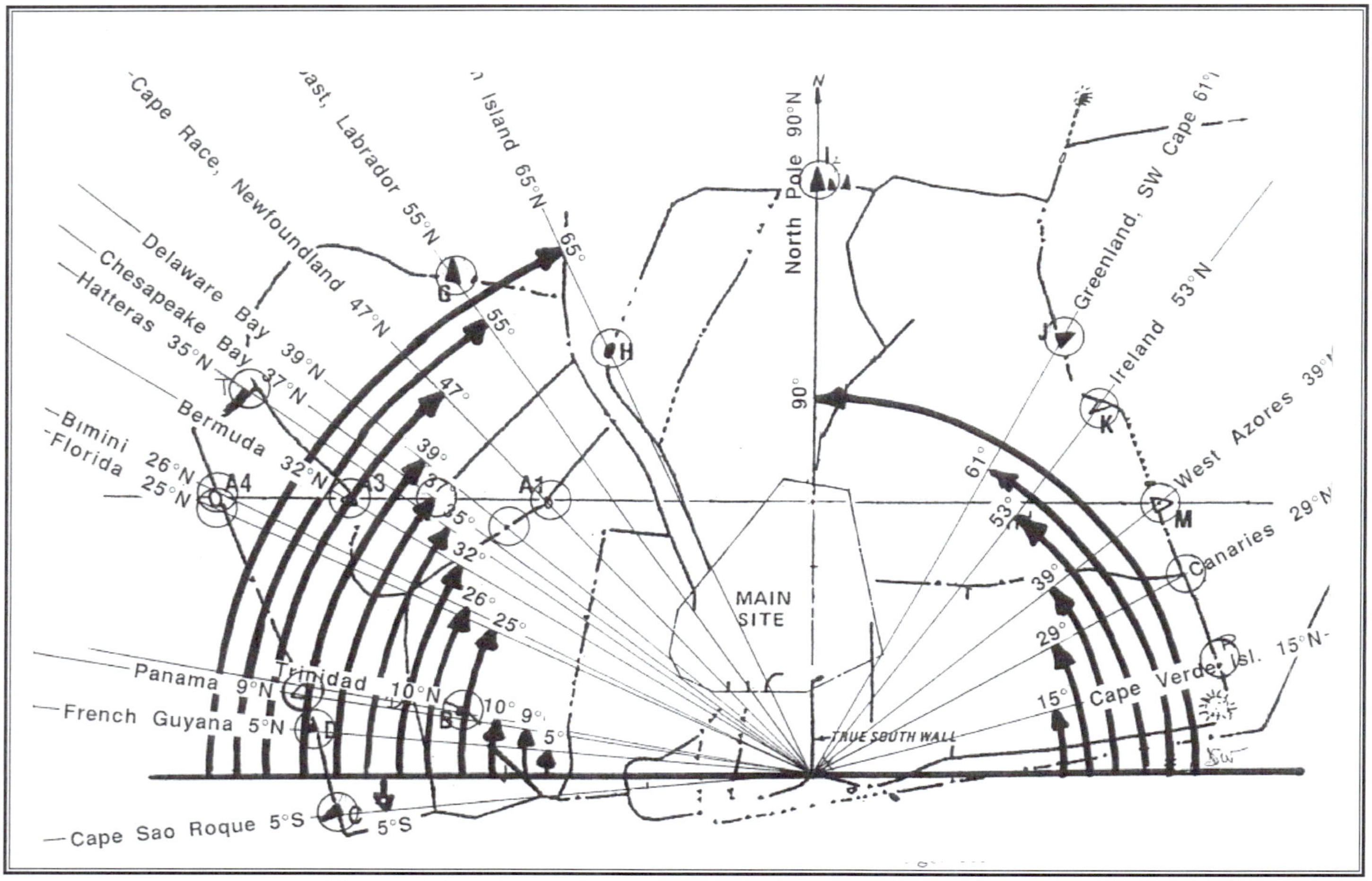

Ground plan of America's Stonehenge. Primary meaning of the Menhirs, seen from viewing point X.

ern and southern portions of the Ocean. These walkways, being water, were never covered with roof stones. The surface of the Sacrificial Table is a microcosm of the North Atlantic Ocean. Similar tables have been found in Portugal. The Speaking Tube is under the Sacrificial Table. Speaking through the Tube resonates and deepens voice sound coming from the small Oracle Chamber below. Probably, powerful personages hidden below the Table taught the latitudes and sailing directions encoded in the monument and enriched themselves by selling safe passages.

From an exhausting technical analysis of the site, which took us six months, we learned that point X at the southern end of the North-South wall was the most important viewing point of the site. All the outlying menhirs, so many of which hold astronomic importance, are identified correctly by latitude, so are shown to have straightforward geographic meanings. Note that the complementary angle of menhir M, the most important stone in America's Stonehenge, makes an angle of 90°-39°= 51°, which is the latitude of Stonehenge in England. This is not just coincidence. According to carbon dating at both sites, both the large stone Saracen Circle (Phase III of Stonehenge) and the eastern half of America's Stonehenge (Phase I of American Stonehenge) were under construction at the same time, 2300 BC. It is clear the two monuments are related to one major event, the discovery of the Americas.

An interesting incident occurred that convinced us of the accuracy of our understanding of the site. Note the slight bend in the Greenland coastline on the Astronomical Alignment map, labeled "Cape Holm." Knowing this is where Greenland was first discovered in c.3300 BC on the Arctic Circle at 67°N from the Northwest Cape of Iceland, there should have been a big stone at this spot, but there was not. However, when we walked the site with its owner Bob Stone the following summer, we found a 14-foot menhir lying there in four pieces, which had been once standing as the tallest menhir at American Stonehenge. When we asked Bob why it had been left off the site ground plan, he replied, "Because it was broken!" Our theory of decipherment of megalithic sites had just been proven correct by its ability to predict the design of an unseen site.

This article is taken from a 30 page report "A Nautical Center for Crossing the Ocean," the tenth of 14 chapters in *How the Sungod Reached America c.2500 BC*, by Wakefield and de Jonge in 2002. Unfortunately, Bob Stone, owner of the site, passed away recently. He spent much of his life researching his site and was helpful to us. We are sorry he is gone. ∎

The authors beside the Sacrificial Table in the Processional Walkway (Fig. 5), seen from the southwest.

Ocean Pendants

(Portugal, Spain, Ireland, and America, c. 2200 BC)
J.S. Wakefield, jayswakefield@yahoo.com

Summary
In quite a few of the megalithic "anta" or "burial dolmen" of Iberia, small inscribed tablets (pendants) of slate have been found. At least one or two of them are now to be seen in most of the archaeological museums in the cities and towns of Portugal and Spain. Photos of them will be seen in tourist brochures and in archaeological publications. They are each unique, but they have common characteristics. Considered anthropomorphic artistic objects, or idols, we show they also have geographic meaning. They represent a crossing of the ocean to the backside of the world, on the other side of the ocean. The pendant accompanied the wearer in burial, to show he/she had made the risky journey to Paradise, and deserved a special place in the Realm of the Dead. Related examples show that they were admired and copied in Denmark, Ireland, Greece, and America during the Bronze Age.

Introduction
The Megalithic Culture of Western Europe lasted from 5500 BC to 1200 BC. The characteristic and well-known features of that culture are visible in the big stone monuments: the passage graves, the dolmens, the stone circles, and the stone rows. The megalithic petroglyphs are less known, but these are very interesting. Several thousands of carvings are identified, and most of these have geographic meanings. They often represent coastlines, islands, and sailing routes. Usually, they are carved rather roughly on the inside faces of upright passage stones or the endstones of passage graves.

An unusual type of petroglyph are to be seen upon the small engraved tablets found in southwest Iberia. Since they have been excavated from passage graves, it is certain they belong to the Megalithic Culture. **Figures 1 and 2** show many of them, reduced from their original sizes of about 3 1/2 inches long (10cm). They are almost always about 3/8 of an inch thick, and usually are slate rock. Their surfaces are polished, and usually have inscriptions only on one side. Usually they have a hole or two at the somewhat tapered top, so are considered pendants. In the limited existing literature, they are referred to as religious idols. They are all unique, but they all share design characteristics. Understanding these objects will contribute to a better understanding of this Culture and its achievements.

It is not known how many of these engraved pendants have been found, but probably there are hundreds. More than 60 are reported to have been found in one passage grave, the Anta 1 do Olival de Pega. We have collected images of quite a few, from archaeologic literature, museum exhibits, and tourist brochures. Many tablets have come from the area surrounding the town of Evora, 100 km east of Lisbon, Portugal. They have also been excavated in the tombs of the tholos type at Los Millares, in southeastern Spain, and numerous other places in SW Iberia.

Background
The Megalithic Culture, starting from 5,500 BC, two thousand years before the first Pharoahs of Egypt, had developed a SunGod religion, and had developed a tradition of building SunGod temples, facing the western ocean, along the coasts of western Europe. Today, these churches are called "passage graves", because burials have been found in them, like Winchester Cathedral, which also has a long passage, and graves in it. Their political and spiritual leaders told them the Earth was a big sphere, just like the sun and the moon. They said that all the known land was surrounded by a sea, and that in the west there was the Empire of the Dead, at the other side of the earth. (As the Sunreligion was later developed in Egypt, Osiris was called the God of this Underworld in the West.)

Impressed by this story, people tried to cross the Ocean. At first, they tried to cross at the Tropic of Cancer, at 23°N, in honor of the Sungod, who came north to that latitude each year, before turning south for the winter. Unfortunately, at that latitude, the courageous sailors died, because that is the latitude of the windless doldrums of the "horse latitudes", where later sailing ship crews ate their horses. Some early "Culture Bringers", as they are called in myth in the Americas, apparently made it across, but they were not heard from again, because the tradewind patterns of the Ocean were not yet understood. Some boats were blown north out of the Doldrums, and, following the birds, discovered the Azores Islands. This discovery was commemorated at the highly decorated megalithic tomb of Gavrinis in c.3600 BC, as explained in our book, How the SunGod Reached America. Interestingly, most of the pendants have been found in Iberia around the latitude of 38°N, the latitude of the Azores Islands, considered the western home of the Sun God after their discovery.

The Pendants: distances
All the Ocean Pendant tablets of Iberia show inscribed crosshatching, triangles, or zigzag lines. The up-down waveform is a universal symbol for water, and is, in fact, the Egyptian hieroglyph for water. Thus many of the pendants are clearly depicting water. We have learned, from our study of megalithic petroglyphs, that the up/down lines are used to encode units of distance that are based upon the distance on the surface of the Earth of one degree of latitude. In Egypt, this unit of one degree was called the moira. The moira was applied to curving distances in the west, as well as the latitudes easily measured with a simple "Jacob's Staff", when moving to the north or south. Today, we use Nautical Miles for navigation, where 1° = 60NM, so one Egyptian moira = 60NM.

Fig.1 Ocean Pendants from various sites and sources in Iberia (see References).

The number of zig-zags on many of the pendants is four, so we see they often show the correct size of the Ocean, which is four multiples of ten degrees, or 40°, or 2400 NM, from Iberia to Newfoundland, or Africa to South America. Usually there are 3 or 4 Big Moira (30 or 40 degrees of latitude) or 6 or 8 half Big Moira, which are correct distances at the different latitudes sailed after the discovery of America. Like the pendants, the Ocean is tapered. The triangles are a stylized modification of the wave/distance motif, and the cross-hatchings are the distance lines laid out, like a fishnet on a globe. After confirmation of land in the west, following Asian explorations in c.2600 BC, and the confirmation of a return route via the known Azores in c.2500 BC, sailors were again venturing to the west, via previously explored southern and northern routes.

The Pendants: religion

Most of the tablets have a centered hole, for hanging the objects around the neck of the hero who went on the dangerous journey across the Ocean. Sometimes there are two holes, like "eyes". The "vee" at the upper portion represents the huge land of Greenland, which had been revered as the westernmost known land in the world for about 600 years. The latitude line at the bottom of the vee is the 60°N latitude line of Cape Farvel, and usually the lines below are inscribed to represent Big Moiras, or 10° intervals.

Clearly these pendants are meant to be anthropomorphic representations of the SunGod, also the God of the Ocean. These plaques certify that the person wearing it, and buried with it, had taken the Journey across the western Ocean to Paradise. These plaques, accompanying the dead, help the dead return to Paradise in the West. The cocaine later put into in Egyptian mummies, which had been obtained in the West, also meant to help the deceased reach Paradise. The obtaining of these drugs was one of the purposes of later voyages to the west, as first suggested by Perry. In some of the pendants, the eyeholes have little rays around them, like little suns, so these may be SunGod images. Note that one pendant has a stick figure (**Figure 3**) of the Sun God crossing the Ocean. The eyed plaques are seen by some reasearchers as the Owl Goddess, a representation of the Mother Goddess, in the very old tradition. Such simultaneous meanings of symbols is not unusual, such as the Christian cross, which is both a symbol of torture and resurrection.

The Pendants: dating

From the petroglyphs it can be concluded that these people knew the size of the North Atlantic Ocean, so we call these artifacts "Ocean Pendants". From this information their approximate date can be determined. By study of other megalithic sites, we learned that America was discovered via the Bering Sea, c.2600 BC. A century later the continents were reached via the Southern Crossing of the Atlantic, between Africa and South America, for the first time (c.2500 BC). In the same century, America was also reached via the Upper North, via Greenland. Since all these pendants relate to the effort of this culture to explore the backside of the Earth, they are all roughly contemporary with one another.

The Pendant of Crato

Figure 3 (left) shows a photo we took, showing a very simple design, so we think it is one of the older pendants. It was excavated by Portuguese archaeologist A. Isidoro in one of the dolmen in the District of Crato, near the town of Portalegre (Alto Alentejo). This town is located 80km NNE of Evora, close to the Spannish border. The site is at the latitude of 39°N, the latitude of the West Azores, also at 39°N. Now it is on display in the Museum of Mendes Correa in Porto, in the north of Portugal.

The petroglyph represents the North Atlantic Ocean, in a stylized way. It is divided into 4 strips of triangles, each corresponding to 15° of latitude. One after the other, the horizontal lines are situated at 0°N (the equator on the bottom edge), 15°N (the latitude of the southern Cape Verde Islands), 30°N (the Nile Delta and the northern Canaries), 45°N (halfway to the pole), and 60°N (the south point of Greenland, no horizontal line). The hole itself perhaps represents Cape Farvel, the south tip of Greenland, known since c.3200 BC.

The upright, shaded triangles each have a width of one Big Moira = 1 0°= 600 NM. The lowest strip has 4 triangles, corresponding to a total width of 4 Moiras = 40°= 2,400 NM. Above it are 4 Y2 triangles, then 5, corresponding to a width of 5 Moira= 50° = 3,000 NM. At the top, there is a strip of 4 triangles again. More important than the exact distances, is the fact that the order of magnitude is correct, and that the middle of the Ocean is its broadest part. Note that each triangle has a width of 1 Moira, and a height of 1.5 Moira, so the shapes are proportionate to distance. The shading of the triangles are done with horizontal. lines, showing they are stylized small latitude lines. In total there are 18 triangles, possibly encoding the destination in the west, the Civilization developing in the Gulf of Campeche at 18°N. At the top of the pendant are 4 horizontal lines on the left, 5 on the right. Possibly these encode the discovery of America by the 5th pharaoh of Egypt, of the 4th Dynasty c.2580-2562 BC.

The Pendant of Pavia

Figure 4 shows an Ocean tablet found in the Dolmen of Pavia, 40 km north of Evora, again at 39°N, the latitude of the West Azores. This big dolmen which was later reused as a chapel was declared as a National Monument in 1910. The unusual design of the pendant shows the edges engraved all around, showing that at this time, they thought there was land all around the Ocean. The double edge is probably covering coastal Ocean over a width of 1 Big Moira, or 10° (=600 NM). At the bottom, three triangles have the same width, so they show the length of the Southern Crossing from Africa to South America, with the wind and current, to be 3 Big Moira, or 30° (= 1,800 NM), which is correct. From this length, it appears they probably landed at the latitude of about 5°N, French Guyana. The fishbone shading on the right edge points upwards, as they are living in the Northern Hemisphere, oriented to the north, but the left side points downward, because the goal of the crossing, Central America, is in the southwest. The edging across the top suggests they know the Upper North route around Cape Farvel, Greenland. The dotted lines, if not accidental scratches, would be showing the holy 23 °N line of the Tropic of Cancer, crossed by a line going south, showing that one must sail southwest from Iberia to accomplish the Southern Crossing, with its length and southern location given by the three triangles.

Fig.2 More Ocean Pendants, with below, ceremonial crooks, inscribed with Ocean motifs.

The Pendant of Sesimbra

Figure 3 (right) also shows a pendant excavated in one of the dolmen near the town of Sesimbra, 30 km south of Lisbon, at the latitude of the West Azores, at 39°N. It is on display in the Archaeological Museum of Setubal. This petroglyph has the same Southern Crossing shown at the bottom, with 3 triangles showing a distance of 3 Big Moira (1,800 NM). The edge at the right is the coast of the Old World, with 6.5 or 7 triangles encoding the Arctic Circle at the holy 67°N (reciprocal of 23°N), where they had to go for the Northern Crossing via Greenland. The thicker edge on the left side is the coast of the New World, with the larger triangles showing that is the important location of he Realm of the Dead (America). The 5.5 or 6 triangles in the west correspond with Cape Chidley, Labrador, at 60°N, entry to the American Coast in the west. In the middle of the Ocean is a stick-figure person, the SunGod or Ocean God, which consists of 3 triangles, also representing the 3 island groups of the Azores. The large triangles point with great emphasis upward, to this figure. The thick horizontal line the figure stands on is the Return Route, with the wind and the current, from Newfoundland via the Azores back to the Old World. The tablet can mean that "our king, who crosses the Ocean is highly esteemed", or it could be more religious, "the SunGod who crosses the waters and visits the Realm of the Dead, and returns to the Land of the Living, is our highest God".

Pendants in Porto

Figure 5 shows an Ocean Pendant that is c.12-14 cm long, in a collection of 15 of similar appearance, but somewhat varying designs. They are in the Museu de Historica Natural, Faculdade de Ciencias do Porto, Portugal, formerly a collection at the University of Porto, now in the Natural History Museum in Porto. You can see how thin these slate tablets are, by looking at the holes at the top. Many of the stones are hung by nylon fishing line in the exhibit, as it appears they are designed to be worn hanging from the neck. Note the "vee" at the top of the stone, a representation of the big land that had been discovered in the north, Greenland, which comes to a point at Cape Farvel at 60°N. The discovery of Greenland had been commemorated by the construction of the huge megalithic Ring complex of Brodgar, Stenness, and Bookan in the Orkney Islands. The three shaded "vee" patterns illustrate that the seas extend in open water for an extended distance on both sides of Cape Farvel, which indeed it does. The checkerboard squares on this pendant are a symbolic chart of the ocean, eleven squares across, and five rows down.

The pendant beside it, also from the Natural History Museum, has an anthropomorphic appearance, now also representing the Ocean God or Sun-God. In the center is a threesided triangle, representing the highly revered three island groups of the Azores. These Islands had been revered as the western home of the Sungod, from their discovery c.3,600 BC until the discovery of further land to the west, as explained in our book, How the SunGod Reached America, c.2500 BC, A Guide to Megalithic Sites. The megalithic tomb most decorated with petroglyphs in the world is the Tumulus of Gavrinis, in the Gulf of Morbihan, Brittany, built in celebration and commemoration of the discovery of the Azores Islands, in the middle of the Ocean.

Many interesting details can be found while looking at the many pendants. For example, the last small reduced pendant image on **Fig.2** does not calibrate distances, but has a hole incised on the right side of the stone (the edge of it is broken away), and a hole on the left. These might represent either Iberia on the right, and Newfoundland on the left, or the Mediterranean Sea on the right, and the Carribbean, on the left, like the carved circles on both sides of the Ocean in the huge petroglyph of Serrazes, also found in mid-Portugal.

Related finds

Figure 2 shows some "crooks" below the pendants. All the images have been greatly reduced, to show the interesting variety, and yet common characteristics of these objects. It is thought the large stone crooks had a ceremonial function. Note they all are inscribed with similar ocean motifs, so the ocean voyages were important. The **top left object of Figure 6** is also a Bronze Age pendant, reported by Archaeology Magazine, found in a 2008 dig in the megaron (Palace area) of Mycenae, in Greece. It bears a petroglyph of a sundisc, so is a SunGod pendant of a probable similar date to these others, perhaps inspired by them. The bronze axehead found in Denmark, in the **center of Fig.6**, from the book by Cooke, carries the same Ocean motifs. It also surely has a similar Bronze Age date, both by the axehead design, and the motifs. On the **right of Fig.6** is a pendant found in County Antrim, Ireland, from the referenced book by Dames. It appears to be an Ocean Pendant, carrying an ogham inscription, which needs decipherment. Like the Iberic pendants, it has continental edges, a 60°N latitude line through Cape Farvel, at the top, and the important 40°N latitude line which runs through the West Azores. This appears to be an Irish version, inspired by the Iberic pendants.

On Figure 6, is an American Indian "gorget", or pendant, reproduced with the photo legend. It has a guaranteed authenticity, as it is reproduced from the 1917 work of the great American archaeologist, Warren K. Moorehead. His book does not discuss the object, except in this note, where he calls the mesh triangles "wigwams". The "snowshoe" is probably a land mass, depending upon the orientation of the stone, and the experience of the sailor. Note the classical appearance of the two fluted columns, each with stone capitals. To the right are photos of fluted columns found off Bimini (Ref.37). Clearly, a classical building is being remembered somewhere. The rectangular pendant shape with two holes in this position is common among American Indian gorgets. Somehow, this one, found in New Jersey, has been inscribed with Old World motifs, so this can be called an American Ocean Pendant, confirming the Trans-Atlantic crossings in the Bronze Age.

Conclusion

It was a daring thing to cross the Ocean to the west. We think early attempts at the Tropic of Cancer probably cost many lives, in the course of learning the tradewind patterns of the Atlantic Ocean. These slate pendants honor persons who successfully made trips across the Atlantic Ocean, some of the greatest sailing adventurers in prehistory.

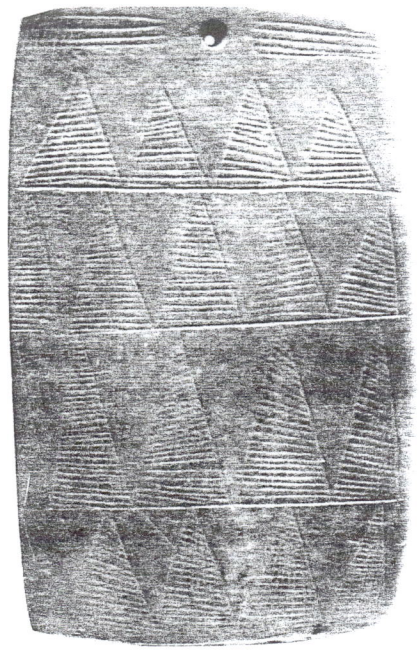 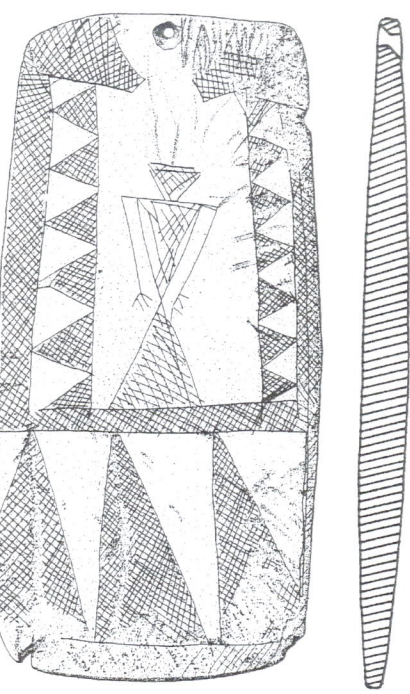

Fig.3 Left: **Ocean Pendant of Crato**, c.12-14 em long, found near the town of Portalegre (Alto Alentejo) in South Portugal at the latitude of the West Azores, 39°N. by archaeologist August Isidoro (Museum of Mendes Correa, Porto, photo by the authors, May, 2007). Right: **Pendant of Sesimbra**, an Ocean Pendant from Sepultura 9 e Sepultura 11 (Ossario), Estampa 19, in Setubal Arqueologica, VolIX-X. (see References)

  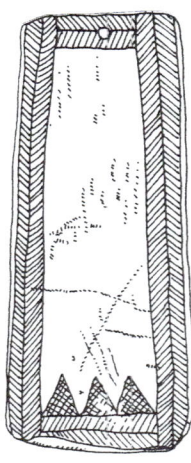

Fig.4 Ocean Pendant, from Anta Capela de S. Dionisio ou Anta de Pavia, Monumento Nacional, Portugal (see References). Below, photos front and rear, of the Anta de Pavia (photo by authors, May, 2007)

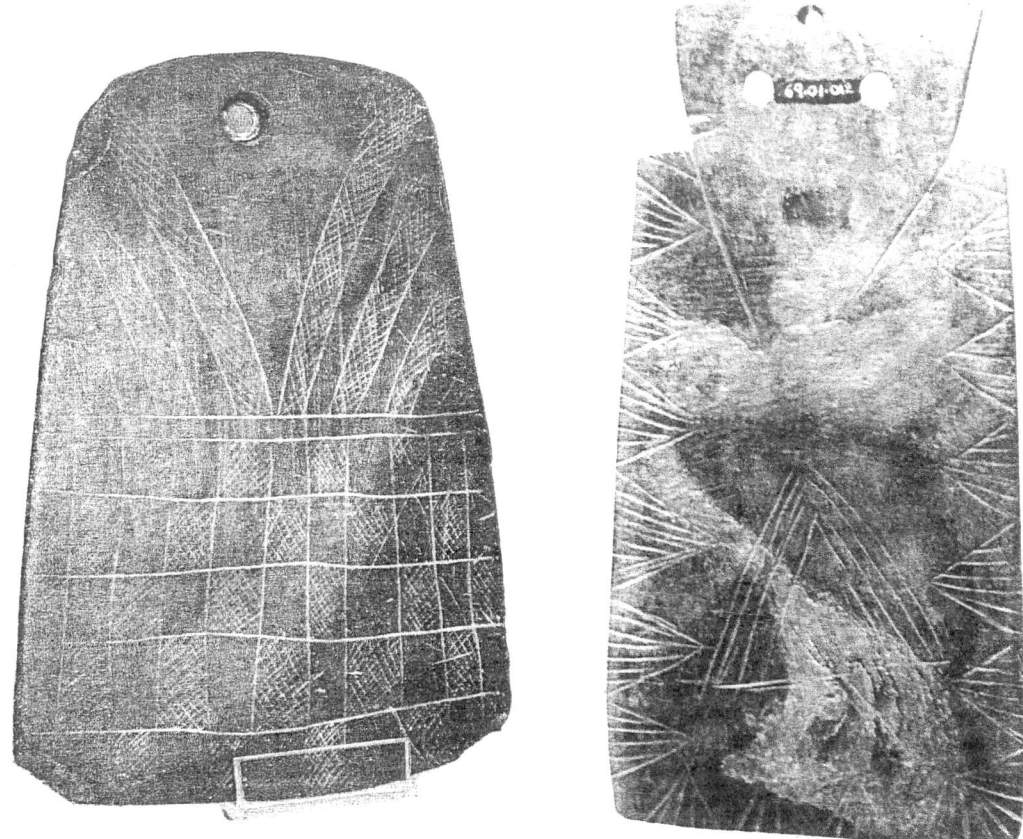

Fig.5 Two **Ocean Pendants of Porto**, the left one is in the collection of 15 pendants exhibited at the Museu de Historica Natural, Faculdade de Ciencias do Porto, Portugal. The "vee" at the top of these pendants is the known land, Greenland, and the squares are a chart of the ocean in latitude lines and distance lines. The 3 center triangles of the right pendant are the 3 island groups of the Azores, in the middle of the Ocean (photos by authors, May, 2007).

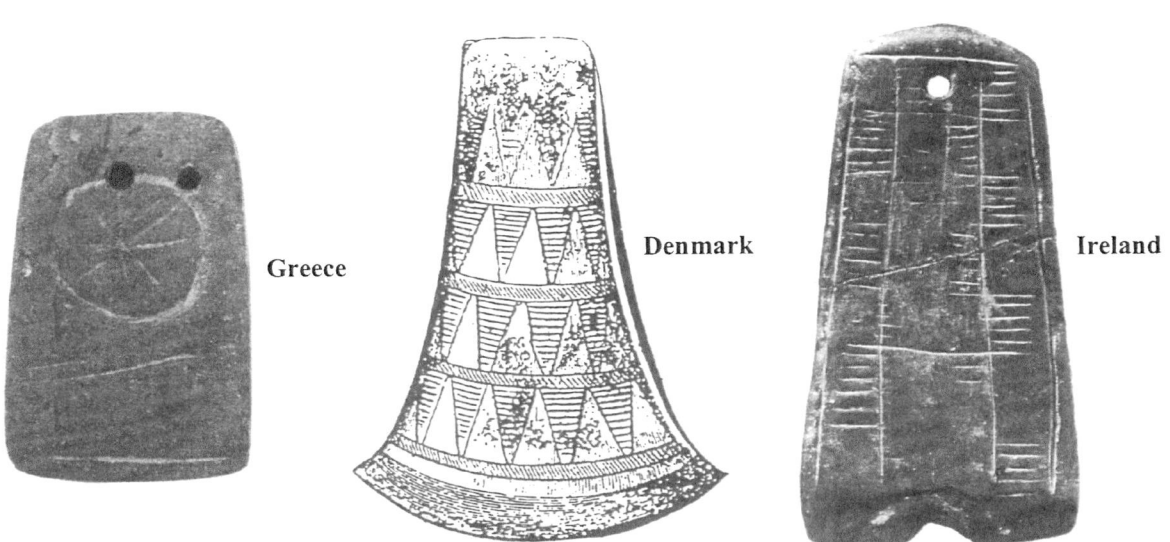

New Jersey, USA

FIG. 37. (S. 1-1.) Found in central part of Sussex County. A gorget of pink, hard sandstone, curiously mottled, being on one side pink and on the other variegated with yellow and green bands. Apparently this stone was considered unusual by the Indians. They had drawn five wigwams near one end, and a snowshoe and other objects at the other end and in the centre. There are four notches on each side, made V-shaped, and six in each end. Collection of Paul S. Tooker, Esq., Westfield, New Jersey.

Fig.6 Related Finds: Upper left, Bronze Age SunGod pendant from Mycenae; Center, an axehead from Denmark; and right, Ocean Pendant with ogham from Ireland. Below, American Ocean Pendant/Gorget from Moorehead, and classical fluted column sections off Bimini, 11/29/69 by C.P. Turolla (Ref.37).

References:

1. Dos Santos, A. P., Megalith Sites in Alto Alentejo, Guias Archeologicos de Portugal, Fenda EdicoesLDA, 1994 (Portugese)

2. DaSilva, C. T., Setubal Argueologica Vols IX-X, Museu De Arqueologia Ethngrafia Do Distrito De Setubal, 1992 (ISSN 0872-3451) (Portugese)

3. Dias, A., and Albergaria, J., Antas de Elvas, Archaeological Circuits, Roteiros Da Arqeologia Portuguesa, Institute Portugues, Sept. 2000 (ISBN 972-8087-74-8) (English)

4. Museum exhibit, Rio Tinto, Andalucia, Spain

5. Museu Nacional de Arquelogia, Lisbon, Portugal

6. Museu de Arqueloga E Etnografia Do Distrito De Setubal

7. Escoural Archaeological Guide, IPPR, 2000

8. Museo Arquelogico Nacional, Madrid, Mysteries of the Ancient World, National Geographic Society, 1985

9. Museum of Guimares, Portugal

10. Natural History Museum, Porto, Portugal

12 Archaeological Museum of Largo do Carmo,

13. Cooke, 1., Mermaid to Merryrnaid. Journey to the Stones, BAS Printers Ltd., Hampshire, 1993, pg.26, (ISBN: 0-9512371-7-9)

14. Dames, M., The Avebury Cycle, Thames and Hudson, 1997, London, pg.25, (ISBN 0-5000-27886-5)

15. Joussaume, R., Dolmens for the Dead, Megalith Building Throughout the World, Guild Publishing, London, 1985, no ISBN

16. Moorehead, W.K., Stone Ornaments Used by Indians in the United States and Canada. Being a Description of Certain Charm Stones, Gorgets, Tubes, Bird Stones and Problematical Forms, Gustavs Library, Iowa, 2005 (original, 1917), page 62 (ISBN: 0-9758914-9-9)

17. North, J., Stonehenge, A New Interpretation of Prehistoric Man and the Cosmos, The Free Press, New York, 1996 (ISBN: 0-684-84512-1)

18. DeJonge, R.M., and IJzereef, G.F., De Stenen Spreken, Kosmos Z&K, Utrecht/Antwerpen, 1996 (ISBN 90-215-2846-0) (Dutch)

19. DeJonge, R.M., and Wakefield, J.S., How the Sun God Reached America c.2500 BC. A Guide to Megalithic Sites, MCS, 2002 (ISBN 0-917054-19-9), also on CD

20. Website: www.howthesungod.com, DeJonge, R.M., and Wakefield, J.S.

21. DeJonge, R.M., and Wakefield, J.S., "The Discovery of the Atlantic Islands", Migration & Diffusion, Vol.3, No.l!, pgs.69-109 (2002)

22. DeJonge, R.M., and Wakefield, J.S., "The Passage Grave of Karleby, Encoding the Islands Discovered in the Ocean, c. 2950 BC", Migration & Diffusion, Vol.5, No.18, pgs.64-74 (2004)

23. DeJonge, R.M., and Wakefield, J.S., "A Nautical Center for Crossing the Ocean, America's Stonehenge, New Hampshire, c.2200 BC", Migration & Diffusion, Vol.4, No.15, pgs.60-IOO (2002)

24. DeJonge, R.M., and Wakefield, J.S., "Germany's Bronze Age Disc Reveals Transatlantic Seafaring, c.1600 BC", Ancient American, Vol.9, No.55, pgs.18-20 (2004)

25. DeJonge, R.M., and Wakefield, J.S., "Ales Stenar, Sweden's Bronze Age 'Sunship' to the Americas, c.500 BC", Ancient American, Vol.9, No. 56, pgs. l6-21 (2004)

26. DeJonge, R.M., and Wakefield, J.S., "The Monument of Ales Stenar, A Sunship to the Realm of the Dead", Migration and Diffusion, Vol.5, No. 19, pgs. 94- 106, 2004

27. DeJonge, R.M., and Wakefield, J.S., "The Rings of Stenness, Brodgar, and Bookan, Celebrating the Discovery of South Greenland", Migration and Diffusion, Vol6, No.24, 2005

28. DeJonge, R.M., and Wakefield, J.S., "Greenland: Bridge between the Old and New Worlds", Ancient American, Vol. II, No. 67, 2006

29. DeJonge, R.M., and Wakefield, J.S., "The Discovery of the Islands in the Atlantic, Stone C-8, Cairn T, Loughcrew, Ireland, c.3200 BC" submitted to Ancient American, fo 1/112009

30. DeJonge, R.M., and Wakefield, J.S. "The Stone Rows of Tormsdale: A Voyage to Central America, The Realm of the Dead; Caithness, NE Scotland c.1600 BC, submitted to Ancient American, Vol.ll. No.70, pgs 28-34, 10/2006

31. DeJonge, R.M., and Wakfield, J.S. "A Return Route across the Ocean, encoded in the Tormsdale Rows; Caithness, NE Scotland, c.l600 BC" submitted to Ancient American, Vol.12 Number 74, pgs.8-12, 8/2007

32. DeJonge, R.M., and Wakefield, J.S. "The Megalithic Megalithic Monument of Lagatjar, The Crossing of the Labrador Sea": Camaret-sur-Mer, Crozon Peninsula, Finistere, Brittany c.1600 BC", Ancient American, Vol.l2, no.76, pgs.32-37, 12/2/2007

33. DeJonge, R.M., and Wakefield, J.S., "Germany's Bronze Age Disc: A Transatlantic Device?", Discovering the Mysteries of Ancient America, Lost History and Legends, Unearthed and Explored, edited by Frank Joseph, New Page Books, 2006, pgs 84-87, (ISBN: 1-56414-842-4)

34. Perry, W.J., The Children of the Sun, Adventures Unlimited Press, Illinois, 2004, originally published in 1923 (ISBN: 1-931882-27-4)

35. Lobell, J.A., "Search for the Mycenaeans", Archaeology, Jan/Feb 2008, Vol.61, No.l

36. Cope, J., The Megalithic European, Harper Collins, London, 2004 (ISBN 0-00-713802-4)

37. Childress, D. H., Lost Cities of North and Central America, 1992, Adventures Unlimited Press, Illinois, p.431, (ISBN 0- 932813-09-7)

38. Peabody, C., and Moorhead, W.K., "The So-called Gorgets", Bulletin 2, Department of Archaeology, Phillips Academy, Andover, Mass. 1906

Ocean Pendants of Ancient Travelers
(Portugal, Spain, Ireland, and America, c. 2200 BC)

by J.S. Wakefield

In quite a few of the megalithic anta or burial dolmen of Iberia, small inscribed tablets (pendants) of slate have been found. At least one or two of them are now to be seen in most of the archaeological museums in the cities and towns of Portugal and Spain. Photos of them will be seen in tourist brochures and in archaeological publications. They are each unique, but they have common characteristics. Considered anthropomorphic artistic objects, or idols, we show they also have geographic meaning. They represent a crossing of the ocean to the backside of the world, on the other side of the ocean. The pendant accompanied the wearer in burial, to show he/she had made the risky journey to Paradise, and deserved a special place in the Realm of the Dead. Related examples show that they were admired and copied in Denmark, Ireland, Greece, and America during the Bronze Age.

Introduction

The Megalithic Culture of Western Europe lasted from 5500 BC to 1200 BC. The characteristic and well-known features of that culture are visible in the big stone monuments: the passage graves, the dolmens, the stone circles, and the stone rows. The megalithic petroglyphs are less known, but these are very interesting. Several thousands of carvings are identified, and most of these have geographic meanings. They often represent coastlines, islands, and sailing routes. Usually, they are carved rather roughly on the inside faces of upright passage stones or the end stones of passage graves.

An unusual type of petroglyph is to be seen upon the small engraved tablets found in southwest Iberia. Since they have been excavated from passage graves, it is certain they belong to the Megalithic Culture. Figures 1 & 2 show many of them, reduced from their original sizes of about 3½ inches long (10cm). They are almost always about an inch thick, and usually are composed of slate rock. Their surfaces are polished, and usually have inscriptions only on one side. Usually they have a hole or two at the somewhat tapered top, so are considered pendants. In the limited existing literature, they are referred to as religious idols. They are all unique, but share design characteristics. Understanding these objects will contribute to a better understanding of this Culture and its achievements.

It is not known how many of these engraved pendants have been found, but probably there are hundreds. More than 60 are reported to have been found in one passage grave, the Anta 1 do Olival de Pega. We have collected images of quite a few, from archaeological literature, museum exhibits, and tourist brochures. Many tablets have come from the area surrounding the town of Evora, 100 km east of Lisbon, Portugal. They have also been excavated in the tombs of the tholos type at Los Millares, in southeastern Spain, and numerous other places in southwest Iberia.

Background

The Megalithic Culture, starting from 5500 BC, 2,000 two thousand years before the first Pharaohs of Egypt, had developed a Sun God religion, and had developed a tradition of building Sun God temples, facing the western ocean, along the coasts of Western Europe. Today, these churches are called passage graves, because burials have been found in them, like Winchester Cathedral, which also has a long passage and graves in it. Their political and spiritual leaders told them the Earth was a big sphere, just like the sun and the moon. They said that all the known land was surrounded by a sea, and that in the west there was the Empire of the Dead, at the other side of the earth. (As the sun religion was later developed in Egypt, Osiris was called the God of this underworld in the west.)

Impressed by this story, people tried to cross the ocean. At first, they tried to cross at the Tropic of Cancer, at 23°N, in honor of the Sun God, who came north to that latitude each year before turning south for the winter. Unfortunately, at that latitude, many courageous sailors died because that is the latitude of the windless doldrums of the horse latitudes, where later sailing ship crews ate their horses. Some early Culture Bringers, as they are called in myth in the Americas, apparently made it across, but they were not heard from again because the trade wind patterns of the ocean were not yet understood. Some boats were blown north out of the doldrums, and, following the birds, discovered the Azores Islands. This discovery was commemorated at the highly decorated megalithic tomb of Gavrinis in c. 3600 BC, as explained in our book, How the Sun God Reached America. Interestingly, most of the pendants have been found in Iberia around the latitude of 38°N, the latitude of the Azores Islands, considered the western home of the Sun God, after their discovery.

The Pendants: distances

All of the Ocean Pendant tablets of Iberia show inscribed crosshatching, triangles, or zigzag lines. The up-down waveform is a universal symbol for water, and is, in fact, the Egyptian hieroglyph for water. Thus many of the pendants are clearly depicting water. We have learned, from our study of megalithic petroglyphs, that the up/down lines are used to encode units of distance that are based upon the distance on the surface of the Earth of one degree of latitude. In Egypt, this unit of one degree was called the moira. The moira was applied to curving distances in the west, as well as the latitudes easily measured with a simple Jacob's Staff, when moving to the north or south. Today, we use nautical miles for navigation, where 1°= 60 NM, so one Egyptian moira = 60 NM.

The number of zigzags on many of the pendants is four, so we see they often show the correct size of the ocean, which is four multiples of ten degrees, or 40°, or 2,400 NM, from Iberia to Newfoundland, or Africa to South America. Usually there are three or four big moiras (30 or 40 degrees of latitude) or six or eight half big moiras, which are correct distances at the different latitudes sailed after the discovery of America. Like the pendants, the ocean is

Figure 2: More Ocean Pendants, with below, ceremonial crooks, inscribed with Ocean motifs. (see references)

tapered. The triangles are a stylized modification of the wave/distance motif, and the cross-hatchings are the distance lines laid out, like a fishnet on a globe. After confirmation of land in the west, following Asian explorations in c. 2600 BC, and the confirmation of a return route via the known Azores in c. 2500 BC, sailors were again venturing to the west, via previously explored southern and northern routes.

The Pendants: religion

Most of the tablets have a centered hole, for hanging the objects around the neck of the hero who went on the dangerous journey across the Ocean. Sometimes there are two holes, like eyes. The vee at the upper portion represents the huge land of Greenland, which had been revered as the westernmost known land in the world for about 600 years. The latitude line at the bottom of the vee is the 60°N latitude line of Cape Farvel, and usually the lines below are inscribed to represent big moiras, or 10° intervals.

Clearly these pendants are meant to be anthropomorphic representations of the Sun God, also the God of the Ocean. These plaques certify that the person wearing it, and buried with it, had taken the Journey across the western ocean to Paradise. These plaques, accompanying the dead, help the dead return to Paradise in the West. The cocaine later put into in Egyptian mummies, which had been obtained in the west, also was meant to help the deceased reach Paradise. The obtaining of these drugs was one of the purposes of later voyages to the west, as first suggested by Perry. In some of the pendants, the eye-holes have little rays around them, like little suns, so these may be Sun God images. Note that one pendant has a stick figure (Figure 3, right) of the Sun God crossing the ocean. The eyed plaques are seen by some researchers as the Owl Goddess, a representation of the Mother Goddess, in the very old tradition. Such simultaneous meanings of symbols are not unusual, such as the Christian cross, which is both a symbol of torture and resurrection.

The Pendants: dating

From the petroglyphs it can be concluded that these people knew the size of the North Atlantic Ocean, so we call these artifacts Ocean Pendants. From this information their approximate date can be determined. By study of other megalithic sites, we learned that America was discovered via the Bering Sea, c. 2600 BC. A century later the continents were reached via the southern crossing of the Atlantic, between Africa and South America, for the first time (c. 2500 BC). In the same century, America was also reached via the upper north, via Greenland. Since all of these pendants relate to the effort of this culture to explore the backside of the Earth, they are all roughly contemporary with one another.

The Pendant of Crato

Figure 3 (left) shows a photo we took, showing a very simple design, so we think it is one of the older pendants. It was excavated by Portuguese archaeologist A. Isidoro in one of the dolmens in the District of Crato, near the town of Portalegre (Alto Alentejo). This town is located 80 km NNE of Evora, close to the Spanish border. The site is at the latitude of 39°N, the latitude of the West Azores, also at 39°N. Now it is on display in the Museum of Mendes Correa in Porto, in the north of Portugal.

The petroglyph represents the North Atlantic Ocean, in a stylized way. It is divided into four strips of triangles, each corresponding to 15° of latitude. One after the other, the horizontal lines are situated at 0°N (the equator on the bottom edge), 15°N (the latitude of the southern Cape Verde Islands), 30°N (the Nile Delta and the northern Canaries), 45°N (halfway to the pole), and 60°N (the south point of Greenland, no horizontal line). The hole itself perhaps represents Cape Farvel, the south tip of Greenland, known since c. 3200 BC.

The upright, shaded triangles each have a width of one big moira = 10° = 600 NM. The lowest strip has four triangles, corresponding to a total width of four moiras = 40° = 2,400 NM. Above it are 4½ triangles, then five, corresponding to a width of five moiras = 50° = 3,000 NM. At the top, there is a strip of four triangles again. More important than the exact distances, is the fact that the order of magnitude is correct, and that the middle of the ocean is its broadest part. Note that each triangle has a width of one moira, and a height of 1.5 moira, so the shapes are proportionate to distance. The shading of the triangles is done with horizontal lines, showing they are stylized small latitude lines. In total there are 18 triangles, possibly encoding the destination in the west, the civilization developing in the Gulf of Campeche at 18°N. At the top of the pendant are four horizontal lines on the left, five on the right. Possibly these encode the discovery of America by the 5th pharaoh of Egypt, of the 4th Dynasty c. 2580-2562 BC.

The Pendant of Pavia

Figure 4 shows an ocean tablet found in the Dolmen of Pavia, 40 km north of Evora, again at 39°N, the latitude of the West Azores. This big dolmen, which was later reused as a chapel, was declared as a National Monument in 1910. The unusual design of the pendant shows the edges engraved all around, showing that at this time, they thought there was land all around the Ocean. The double edge is probably covering coastal Ocean over a width of one big moira, or 10° (=600 NM). At the bottom, three triangles have the same width, so they show the length of the Southern Crossing from Africa to South America, with the wind and current, to be three big moiras, or 30° (= 1,800 NM), which is correct. From this length, it appears they probably landed at the latitude of about 5°N, French Guyana. The fishbone shading on the right edge points upwards, as they are living in the Northern Hemisphere, oriented to the north, but the left side points downward, because the goal of the crossing, Central America, is in the southwest. The edging across the top suggests they know the upper north route around Cape Farvel, Greenland. The dotted lines, if not accidental scratches, would

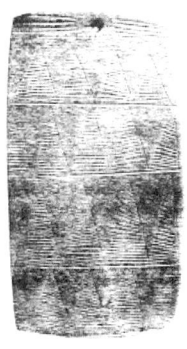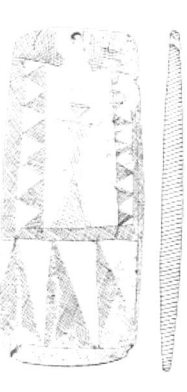

Figure 3: Left: Ocean Pendant of Crato c.12-14 cm long, found near the town of Portalegre (Altp A:emtekp) in South Portugal at the latitude of the West Azores, 39 degrees N, by archaeologists August Isidoro (Museum of Mendes Correa, Porto, photo by the authors, May, 2007). Right: Pendant of Sesimbra, an Ocena Pendant from Sepultura 9 e Sepultura 11 (Ossario), Estampa 19, in Setubal Arqueologica, Vol 1X-X. (see references)

be showing the holy 23°N line of the Tropic of Cancer, crossed by a line going south, showing that one must sail southwest from Iberia to accomplish the Southern Crossing, with its length and southern location given by the three triangles.

The Pendant of Sesimbra

Figure 3 (right) also shows a pendant excavated in one of the dolmen near the town of Sesimbra, 30 km south of Lisbon, at the latitude of the West Azores, at 39°N. It is on display in the Archaeological Museum of Setubal. This petroglyph has the same Southern Crossing shown at the bottom, with three triangles showing a distance of three big moiras (1,800 NM). The edge at the right is the coast of the Old World, with 6.5 or 7 triangles encoding the Arctic Circle at the holy 67°N (reciprocal of 23°N), where they had to go for the Northern Crossing via Greenland. The thicker edge on the left side is the coast of the New World, with the larger triangles showing that it is the important location of he Realm of the Dead (America). The 5.5 or 6 triangles in the west correspond with Cape Chidley, Labrador, at 60°N, entry to the American Coast in the west.

In the middle of the Ocean is a stick-figure person, the SunGod or Ocean God, which consists of three triangles, also representing the three island groups of the Azores. The large triangles point with great emphasis upward, to this figure. The thick horizontal line the figure stands on is the return route, with the wind and the current, from Newfoundland via the Azores back to the Old World. The tablet can mean that our king, who crosses the ocean is highly esteemed, or it could be more religious, the Sun God who crosses the waters and visits the Realm of the Dead, and returns to the Land of the Living, is our highest God.

Pendants in Porto

Figure 5 shows an Ocean Pendant that is c. 12-14 cm long, in a collection of 15 of similar appearance, but somewhat varying designs. They are in the Museu de Historica Natural, Faculdade de Ciencias do Porto, Portugal, formerly a collection at the University of Porto, now in the Natural History Museum in Porto. You can see how thin these slate tablets are, by looking at the holes at the top. Many of the stones are hung by nylon fishing line in the exhibit, as it appears they are designed to be worn hanging from the neck. Note the vee at the top of the stone, a representation of the big land that had been discovered in the north, Greenland, which comes to a point at Cape Farvel at 60°N. The discovery of Greenland had been commemorated by the construction of the huge megalithic ring complex of Brodgar, Stenness, and Bookan in the Orkney Islands. The three shaded vee patterns illustrate that the seas extend in open water for an extended distance on both sides of Cape Farvel, which indeed it does. The checkerboard squares on this pendant are a symbolic chart of the ocean, eleven squares across, and five rows down.

The pendant beside it, also from the Natural History Museum, has an anthropomorphic appearance, now also representing the Ocean God or Sun God. In the center is a three-sided triangle, representing the highly revered three island groups of the Azores. These Islands had been revered as the western home of the Sun God, from their discovery c. 3,600 BC until the discovery of further land to the west, as explained in our book, How the SunGod Reached America, c. 2500 BC, A Guide to Megalithic Sites. The megalithic tomb most decorated with petroglyphs in the world is the Tumulus of Gavrinis, in the Gulf of Morbihan, Brittany, built in celebration and commemoration of the discovery of the Azores Islands, in the middle of the Ocean.

Many interesting details can be found while looking at the many pendants. For example, the last small reduced pendant image on Fig.2 does not calibrate distances, but has a hole incised on the right side of the stone (the edge of it is broken away), and a hole on the left. These might represent either Iberia on the right, and Newfoundland on the left, or the Mediterranean Sea on the right, and the Caribbean, on the left, like the carved circles on both sides of the Ocean in the huge petroglyph of Serrazes, also found in mid-Portugal.

Related finds

Figure 2 shows some crooks below the pendants. All the images have been greatly reduced, to show the interesting variety, and yet common characteristics of these objects. It is thought the large stone crooks had a ceremonial function. Note they all are inscribed with similar ocean motifs, so the ocean voyages were important.

The top left object of Figure 6 is also a Bronze Age pendant, reported by Archaeology Magazine, found in a 2008 dig in the megaron (Palace area) of Mycenae, in Greece. It bears a petroglyph of a sun disc, so is a Sun God pendant of a probable similar date to these others, perhaps inspired by them. The bronze axe head found in Denmark, in the center of Fig.6, from the book by Cooke, carries the same Ocean motifs. It also surely has a similar Bronze Age date, both by the axe head design, and the motifs. On the right of Fig.6 is a pendant found in County Antrim, Ireland, from the referenced book by Dames. It appears to be an Ocean Pendant, carrying an ogham inscription, which needs decipherment. Like the Iberic pendants, it has continental edges, a 60°N latitude line through Cape

Fig.4 Ocean Pendant of Pavia, from Anta Capela de S. Dionisio ou Anta de Pavia, Monumento Nacional, Portugal (see References). Above: Photos front and rear, of the Anta de Pavia (photo by authors, May, 2007)

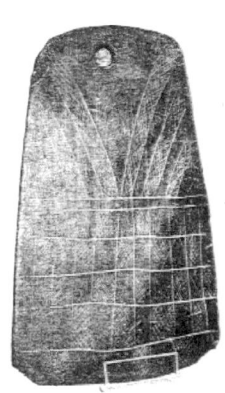 

Fig.5 Two Ocean Pendants of Porto, the left one is in the collection of 15 pendants exhibited at the Museu de Historica Natural, Faculdade de Ciencias do Porto, Portugal. The "vee" at the top of these pendants is the known land, Greenland, and the squares are a chart of the ocean in latitude lines and distance lines. The 3 center triangles of the right pendant are the 3 island groups of the Azores, in the middle of the Ocean (photos by authors, May, 2007).

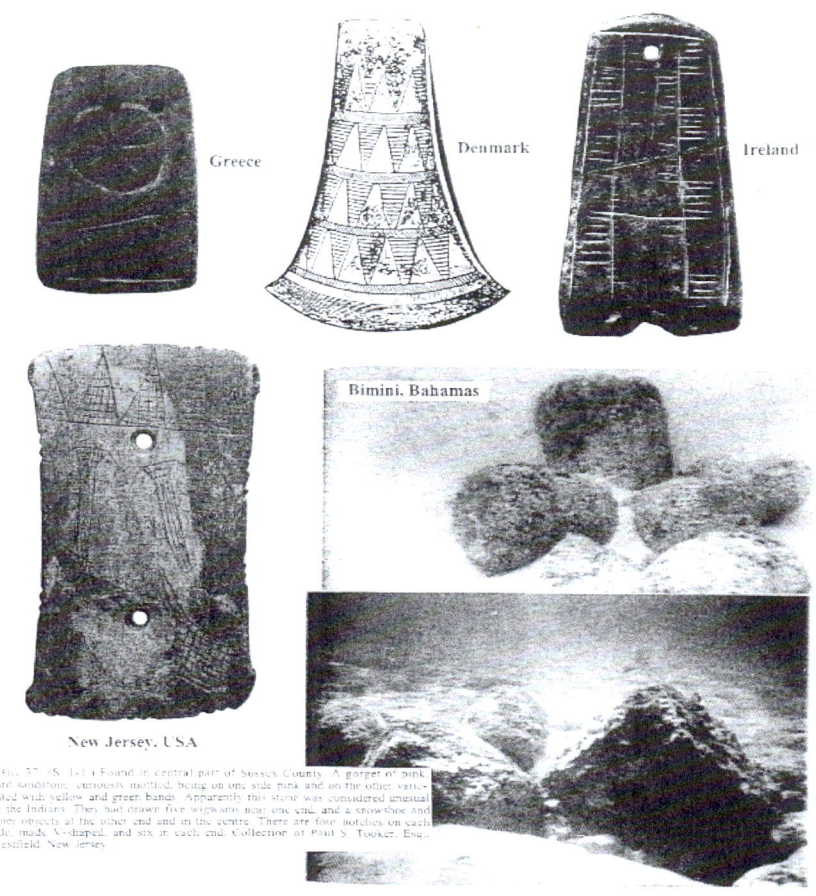

Fig.6 Related Finds: Upper left, Bronze Age SunGod pendant from Mycenae; Center, an axehead from Denmark; and right, Ocean Pendant with ogham from Ireland. Below, American Ocean Pendant/Gorget from Moorehead, and classical fluted column sections off Bimini, 11/29/69 by C.P. Turolla (Ref.37).

Farvel, at the top, and the important 40°N latitude line which runs through the West Azores. This appears to be an Irish version, inspired by the Iberic pendants.

Below, on Figure 6 is an American Indian gorget, or pendant, reproduced with the photo legend. It has a guaranteed authenticity, as it is reproduced from the 1917 work of the great American archaeologist, Warren K. Moorehead. His book does not discuss the object, except in this note, where he calls the mesh triangles wigwams. The snowshoe is probably a land mass, depending upon the orientation of the stone, and the experience of the sailor. Note the classical appearance of the two fluted columns, each with stone capitals. To the right are photos of fluted columns found off Bimini (Ref. 37). Clearly, a classical building is being remembered somewhere. The rectangular pendant shape with two holes in this position is common among American Indian gorgets. Somehow, this one, found in New Jersey, has been inscribed with Old World motifs, so this can be called an American Ocean Pendant, confirming the Trans-Atlantic crossings in the Bronze Age.

Conclusion

It was a daring thing to cross the Ocean to the west. We think early attempts at the Tropic of Cancer probably cost many lives, in the course of learning the trade wind patterns of the Atlantic Ocean. These slate pendants honor persons who successfully made trips across the Atlantic Ocean, some of the greatest sailing adventurers in prehistory. ∎

Bronze Age Ocean Pendants
The Recording of Geographic Information by Bronze Age Sailors
by Jay S. Wakefield

In my book, *Rocks&Rows*, and in *Ancient American*, Vol. 14, Issue #88, September 2010, many Iberian pendants are illustrated. They have been found in passage graves, mainly located in the Evora area, and along rivers in Portugal. Most may be seen in museums. They are illustrated on restaurant menus and tourist brochures in Portugal, and in a few archaeological works which are referenced in *Rocks&Rows*.

I always assumed I would never actually see an Iberian pendant outside museum cases. It took a lot of coaxing to get the glass case top lifted in one museum, so we could get photos without ourselves appearing in the reflections. Years later, one was offered on Ebay. I was the lone bidder. Later, I bought three more direct from the collector. The four recently acquired plaques are shown in the accompanying photographs.

I have learned that a Professor of Archaeology, Katina T. Lillios, has studied these plaques for a lifetime, and written a book on them, entitled *Heraldry for the Dead, Memory, Identity, and the Engraved Stone Plaques of Neolithic Iberia*, 2008, University of Texas Press. In her acknowledgements, she describes how the Archaeological Institute of America awarded her an Archaeology of Portugal Grant in 2003 to study and photograph the hundreds of plaques in Lisbon Museums (not that many are on exhibit). In 2004, she recieved an Arts and Humanities Initiative grant from the University of Iowa, which funded the technical support that helped produce the electronic database of the records and images of over 1,300 plaques, called the Engraved Stone Plaque Registry and Inquiry Tool (ES-PIRIT). The work involved many archaeologists, students and graduate students, and other professors of various disciplines, and included "spatial analyses," and "statistical analyses."

In May 2012, I emailed her at the Department of Anthropology of the University of Iowa. I said I had run across a recommendation to her book by an archaeologist in a museum in Iraklion, Crete, and I had much enjoyed

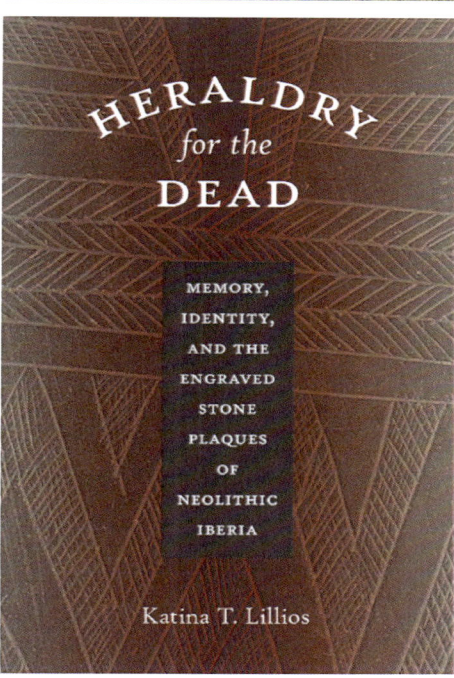

her book. I complimented her on the many insightful observations I found in the book, such as the "plaques might differentiate those who traveled from those who stayed closer to home," that "the number of horizontal register lines was important," and that the "vocabulary of the plaques consists of a relatively limited set of repeating design elements." She noted correctly that "the base designs are 'squeezed' very close to the top," that a "shared and rigourously followed set of rules" was followed. She also noted that the plaques were "a medium for record-keeping and memorializing," that "the motifs had ... rich expression in Bell Beaker pottery," and that the "plaques were closely linked to the identity of the dead." She says that "after the plaques ceased to be used stone axes were ... replaced by copper axes." All of this is in agreement with our explanation of the plaques in *Rocks&Rows*.

I chose not to explain to her that the graphics represented prehistoric latitude and longitude lines, and the plaques all illustrated the size of the Atlantic Ocean, with Greenland at the top, sometimes in the anthropomorphic form of the Ocean Sungod. Of course, these plaques were not mass produced, but each was custom made, unique, and stylistic. Each plaque was possessed by a sailor in the transatlantic copper trade, and his heroic status accompanied him into his tomb and the afterlife. All she was missing was an insight by a mathematician, Reinoud de Jonge, which made sense of the whole issue. The Bell-Beaker people she was referring to are acknowledged for having introduced copper and metal tools to Britian, through the Isles of Scilly, and Southern Cornwall.

What I found most interesting in her book is on page 21 and 22, where she says Argentine paleontologist Florentino Ameghino (1854-1911) had included a discussion of the Portuguese plaques in his study of the prehistory of La Plata, Argentina (Ameghino 1879, 1880). He "saw clear parallels between the engravings on the Portuguese plaques and those on stone plaques from the Rio Negro region of Patagonia":

"We find these signs to be absolutely identical to those that are found on some slate plaques of Portugal that the distinguished Portuguese geologist don Carlos Ribeiro has informed us about. (Ameghino 1880:273)."

Lillios says: "Ameghino also saw in the abundant inscriptive art of the Americas, including the engraved plaques of Argentina (and by implication the plaques of Portugal), "a complete system of ideographic writing that awaits decipherment and obscures facts of great importance" (Ameghino 1879:218-219). No prehistorian followed up on Ameghino's intriguing suggestion, and few scholars seemed to know about it. ... The geologist Carlos Ribeiro (1813-1882) briefly described the plaques in *Noticia de Algumas Estacoes e Monumentos Pre-Historicos* (1978-1880)."

We are looking for hard evidence that Iberian or Minoan sailors obtained tin via the La Plata region of Argentina, as indicated so far by a little petroglyphic evidence, the historical record of a pathway to the coast, the megaliths of Argentina and Paraguay, and the history of Tiahuanaco. Through Google, I have not been able to find the works of Ameghino or Ribeiro. So I asked Professor Lillios if she had any images of the Argentinian plaques. She replied that she "could not find figures/illustrations" in these articles, but that "if I should run across the images for the Argentinian plaques, I will know to forward them to you." I hope they come to light somehow, as they would connect the two sides of a transoceanic tin trade. ∎

Crossing the Atlantic via the Azores
(Stone Rows of Kerlescan, Menec and Kermario, Carnac, Brittany, c.1900 BC)
by Dr. R.M. de Jonge & J.S. Wakefield

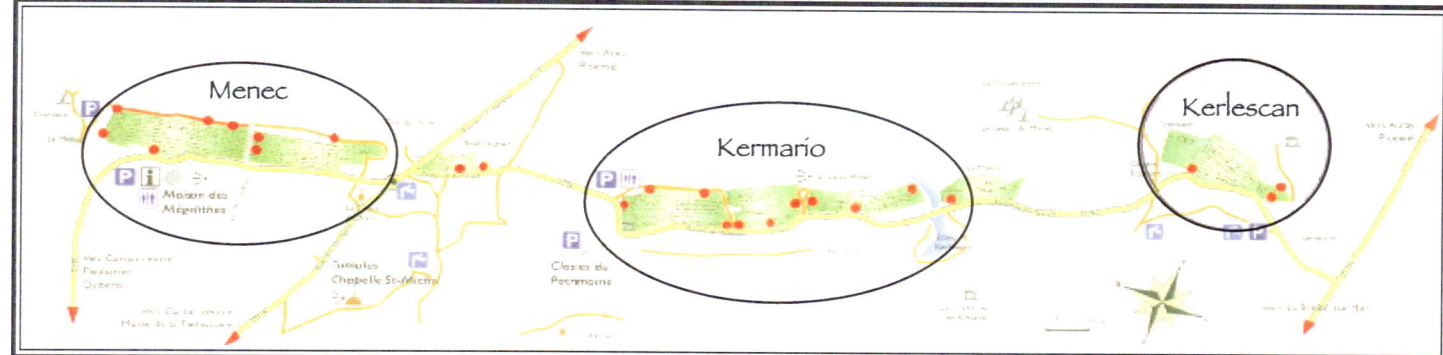

The tail ends of the stone rows of the "Royal Avenue" in the east, near the house. (Kerlescan, Brittany, taken in May, 2005)

The true N-S row of the U (representing Europe and Africa), view south. (Kerlescan, Brittany, taken in May, 2005, Reinoud de jonge in the photo)

The three stone row sets at Carnac are the largest megalithic monuments in the world, constructed of approximately 3,000 large stones, spread over 3 miles. They run across a rolling landscape near the sea, north of the Gulf of Morbihan, in an area with the largest number of megalithic monuments in the world. This area was probably the center and homeland of the megalithic culture. The meaning of the rows was lost after the end of the Bronze Age (1200 BC), so throughout the Celtic Iron Age, and after the Roman Gallic War, the site was as mysterious as it is today. So these enormous sites have been a tourist site for three thousand years, now drawing visitors from all over the world. Roads and farm buildings have been built among the stones. Today the rows are mostly fenced off, with observation towers built midway along the rows. There have been no reasonable explanations of these sites proposed, and the literature is very thin. Our study of these sites shows that they were very precisely designed, with very clear intentions behind the enormous labor involved in their construction.

KERMARIO

Kermario, the middle set of rows, is a poorly preserved monument. The rows have a length of more than one kilometer, with 1181 menhirs. About in the center of the construction is a bend in the rows, at a now-flooded dip called the Ravin de Keroquet. The height of the menhirs slowly increases from about 0.5 meter in the east, to more than 3 meters in the west. In the last 100 meters the sizes of the menhirs are very big, emphasizing again the south-western direction, toward the Azores. The 7 alignments of the central part of Kermario all point 28°WSW, to Santa Maria, the eastern island of the East Azores.

Dating these rows is complicated. Comparing Kermario with the other row sets, you see that in Kermario has no stone circles at the ends of the rows, and that south of the alignments the makers added extra rows at different angles. In its design, Kermario is more primitive than Kerlescan to the east or Le Menec on the west Since the monu-

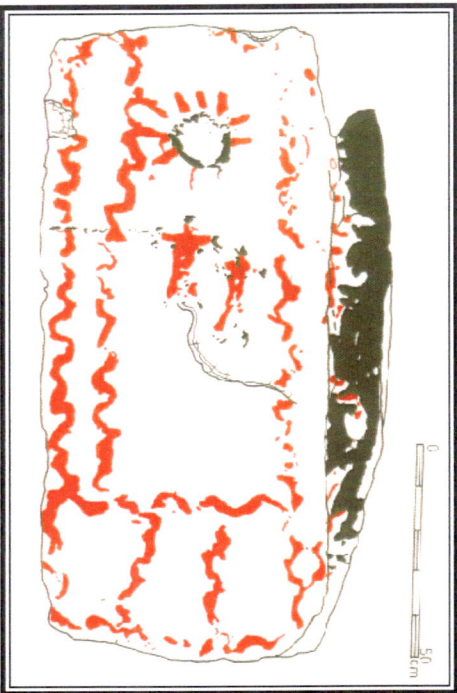

Petroglyph of the Atlantic Ocean, with the Southern Crossing shown as 3 boxes (10 degrees ea.) at the bottom. The Sun God Ra shines down upon the Egyptian gods Horus and Osiris, crossing their difficult windward route, the Royal Crossing: via the Azores to Newfoundland, the Tuat, the Realm of the Dead in the West, at the other side of the great waters, in the land where the sun goes down. Red ochre, Porto University, Portugal, from E. Shee Twohig, "The Megalithic Art of Western Eruope" c.1900 BC)

ment is pointed toward the Azores Islands, which were so important in sailing back to the east with the tradewinds. Kermario surely was built after the discovery of America via the Atlantic. c.2500 BC. Probably, Kermario is contemporary with Stonehenge III in South England, dating from c.2000 BC. The Rows of Kerlescan were built on the east side, probably to incorporate design improvements, probably 100 years later, c.1900 BC, and soon thereafter the Rows of Menec were added on the west side, to include new information that needed to be recorded. These details can be seen in the other row sets.

KERLESCAN

Built next Kerlescan, the eastern set, the right consists of 352 "menhirs" (standing stones), in 13 rows, and a U-shaped "stone circle" of 46 menhirs on the west end. While the rows appear chaotic, we have found that this is a straightforward monument, because its numeric encodings of angles, latitudes, and distances are stored in single digits, a stone for each digit. The rows can be seen as a big arrow, pointing to the U-shaped stone "circle" at the end of the rows. One can also vizualize this entire monument as an arrow, pointing along the 47° latitude line to the west to Cape Race, Newfoundland, the easternmost point of North America, also at 47°N. During the time of the megalithic culture, people were curious about what was on the other side of the Earth, at the other side of the big ocean. Because of the opposing winds and current of the Gulfstream, no one could sail this route directly to Newfoundland. They had been able, however, to reach the Azores, as commemorated in the nearby Tumulus of Gavrinis c.3600 BC. Until the discovery of the Americas, eleven hundred years later (c.2500 BC), the mid-ocean Azores were the most westerly known islands in the ocean to the west, and had been revered as the western home of the SunGod. After the discovery of the Americas, however, these islands became the focus of the return route back to the Old World.

Cape Finisterre, the NW tip of Spain, is located north of the Azores, so the uppermost Row I represents Cape Finisterre, literally. From Cape Finisterre, people would sail to the Azores, and hoped to welcome their New King arrive from the "other side of the waters". Below Row I are 9 rows of menhirs. These 9 rows represent the nine islands of the Azores. On the West Azores the new King will arrive after the long crossing from Newfoundland, as do nearly all the returning ships from the New World.

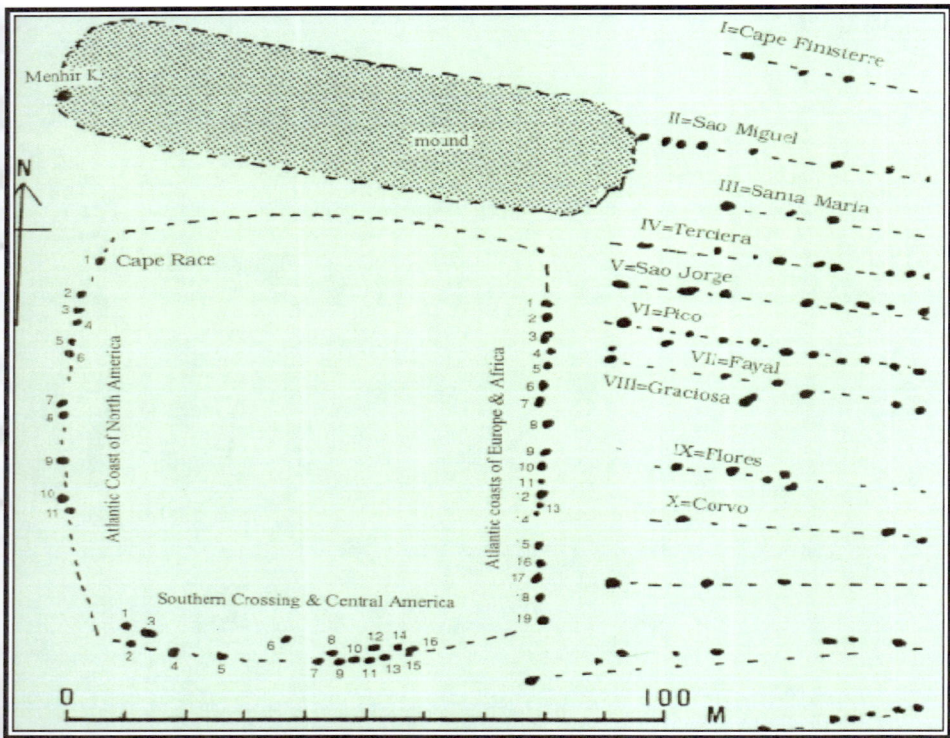

The Western U stones of Kerlescan, with the mound on the north side, and the rows of the monument identified by its associated island, as discussed in the text. (Lines and number added by the authors.)

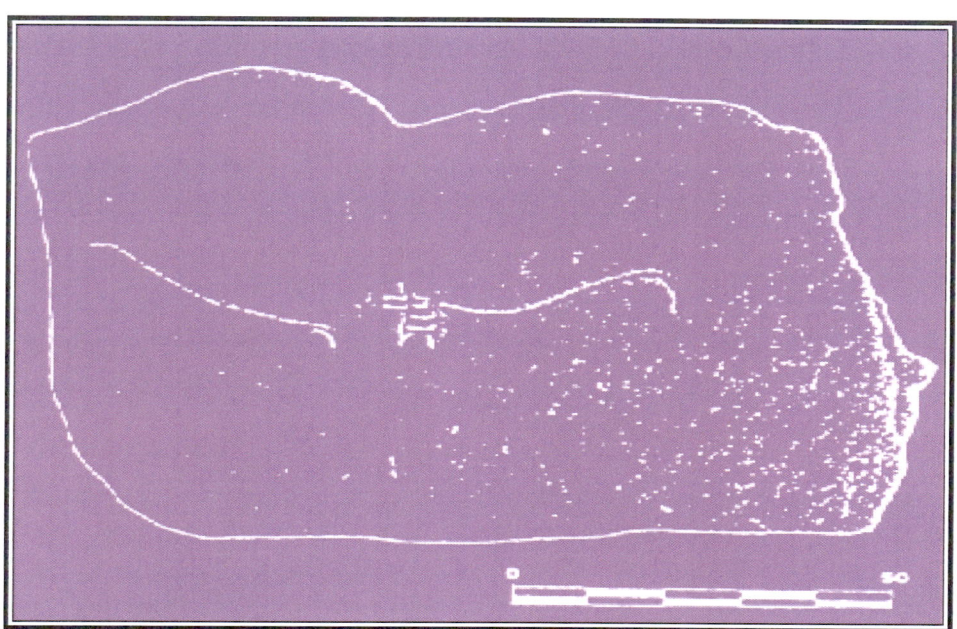

The Sun God Ra (in the middle, as a 9-stick figure, also the 9 islands of the Azores) involved in the difficult "Royal Crossing" of the Atlantic Ocean. Note the coast of Iberia to Cape Finisterre as a small curve at the right side. (Portillo de las Cortes, Guadalajara, Galica, western Spain, c.2000 BC). (From Twohig, Ref.34)

The U-shaped stone circle symbolizes the North Atlantic Ocean. The stones along the east side of the U represent the coast of Europe and Africa, the stones in the south side of the U, the coast of South America, and the U stones in the west, the coast of North America. This east side has a vertical row of stones, which is a straight meridian along the coast of the Old World, where the monument of Kerlescan is situated. This row has 19 menhirs, corresponding to the degree of latitude of the Gulf of Campeche in Central America, the Realm of the Dead, at 18-20°N. This is the place where the new King can be found! An important government delegation will travel to that far-off country to accompany the King on his return voyage to the Azores. The bowed south side of the U represents the long crossing to the Realm of the Dead, along a southern, far-away, curved latitude. This south side represents the journey to the Realm of the Dead, literally. Some of the menhirs at the bottom of the U-shape may be indicating large islands reported off the coast of Venezuela, along this east-west route, from Isla Margarita to Aruba. The curved west side of the U is where one has to sail to return. This represents a far-away, curved meridian along the coast of the big continent at the other side of the Ocean, North America.

An oblong burial mound lies above the full width of the U. It is a royal vault, about 75 meters long, 20 meters wide, and nowadays only c.1.5 meters high. In view of its position above the stone circle, this burial mound, and with it the whole monument, deals with the return of the King from the Realm of the Dead.

Only the gods would be able to reach Cape Race by going west, and therefore this is a "Royal Crossing". The Sungod is actually shown doing this crossing in a number of petroglyphs from Portugal. This mid-ocean route is shown with the 9 islands of the Azores, as the home of the 9-stick figure of the SunGod. All sailors returning from the west will return from Cape Race, Newfoundland, to these west Azores, however, because the Gulfstream and the tradewind patterns of the earth have become understood during the last few thousand years of sailing expeditions. Now everyone at the "other side of the waters, in the land where the Sun sets, will return via the West Azores, using this Royal Crossing with the wind from west to east.

MENEC

The Rows of Menec also have a length of about one kilometer, with 1061 menhirs. Roughly in the center, the rows are bent. The rows form an Arrow of a kilometer length, pointing to the west. The Eastern Rows point between 25.5° and 23° WSW, which is from the Menec to Sao Miguel, the main island of the East Azores, c.25° WSW. The Western Rows point between 19° and 17.5° WSW, which is from the Menec to Pico, the main island of the (Central) Azores, c.18.5° WSW. The Western Rows have twice as many menhirs as the Eastern Rows, so the western direction is strongly emphasized. This is confirmed by the height of the menhirs, which slowly increases from less than 1 meter in the east, to 2.5 meters in the western ends of the rows.

The two stone circles of the Menec both represent the spherical Earth. The menhirs on their edges symbolize "land", the lacking of them "water", so they are mostly ocean. At both circles menhirs are present both on the eastern edge and on the western edge. Both circles deal with the crossing of the Ocean, from east to west. The 12 rows of menhirs represent the crossing via 12 islands: Lanzarote, the eastern Canary island, the 2 islands of Madeira, and the 9 islands of the Azores. The important Western Rows of the Menec represent the long crossing from the West Azores to Newfoundland (c.2050 km).

The pear shaped East Circle of the Menec symbolizes the spherical Earth. On the east side is Western Europe, in the west is North America, and in between are the islands in the

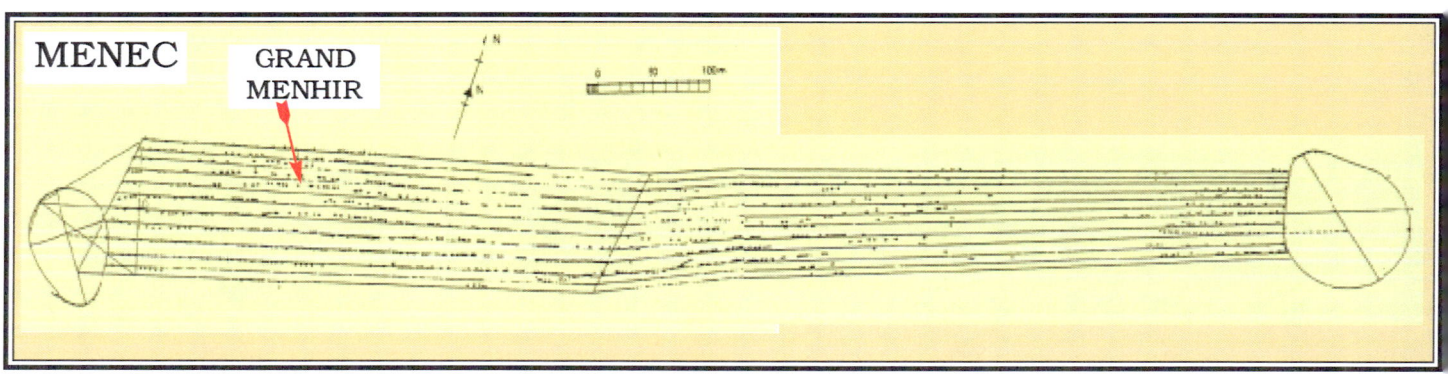

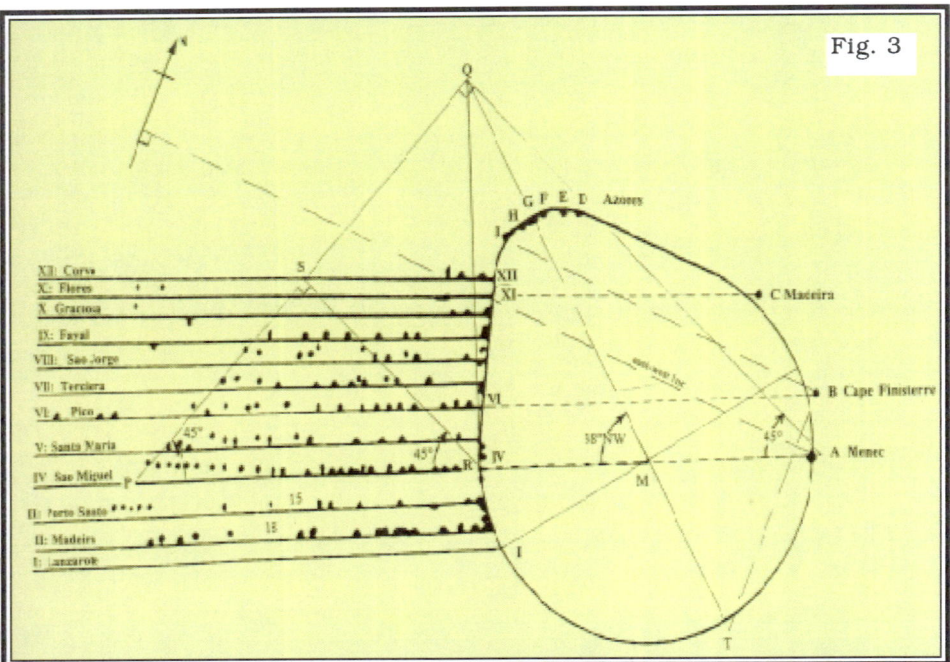

Fig. 3

Above: The East Side of Menec. It describes the crossing from the Menec (A) via Cape Finisterre (B), and the crossing via Madeira (C), to the 2 islands of the West Azores (rows XI and XII). (Menec, Carnac, Brittany, c. 1900 BC)

Right: The end of the Western Menhir Rows, and the West Circle of the Menec. At the edge of the Circle are two clusters of menhirs. Group A represents Brittany, and the 3 groups of the western cluster are 'at the other side of the sea'. (Menec, Carnac, Brittany, c. 1900 BC)

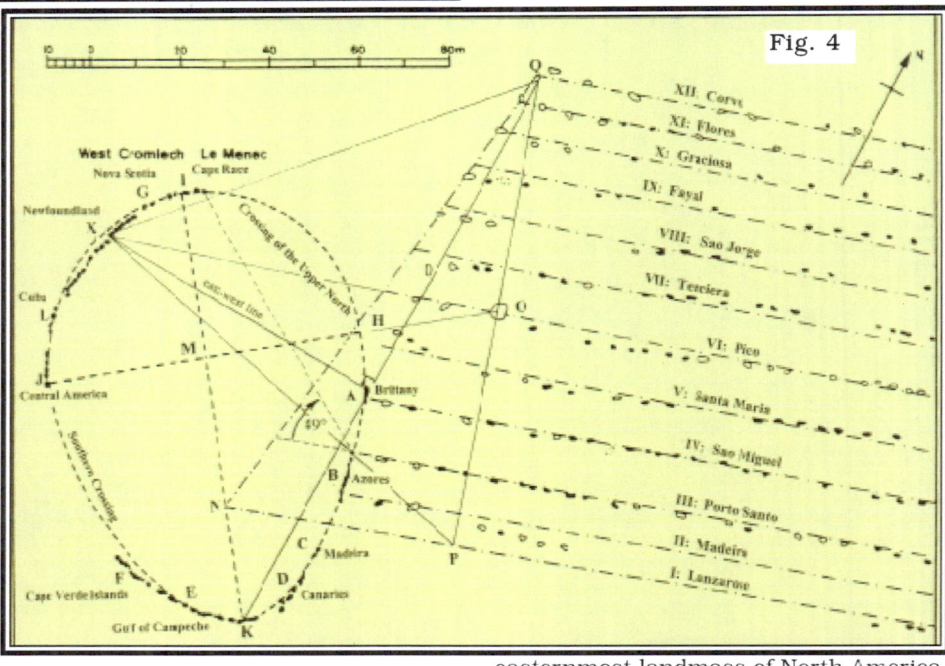

Fig. 4

Ocean. The many big menhirs in row II show the important goal in Central America. This row has 18 menhirs, corresponding to the civilization the Gulf of Campeche, the center of the Realm of the Dead, at 18°N. Row III has only 15 stones, encoding a less important goal, the north coast of Honduras, at 15°N. But here, on the east side of the Menec, the first goal is the Azores. For that reason there are besides rows II and III, 9 other rows IV-XII.

On the east side of the East Circle, the huge menhir A represents Menec in Brittany, the monument where we are standing. The menhir is situated at the very start of important row IV. All eastern rows of Menec with 361 menhirs, and especially row IV, point 25° SW to the main island of the East Azores, Sao Miguel. That is the first goal. Menhir B is situated at the very start of central row VI. It represents Cape Finisterre, the NW cape of Iberia. It is the most logical point of departure for crossing to Sao Miguel, because Cape Finisterre is located more to the west than Menec, and it is closer to the Azores.

The East Side of Menec provides the routes from Cape Finisterre and Lanzarote to the West Azores. Routes beyond these islands are not given here, because the East Circle and the long eastern rows symbolize the Old World and the crossing to the West Azores. The menhir rows of Menec run from east to west. In principle, the meanings of the rows at the East Side are valid for the whole monument. So, the 12 rows represent the 12 islands of the crossing of the Ocean from NW Africa, via the West Azores, to Newfoundland.

The long rows of menhirs connect to the important West Circle of the Menec. Here the menhirs in the rows are biggest. They have an average diameter of about 1.5 meters, and a height of c.2.5 meters. The West Circle is symbolic for the southern part of the Ocean. The bottom part of it is narrow, because people knew the Southern Crossing between Africa and South America. The East Circle is symbolic for the northern part of the Ocean. The top part of it is narrow, because people knew the Crossing via the Upper North, via Iceland and Greenland. However, both crossings are not important in the monument, because the Menec is a great Arrow, pointing to the Azores.

The 9 menhirs of group B at the east side of the egg represent the 9 islands of the Azores. The western cluster at the other side of the west circle now represents the East Coast of North America, at the other side of the Ocean. So, the enormous Arrow of the Menec now points to Newfoundland, at the same latitude as Brittany, at 49 N. Newfoundland is the easternmost landmass of North America, now it is represented by the central group of menhirs around point X.

The great crossing from the West Azores to Newfoundland, against the wind and the current, is the most important subject of the monument of the Menec. This long and difficult voyage is represented by the Western Rows. These contain twice as many menhirs as the Eastern Rows, the menhirs are on the average twice as big, and the end of the rows is about twice as broad as the start, at the East Side. The Great Secret of this crossing, is indicated by the enormous Arrow of the Menec! This Arrow points to the western cluster, X, Newfoundland. The 18 menhirs of group

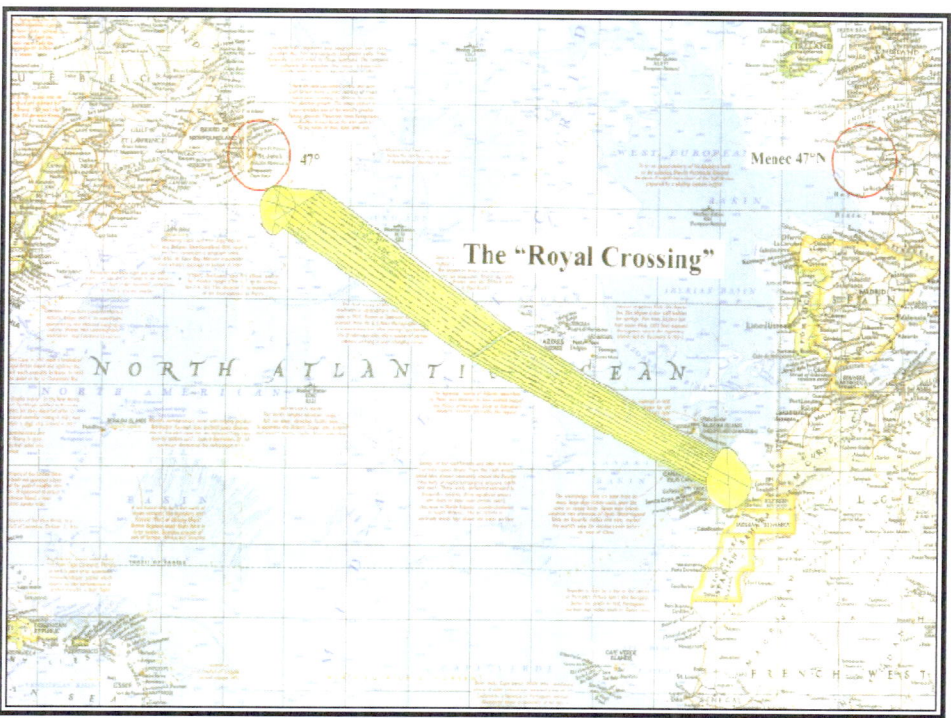

X also correspond to the sailing distance, 18dl= 2000km (1dl= 1°of latitude= 111km).

Directly below the SunGod Ra were two other gods, Horus and Osiris. In a symbolic way, the East Circle is the Empire of the Living, of the Sungod Horus, and the West Circle is the Realm of the Dead of the moongod Osiris. But the course of these gods over the waters was the important focus of this monument, so the rows have much larger and more stone than the circles. This was all the work of the Earthgod Maat, creator of the East and West Circles.

The Western Rows of the Menec represent the long crossing from the West Azores to Newfoundland (c.2050 km). However, this crossing is against the governing winds and currents. The megalith builders could no sail this difficult windward route. They had learned to cross to the west by the Route of the Upper North, or by the Southern Crossing, in accord with the tradewind patterns. In the time period when the Menec was built, their vessels had been returning from Cape Race Newfoundland to the Azores for about 600 years. They thought nobody could accomplish this direct crossing in the western direction, except the SunKing who traveled west every afternoon to the sunset.. So they believed it was a "Royal Crossing". It is carved into an Egyptian temple that the SunGod has said "The New King will appear in the Realm of the Dead in the west, at the other side of the waters, in the land where the sun sets".

In these monuments, there are a lot of details about sailing to and from the Azores, which was discovered to be the best return route across the ocean. It may seem odd to you that all this complexity is embedded in the site designs, built at great labor for mnemonic use. No one on earth does this anymore. This monument was built deep in the past, when man could not write. It must not be thought to be beyond their capabilities just because it seems strange to us. With these devices, geographic knowledge was successfully passed, over 800 years, to subsequent generations. ∎

Photo of fallen Menhir "C", looking east from the West Circle, up row VI (left), and row V (right). Menec, Carnac, Brittany, c. 1900 BC

References:

1. Burl, A., From Carnac to Callanish, The prehistoric stone rows and avenues of Britain, Ireland and Brittany, Yale University Press, 1993 (ISBN 0-300-05575-7)

2. Giot, P.R., La Bretagne, des Megalithes, Ed. Ouest France, 1995 (ISBN 2-7373-1388-0) (French)

3. Briard, J., The Megaliths of Brittany, Gisserot, 1991

4. An Approach to Megalithic Geography, Association Archeologique Kergal, Booklet No.20, 1992 (ISSN 0220 5939)(1SBN: 2902727.20.8)

5. Jonge, R.M. de, and IJzereef, G.F., De Stenen Spreken, Kosmos Z&K, Utrecht/ Antwerpen, 1996 (ISBN 90-215-2846-0) (Dutch)

6. Jonge, R.M. de, and IJzereef, G.F., Exhibition: The Megalithic Inscriptions of Western Europe, 1996

7. DeJonge, R.M., and Wakefield, J.S, How the Sungod Reached America, A Guide to Megalithic Sites, MCS Inc., 2002 (ISBN 0-917054-19-9)

8. Bailey, J., Sailing to Paradise, Simon & Schuster, 1994

9. Giot, P.R., Prehistory in Brittany, Ed JOS (ISBN 2-85543--123-9)

10. Batt, M., and others, AuPays des Megalithes, Carnac-Locmariaquer, Jos, 1991 (French)

11. Bailloud, G., et.al., Carnac, Les Premieres Architectures de Pierre, CNRS Edition, 1995 (ISBN 2-85822-139-1)

Bronze Age Colonies in the Azores and Canaries

by Jay S. Wakefield

Azores Islands

The Azores are nine semi-tropical volcanic islands on the Mid-Atlantic Ridge. They arose from the collisions of four continental plates that are 1000m below sea level. They lie on the south edge of the Gulfstream. They feel like an Atlantic Hawaii, but the Hawaiian Islands are at latitude 20°N, while the Azores are much further north at 37-39°. They get a lot of rain and warmth from the Gulfstream, especially the western islands of the group. It is surprising to see hydrangeas growing wild, as they need so much water, when grown in the States. The islands are Portuguese, and, unlike Hawaii, have no Japanese or Philippinos. Also unlike Hawaii which has lots of beaches, sheer cliffs dominate the coasts of the Azores islands, as they are constantly eroded by NE and westerly winds.

San Miguel, the largest of the eastern two islands, lies at 37°N. Its major city, Ponta Delgada, is where your SATA Air (SATA.pt) flight from Madrid will land. The island is popular with European tourists, with its remarkable green and blue lakes. The five Central Azores include the islands of Pico and Terceira, where the ruins of Bronze Age colonies are found, at 38°N. The western two islands, Corvo and Flores, are at 39°N. The modern sailing guide provides the recommended route for small sailboats heading for Europe: sail up the American coast to 39°N, then sail east on that latitude until you find the West Azores. These yachts will be found doing their repairs and reprovisioning at the harbor of Horta on the central island of Faial. Across the small channel from Horta, the sailors will be admiring the towering volcanic peak Pico, at 7,713 feet, on the neighboring island of Pico. Probably without knowing it, below the volcano, they will be looking at the small port of Madalena, where reportedly 200 pyramids have been found.

Many Bronze Age (6500 BC-1200 BC) monuments and artifacts have the number 23 carved into them, or their stone counts. For example, the cairn of Gavrinis, on the Brittany coast of France, the "most decorated" passage grave, is built of 39 huge stones. Twenty three of them decorated with petroglyphs from floor to ceiling, but there is a gap at the 23rd stone, which is a white quartz stone. The axis is oriented 38° off true north. This monument was built, according to archaeology, c.3600 BC, and clearly it was built to celebrate and commemorate the discovery of the Azores, which were found at 38°N and 39°N. We think that ancient navigators sailed west at 23°N, the Tropic of Cancer, the furthest north the sun travels before going south again, changing Summer to Fall. They were trying to find where the sun went every night as it traveled west, to the unknown backside of the Earth. Unfortunately, this course brought them into the windless "doldrums", or "horse latitudes", where Age of Discovery sailors ate their horses. Heroic Bronze Age sailors must have died on this route. Apparently some were blown to the north, and then followed birds to the Azores Islands. Since the tradewinds blow from the west onto the coast of France, sailing to these islands directly from Europe is difficult. It took a thousand years for sailors to learn the tradewind patterns of the Earth. The patterns had to be learned all over again during the "Age of Discovery", with the re-discovery of the Azores claimed by the Portuguese in 1427.

Photo 1: Perched Stone with petropot carved into the top. Located a the start of a rough roadway (ceremonial pathway?) up to Grota d Medo site above Angra, on island of Terciera, Azores Islands. Balanced stones, perched stones and petropots are commonly found in Bronze Age sites

Photo 2: One of maybe a dozen boulders on the Grota do Medo hilltop with these slot cuts, seen commonly n European Bronze Age sites. The slots had wood hammered into them, then the wood was swelled with a water soak, splitting the stone. Some of the stones failed to crack

In 1749 a pot of Carthaginian coins dating to c.200 BC were found washed out by a storm in the foundation of a building on the island of Corvo. This brought the first brought attention to Carthaginian knowledge of the sailing route. Among them were 2 gold coins and 5 bronze coins from Carthage, and 2 bronze coins from Cyrene. They were given by numismatist Enrique Florez to Johan Podolyn, who published a report about the find in 1778 in the Publications of the Royal Society of Sciences and Letters in Gothenburg. More recently, Carthaginian hypogea have been found in multiple places. A full sized bronze statue of horseman with outstretched arm pointing west tumbled down a slope when parts of it were being retrieved for a Portuguese king. The retrieved parts were later lost in the great Lisbon tsunami of 1755. No one knows who built the statue, or where the bulk of it lies. The Spanish galleons from Mexico and Panama used the Azores route for gold bearing ships, just as the route had been used in a previous era for copper bearing ships. The principal harbor during both eras, and base in the Azores, was Angra, on the central island of Terceira. Angra features some of the major Bronze Age ruins to be found in the islands.

The harbor at Angra is formed behind a 1 km diameter tuff-cone resulting from a basaltic submarine eruption called "Monte Brasil". My Dutch friend, Reinoud de Jonge and I toured the huge Spanish fortifications, and the WWII British anti-aircraft guns on top. In a "military zone" on the north side, we walked old Spanish walls to view old man-made "caves" above the seacliffs. The caves are thought to be Carthaginian ritual centers dedicated to Tanit or Asherah, Goddess of the Sea. Today they show water channels cut in the lava, leading to watering holes for Spanish horses, and one is a water reservoir. There is a small sand beach at Angra, and a town of major buildings, and tourist hotels. Part of the European Union, the roads are good, and driving is on the right, but the streets are narrow and on this populated government-center island of Terceira, there are a lot of cars parked along the roads.

Above Angra do Heroismo (Angra of the heroes), is located a site labeled on the map "Grota do Medo", up the red road, not the freeway, up the hills behind town. At the top of the steep hill, where the road levels out, there are two houses, and on the left, a farm gate. A farmer opened the gate for us, and told us to walk toward the woods on the track beside his field. A path appeared rising into pine woods on the left, and soon we were finding boulders with unreadable weathered petroglyphs on them, and boulders with slots cut for wooden splitting wedges (PHOTO 2). The path crossed a powerline, and then, near the crest, the Perched Boulder PHOTO 1 appeared before us. Right on the top of it appeared a perfect petropot. These are usually found in Iberia above ceremonial pathways, on the top of prominent boulders (REF.9, www.rocksandRows). The pathway continued, with brush clearings, the first steps in an early archaeological effort. At the top of the hill was a megalithic stone structure (PHOTO 3), and nearby another, smaller structure(PHOTO 4).

There are stone walls, stairs, steps, and stones arranged as "chairs". We explored the fields and stone fences around these woods, and found many petroglyphs, and ancient walls. Particularly impressive was a petropot that was carved into one of the stones in a cow field, that had the harbor of Angra in the view below. Clearly the hilltop site has been respected and saved although there are no signs to it or about it, and no mention of it at all in the tourist literature. In the rocks on the eastern steep hillside, where there are stone stairs and passageways, there is a full-size stone bull, with a prominent concentric carved eyeball, evoking thoughts of Minoan bull jumping or Egyptian Apis bull worship. From the slot cuts, to the petropots, stone buildings, and huge stones in stone walls, it was a European site to us.

On the other side of the island of Terceira, there is a town named Sao Bras, just off the cross-island freeway. Actually quite a way above the town, past a small group of houses called "Baldio", you come to an area labeled on the map as "Biscoito da Fontinhas". Allthough Portuguese, it is actually easier to get around here than in Portugal, as quite a few folks know some English. That is because when the whaling industry died, there was quite a diaspora to Brazil and New England. That is why the SATA flights originate in Boston, full of American Portuguese, returning to visit relatives. (The fellow next to me in the airplane was returning from Hollywood to stay again in the house a grandmother had left him.) At the

Photo 3: Megalithic stone structure on the hilltop at Grota do Medo, above Angra

Photo 4: A smaller stone structure at Grota do Medo

Photo 5: One of many similar photos of approximately half a mile trackway previously described as near Sao Bras, but actually up on the hilltop above that town in an area labeled "Biscoito da Fontinhas" above Baldio. Along the route was a stone well structure, and at the end of the road were many stone walls 4-6 foot in height throughout the woods. We could not determine the extent of the walling. The trackway starts at a 12 foot diameter concrete platform labeled "CAMINHO PRIMITIVO", with a two wheel cart axle on it.

top of the hill, you will run across a big concrete platform labeled "CAMINHO PRIMITIVO", which has two big wooden wheels with iron rims between a big wooden axle, from an old wine cart. PHOTO 5 shows the

Trackway that runs half a mile through the woods, over mostly level ground. It ends in a seemingly endless complex of stone walls in the woods on a hilltop. The locals think these trackways were made by medieval wine carts, maybe when the lava was molten or soft. On Malta, and other sites where trackways are found, including Spain, Turkey, and Sardinia, there is a suggestion that the tracks were made by poles dragged by animals, or carts carrying heavy stone blocks. There can be no doubt they are very old. PHOTO 6 shows a long trackway behind the airport that goes under a wall. Another piece of trackway can be seen under a highway bridge on the western side of the island at a town called Santa Barbara, where the tracks run under the town walls. We found another trackway in beachrock on the east end of the island south of Porto Martins. This was a light track (not so deep), and even more curious in its origin.

An elevated ridge of eastern Terceira named "Serra do Cume", has been written up by a psychologist named Maria Costa (Refs. 13,20). The first day we tried to explore this area, it was enveloped in deep fog. It was a surprise to come back a few days later when it was clear, and find the rock outcrops with all the petroglyphs and petropots and big rock walls across the fields illustrated in her book. It is unfortunate that the rocks are so weather eroded.

Reinoud and I do enjoy exploring on our own, and sometimes find things others have not noted, despite their being 4,000 years in the past. We are attracted to big stone outcrops on the tops of heights, places that have not been altered by people. On a farmed conical hilltop overlooking the large container and cruise ship port of Praia, east of Serra do Cume, we found a huge boulder at the top of the hill, which was flat on top at about chest height (PHOTO 7). Carved into the top of it was a big carved square full of water. We had seen one just like it up on the Serra. I have also seen a similar square flat bowl in the Pacific, in the Marquesas Islands, square, and the same size, at a hillside site with red rock chairs for only royalty. Our guide, Mark Eddowes, called the "French Polynesian Expert" by the National Geographic Magazine, said that they were filled with water, and served as mirrors. Perhaps, like mummification, mirrors are a concept that spread worldwide during the Bronze Age.

I should note that on the far western side of Terciera, past the village of Serreta, is a road down to a point of land called Ponta do Queimado. In the deep forests near the point are "more than 2-3 square kilometers" of stone ruins. The walls are so extensive in the woods that you can see no ending of them. You would need a full day or more to properly check this site out. There are no signs, and no indications at all of who built all the walls, terraces, and ruins. Old walkways or "roads" run through them. "The place is not classified or registered in any civil documents" -Costa, Ref.20. We walked down a pathway through them for quite a distance, then returned to the car, thinking we needed David Childress over here to check out this "Lost City", his favorite subject. PHOTO 8 takes us back to the Azorean island of Pico, at the ferry port of Madalena.

This pyramid, or "Maroicos" as they call them, is surrounded by a city park, with recreational facilities, including tennis courts. It is a rectangular stepped pyramid on a hill or mound, described as of "origem obscura" (obscure origin) by the archaeologist Manuel Tomas, in his bronze plaque at the foot of the pyramid. It has an interesting design, as its steps spiral up from the base, then the spiral terminates, and there is a square step around

Photo 6: This trackway runs parallel to and just upland of the road that runs on the ocean side of the airport on Terceira. Like the trackway on the hilltop, this is surprisingly long, maybe 1/3rd of a mile. In this photo it goes under a wall. It does connect with an asphalt roadway at both ends. There is another, shorter trackway, nearby, running just alongside the smaller road along the ocean cliffs. The locals have the theory that these were created by the wheels of winecarts, perhaps running over lava that was hot and still soft

Photo 7: My friend Reinoud de Jonge looking at a mirror square atop a conical hill overlooking the cruise ship terminal port of Praia, Terceira, central Azores Islands

Photo 8: This well maintained pyramid is labeled the "Jardim dos Maroicos", in a central park of the port of Madalena, Pico Island, Azores Islands. It is unusual in its design, with two or three spiraled tiers, and one at the top is circular, as can be seen in the photo, and a twelve foot wide, eighty foot long tongue pointing to the SW

the top. The monument is about 20 feet tall (6.2m). Its long sides orient to true north at about 39°, which is the latitude of the site. The unique tongue of stone is 6.6m wide, 1.77m high, with an angle of 228°SW (corrected for the deviation here of 8°w). Is this the winter solstice angle at 38°N? The middle step, on the south side where the spiral ends, is expanded into a wider ceremonial terrace of 2.3m (showing in lighter color in the photo). Most of the steps have a width of less than a meter. I find it interesting that the 4800-4500 BC cairn of Barnenez on the north coast of France also has a south-side middle step with an expanded ceremonial terrace of 2.4m (www.rocksandrows).

On the Internet, you can read claims that there are "200" pyramids around Madalena, while others claim "125". Driving the backroads around town, through the stonewalls sheltering the grape vines, and the houses built of stones, you find at least dozens (see PHOTO 9) of pyramid-type structures, in various states of ruin. Some have houses or garages or sheds built into them, or next to them, or built of their stones. I do not see how one could count them, how small a pile of rocks make a ruin? Surely there were quite a few pyramids built, but a systematic groundplan and archaeological survey needs to be done. Nuno (Ref. 19) reports that APIA (Portuguese Association of Archaeological Research) studied them, and noted that "around 70 of the maroicos appear to have been built aligned to the summer solstice, and that some of them have narrow corridors, chambers, and doors." Unfortunately UNESCO scientists said the APIA conclusions of construction before the 15th Century were premature and fanciful, and designated only the vineyards of Madalena as a World Heritage Site in 2004.

Canary Islands

When the Portuguese "discovered" the Canary Islands in 1427, they found large, strong, white, blond non-Christian people living there they called "human stock" (Ref.24). These people were divided into nine kingdoms around the coasts of Tenerife, surrounding common goat pastures up on central Mt. Tiede (12, 198 feet). My friend Bob List and I tried to go up to the park at the caldera, but the roads were blocked by snowbanks and park police (late February 2016).

The Pope had declared that the title to new lands could be claimed through discovery, as long as there were no Christain people living there. (This also applied to America, by the way.) These non-Catholic "Guanche" were seen as a lesser class of beings, and so they used them as slaves, and sold them sold in the slave markets of Lisbon, Seville, and Valencia. These people, some called "Guanche", some by other names, inhabited the Canaries, as well as the Azores and Madeira. All of them received the same treatment as slaves, whether from the Portuguese in the Azores, or the Spanish in Madeira and the Canaries. In Heyerdahl's museum in the Canaries, there is a painting of these people trying to fight off the first Spanish conquistadores landing at the beach with sling stones. Remember that the slingers of the Balearic islands were so reknown for their slinger skills, that they formed a division of Hannibal's Carthaginian army that crossed the Alps. There is a suggestion that these Guanche were related to the Berbers of North Africa. (My opinion is that both were descended from the same Bronze Age culture.)

In their first battle with the Spanish, the Guanche led the armored Spanish up a trail, where the Spanish stretched out single file. When they encountered a Guanche herd of goats, they put their armor in

Photo 9: This is one of the least dilapidated of the reported "200" pyramids in various states of destruction among the farms and wine walls around the town of Madalena on Pico Island. There are a dozen or two of these strutures easily seen, driving the village roads

Photo 10: Five-tier pyramid "El Guincho" near Los Cancajos, on La Palma Island, Canary Islands. It has a staricase cut into the side, like other pyramids seen in Thor Heyerdahl's Arhcaeological Park on Tenerife Island.

their carts, and caught goats for dinner. Then the athletic Guanche impaled their eyeballs, testicles, and bellies with their wooden poles, and won the battle. A museum painting shows the Spanish cavalry later wiping out every living person in a Guanche valley village. A story goes that a prominent Spanish gentleman colonist in the Canaries had an affair with a Guanche princess. His wife reportedly got even by seducing Columbus when he brought his ships to the harbor, preparing for one of his voyages to America. The story ends with the comment that she then had all the Guanche males still living on the island put to death.

Nowhere in these islands is there active archaeology in progress. Permit applications have been submitted, but none approved. The President of the Portuguese Archaeological Society, Ribeiro Nuno (Ref.19), who claims a Megalithic Culture presence on these islands, says "Archaeology has not yet begun". He has published scientific articles, and presented to international archaeological conferences. He claims he has received "great acceptance" among the international scientific community. I am tempted to speculate that these Catholic-raised administrators must wonder who made these pyramids, trackways, petroglyphs and so on. They must fear that if archaeology were to show that they were built by an early Christian people, what other country today might be able to lay a valid claim to the ownership of the islands? Remember that their perspective is that Jesus and his people began the world, not that there was an earlier Bronze Age world thousands of years before there was Christianity.

Unfortunately, despite the early reports of giant mummies, only small mummies were on exhibit in the Santa Cruz museum we visited. On the SW end of the Canary Island of Tenerife there are the extremely tall "Cliffs of Gigantia". There is a lot of evidence around the edges that at least some of the Guanche were very large. A statue in the city square of Santiago, in western Tenerife, has a huge bronze statue of a guanche warrior, and a museum exhibits a huge bronze head. Unfortunately, the Spanish prefer their conquestadores to be bigger than they were, so even at the entry to Thor Heyerdahl's museum, there are two bronze statues of equal stature.

The seven Canary Islands, off the coast of Morocco at 28 degrees north, are also volcanoes in the Ocean, but they receive hot winds off the Sahara Desert, so are not wet, but are hot and dry. The eastern islands are so close, they say they can be seen from the African coast on a clear day. The rugged and green western island of La Palma had some pyramids, but most are gone. PHOTO 10 shows the best one left. Note that it has an ascending staircase built into the west side of it, like the six step pyramids at the pyramid park of Thor Heyerdahl on Tenerife. Studies in 1991 by the Archaeology Department of La Laguna University carried out the first excavation at the site, and the Canary Islands Astrophysical Institute determined that the pyramids were aligned to the winter and summer solstices (Ref.27). The stairways up the pyramids suggest a "rising sun" ceremony on the morning of Solstice.

At the northern end of La Palma, in the area of La Zarza many petroglyphs are to be found on boulders and at cave entrances. Some of these (see PHOTO 11) are dead ringers for the petroglyph carvings in Gavrinis, on the coast of France, and others are similar to petroglyphs seen at Loughcrew, in Ireland. There can be no question that these were created in the traditions of the same Bronze Age people. PHOTO 12 shows a portion of the large pyramid and plaza complex at the "Piramides de Guimar Ethnographic Park" founded by Thor Heyerdahl and his friend Fred Olsen. An entry fee of 20E brings a lot of revenue to the site, which is elaborately built of stone and glass, with multiple buildings, wired for music, and has a "poison plant garden", lots of botanical displays and south seas relics of Thor Heyerdahl's expeditions. Thor is shown in a movie, where he says that "what struck him most about the site was the plazas between the pyramids, like in Mexico."

There must have been a lot of people to support a complex of this size, but there are no estimates of the former population size, or any explanation of the extensive (ancient?) terracing on the mountainsides around the site. PHOTO 13 shows a pyramid in a complex on the other side of Tenerife, not far from the town of Icod, taken from the parking lot of the public library of the tiny village of Santa Barbara. PHOTO 14 is another pyramid at the same complex of plazas, pyramids and walls, now being farmed. Note this pyramid has an unusual five-sided design. We looked for "La Suerte" pyramid reported by Coppens (Ref.25), and small reported ruins of several others, but did not find them. On the nearby governing island of Gran Canaria are caves with Guanche paintings in them, shown on the internet before and after repainting. They

Photo 11: One of many petroglyphs found on boulders and in caves in the area of "La Zarza" on the north end of La Palma Island, in the Canaries. This design is identical in style to the extensive glyphs in the Cairn of Gavrinis, on an island in the Gulf of Morbihan, on the coast of Brittany. Other petroglyphs have patterns similar to the daisy-circle gllyphs found at Cairn-T at Loughcrew, Ireland

Photo 12: This is one of the pyramids in the multiple pyramid/plaza/walls complex named "Piramides de Guimar Ethnographic Park", founded by Thor Hererdahl and his friend Fred Olsen, who owned the shipping line still serving the Canary Islands, and connecting them with Spain. This site is in the town of Guimar, on the east side of the island, south of Santa Cruz

Photo 13: This is a pyramid in a different Guanche Kingdom, at a place called "Santa Barbara", up a small road from Icod on the western side of the north coast. Actually, this photo is taken from the parking lot of the public library. The entire complex of pyramids and plazas is being farmed. We were being watched by the farmers, who waved as we took photos.

Photo 14: This is the five-sided six story pyramid at the Santa Barbara site, east of Icod.

are highly geometric. Guanche "pintadera" were "small and unique wooden or clay seals worn on a leather thong necklace and thought to be useful in the afterlife" (Coppens, Ref.25). A small museum collection of original Guanche pintadera in Santa Cruz (Ref.28), recalled patterns seen in Iberic pendants. Another cultural cross-connection is given by Coppens (Ref.25): "medical anatomist Elliot Grafton Smith reported the discovery of a Guanche mummy that had been subjected to typically Egyptian mummification procedures of the 26th Dynasty. For all the reasons given above, I conclude that there is convincing evidence that the seafaring people of coastal Europe, with a Minoan and Egyptian component, colonized all these islands during the Bronze Age, in support of their trans-Atlantic trading voyages. ■

Maritime Petroglyphs of the Beaker Colony of Benohare (La Palma Island, Carary Islands)
Photos taken 3/25/17 by Jay S Wakefield

Whale petroglyph, La Zarza, La Palma

Ship petroglyph, La Zarza, La Palma

Axehead in petroglyph, at La Zarzita (on the road LP-1, in the north island), La Palma

Similar axeheads in petroglyphs of Gavrinis Cairn, Brittany, France)

Chart of sailing voyage, at Petroglyphs La Castellana (in gulch below road junction), Santo Domingo De Garifia, La Palma

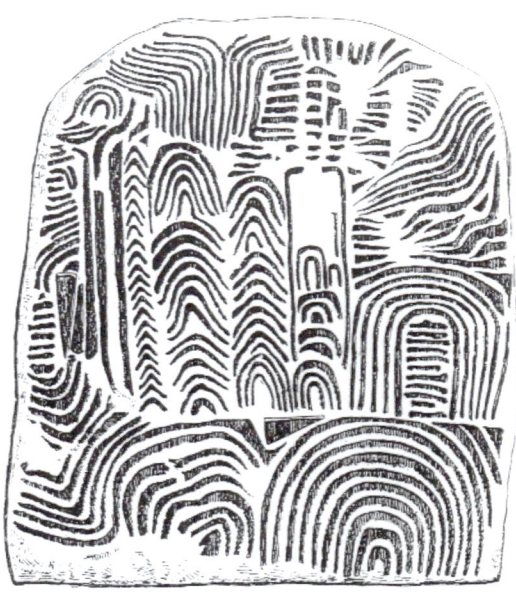
Large 8ft passage stone in Cairn of Gavrinis, Brittany, FR

Degrees of distance lines on pots at Mus. of Archaeology Bena Hoarito, Frachada Del Instituto Museo De Las Culturas del Llano, Los Llanos de Aridane, La Palma

Egyptian pots with similar design pattern, Egyptian Museum, Munich

Pyramid "El Guincho", at los Cancajos (just north of La Palma Airport)

Smaller pyramid at San Simon, La Palma (south of Airport, below road LP-2)

The Sillustani Necropolis in Peru

by Jay Wakefield

The beautiful Sillustani site at 13,000 feet is on a promontory (Photo 1) in Lake Umayo, 32 miles west of the town of Puno on Lake Titicaca in Peru. One can easily see that the stunning setting would have been considered a special sacred place. It is up the lake from the ancient lakeside metropolis of Tiawanaku. It is a 110-acre plateau of sandstone with blocks of volcanic stone and scattered ruins. The site was studied by anthropologist Adolph Bandelier, whose report appeared in *American Anthropologist* in 1905. He describes that he "found at least 95 buildings, more than 80 circular, not including scattered walls, and so-called 'sun circles' of which there are at least five."

These are tombs of the nobility of the Tiwanaku culture of the Bolivian Antiplano, yet the site contains some features typical of European megalithic culture. These features were first noticed as European by archaeologist E.G. Squier, who became the U.S. Commissioner to Peru in 1863. His report in the *American Naturalist* in 1870 (Ref. 17) says, "The point I am illustrating is the close resemblance if not absolute identity of the ... Sillustani Sun-Circles ... with those of the other continent."

The Antiplano is a high plateau between mountain ranges. Within its basin is one of the largest lakes in the world, Lake Titicaca. To the south are the famous tin mining areas and the "silver mountain" Mt. Potosi. The area is approached from the east via the Parana River, running along the southern border of Paraguay and draining into the bay of Rio de la Plata on the coast. The vicuna and guanaco and the llama and alpaca were being domesticated here about 5,000 BC, along with potato farming on the shores of the lake. The Tiwanaku culture developed in five phases from about 2500 BC to 1200 AD, over four thousand years. Starting in the Antiplano, the culture later expanded greatly in the Andes to the north and south, culminating in the 200-year Inca period.

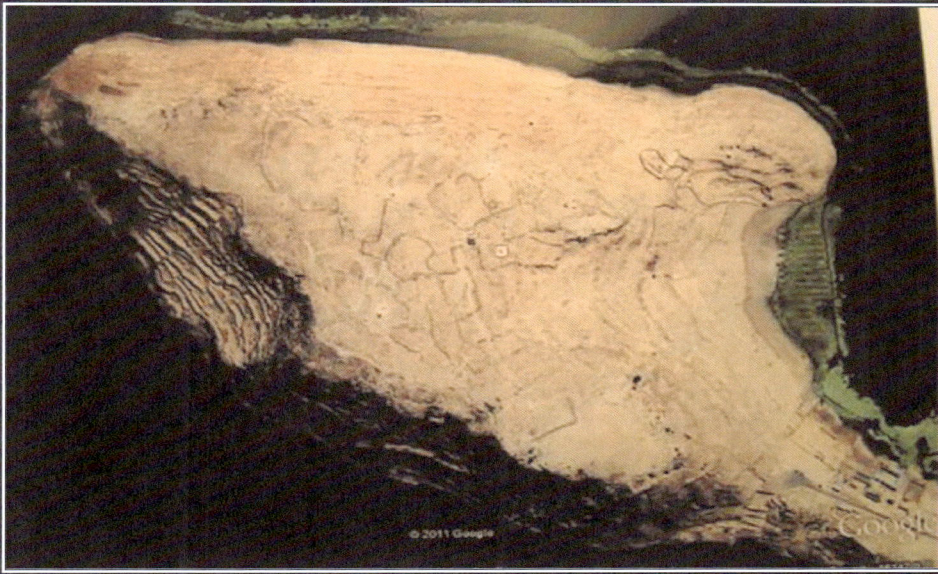

Photo 1: The promontory of Sillustani in Lake Umayo, 32 miles west of Puno, Peru

Photo 2: "Takanas" produced by a huge farming population around Lake Umayo

Satellite photography (Photo 2) shows intense ancient agricultural development, revealing the presence of huge farming populations "of millions of people" in the past (Ref. 6). Farming terraces built of stone are seen almost everywhere climbing the hillsides. These "ladders" in the mountainsides are known as "takanas." They consist of carefully layered soil, sand, and rock, inclined so they will irrigate the lower platforms. Llama and alpaca herding provided meat, textiles, and transport. Three hundred potato species were developed and over 200 corn species. A system of raised-field agriculture was developed called the "suka kollis" and "camelones" (camel backs), which raised the farm productivity by more than twenty times (Photo 3). The beds were built up of layers of sand and soil on beds of rock interspersed by fingers of water-filled canals. Due to the altitude, the climate often has very hot days and freezing nights. The water of the camelones provided moisture and humidity to the plants during the hot days and in the cold nights provided vapor, which protected the plants from freezing. They were able to preserve their foods by dehydration and store them in government-built storage facilities.

These advances transformed the villages around Lake Titicaca into a vast empire of 600,000 square kilometers with a central metropolis of ostentatious temples and palaces. Today, a small town called Tiwanaku has grown up around the ruins of the former Tiwanaku metropolis.

The huge but much dug-out "Piramide de Akapana" once had in it an underground temple in the shape of the Andean Cross. A great treasure of gold objects is reported to have been removed by the Spaniards. The impressive Templo de Kalasasaya ("temple of the stones standing up") has been extensively reconstructed by archaeologists. The famous "Gate of the Sun" has been moved up onto it. It once held the gigantic anthropomorphic figure now featured in the new site museum, the Pachamama Monolito (Mother Earth Monolith). In many of the low-relief icons, fragments of gold nails are seen, showing that they were once covered with gold plating. The smaller Templo Semisubterraneo has a stone pillar standing in the center of it and 175 limestone heads in the four surrounding walls. Interestingly, most of the heads have Middle Eastern-looking turban headgear, and some have beards.

Photo 3: "Suka Kollis," agricultural raised-bed farming

The nearby Piramide de Puma Punku is about ten feet high, surrounded by stone walls. The remaining stones on top appear to have been tumbled about in the mud by the force of a tsunami from nearby Lake Titicaca. We are studying these stones because of the machine-tool flatness of some of the stone surfaces and the perfectly square ninety-degree inner corners cut into many of the stones. The stones have many types of "key cuts" for fastening adjoining stones with poured metal clamps as is seen in Old Kingdom Egypt. As in Egypt during the Bronze Age, the Tiahuanacos developed irrigation hydraulics, construction of monumental edifices oriented to astronomical movements and Cardinal Points, stone carvings, paved bridges and roads (later attributed to the Incas), bronze metallurgy, an advanced calendar, cranial deformation, cranial surgery, ceramics, weaving, and a solar-based religion. Its ideological, technological, and scientific development influenced other parts of the South American continent, as seen in the widespread dispersion of the "God of the Staff," the figure seen on the "Gateway to the Sun" repeated in Moche pottery.

There is evidence for a variety of overseas visitors or immigrants during the Bronze Age. "The Spanish chronicled many legends of 'Viracocha' ('foam of the sea'), a bearded white man of large stature in a long cloak with authoritative demeanor, who suddenly appeared from the south. He gave men instructions on how they should live, speaking to them with great kindness and admonishing them to be good and do no damage or injury to one another, but love one another. Wherever he passed he healed and taught" (Ref. 15).

Sumerians must have been among the "culture-bringing" visitors. A huge pyramid of earth rises from the plain on the other side of the valley. We drove

Photo 4 (above): A "Chulpa" at Sillustani

Photo 5 (right): Backside of a "Chulpa," showing use of hollowed stones. The Dunn-McAllen Flute Theory suggests the hollowed stones resonated, helping the tower produce a flute tone in the wind.

Photo 6: Tomb with Lake Umayo and Isla Mesa in the background

Photo 7: Rick with his hand on a standing stone, some circular tombs in the background

Photo 8: Stone circle with collar of stones

nearby, but locals forbid access. A large stone statue of a man had been found in front of it, called the "Pokotia Monolith." Symbols on the side and rear of the figure have been deciphered by Dr. C. A. Winters as Sumerian language, naming the statue as a Diviner named Putaki, an oracle to be esteemed for his wisdom. Dr. Winters thinks that the Antiplano is the "Tin Land of the West" and the "Sunset Land" or "Mountains of the Sunset" mentioned in Sumerian inscriptions.

We saw a ceramic bowl called the "Fuente Magna" brought in by a Bolivian farmer (his "pig bowl") in the Gold Museum in La Paz, which has small triangular cuneiform symbols in the rim. Dr. Winters has deciphered it as Proto-Sumerian or Minoan–A writing, also about oracle worship. Harold Wilkins (1956) reports that "Cieza de Leon recorded in 1535 that Indians exterminated some very old, bearded, white skinned people who had taken refuge on an island in Lake Titicaca many centuries before the Spaniards. . . . The old Spanish missionaries found these Indians possessed a very ancient form of ideographic writing. Some of the ideograms (seen on Moon Island) correspond with those found in the Canaries, and among the Touaregs of North Africa, and Old Phoenicia"

Other evidence for early European visitors to South America has been showing up in recent years. A huge stone circle, the "Amazon Stonehenge," just north of the mouth of the Amazon has recently come to attention. There is a "National Park Los Menhirs" south of the Rio de la Plata in Argentina with 114 standing stones in the park. I read that one can easily paddle up the Parana River to Asuncion, Paraguay, and proceed upriver from there to the Antiplano of Bolivia and Mt. Potosi, the mountain of silver and tin. A big dot at the latitude of Rio de la Plata is shown on the earliest map of the Atlantic Ocean, carved into a stone in the end chamber of the Passage Grave of Kercado in Brittany (*How the Sun God Reached America c.2500 BC*, p. 7-3). Bolivian archaeologist Denise Schann and others have found over 250 large earthworks, causeways, canals, and field systems in an uninhabited area of 150 square miles in the eastern lowlands of Bolivia. "Not a week goes by that we do not find more." The government of Bolivia is discussing establishing an "eco-tourism park" there, hiring the native peoples as guides, and planning a controversial new road that is estimated will bring 400 trucks a day to a Pacific port.

The Sillustani site is famous for its open circular towers of finely fitted stones called "chullpas." Bandelier quotes a definition of "chullpa" from a translation: "a sack or bag of grass in which the bodies were placed for sepulcher (burial vault)." Wikipedia describes the site as a pre-Incan burial ground, with the chullpas housing the remains of complete family groups, probably nobility. All the tomb openings face east. It notes that "many of the tombs have been dynamited by grave robbers." Chullpas are not unique to Sillustani and are found all around the Antiplano in small groups or singly, though most are rectangular not circular. Photo 4 shows a Sillustani chullpa from the ESE, measured by Bandelier to be 35 feet high with a base diameter of 24 feet and a top diameter of 28 feet. Photo 5 shows a chullpa from the back side, showing most of the exterior wall collapsed, probably due to an earthquake. David Childress and his wife Jennifer are in the foreground. Note that the wall stones of the tower are hollowed out, including all the ones that have fallen down and are lying about. None of us had ever seen stones hollowed out like this. World Explorer Magazine once pro-posed the theory that these tow-ers functioned as wind flutes, like giant Andean panpipes. Chris Dunnhas proposed that they functioned as flutes powered by volcanic gases escaping from fissures below. A new theory emerged, called the Dunn-McAllen Flute Theory, that the hollowed stones were res-onant cavities that produced a more pow-erfully tuned flute. That these chullpas may have been intentionally pitched is support-ed by acoustical lab measure-ments on 73 ceramic "Whistling Vases" that had been made by nine Pre-Columbian cultures (Ref. 16). They found the pots were grouped acoustically by cul-ture. The earlier (Mochica, Vicus, Galli-nazo) pots were pitched in the lowest range, 1200-1300 cycles per second; the Chan-cay and Recuay were pitched at 2000-2100 cps; and the Chimu and Inca were 2600-2800 cps. In these cultures, like our own with its rock bands, movie music, or elevator music, rich chords ap-parently were used as mind-altering in-struments, setting up sympathet-ic vibrations that led to psychological or psy-cho-spiritual effects in the human body. Archaeology Magazine reports that the tunnels beneath the Chavin de Huantar ruins on the Pacific coast of Peru are being studied by a team of archaeolo-gists, anthropologists, and acoustic ex-perts from Stanford's Center for Computer Research in Music and Acoustics. "The maze of tunnels and al-coves ... are capa-ble of disorienting people through tricks of sound." The re-

Photo 9: Hilltop stone circle in European Megalithic Period style

Photo 10: Pairs and single standing stones possible astronomic sighting stones

Photo 11: Fallen and broken-shaped standing stone pair
What might be carved on the backside?

searchers found 20 deco-rated trumpet shells in one of the gal-leries. "They are trying to find out if the tunnels were deliberately designed to en-hance the sound of voices or musical in-struments such as the flute." I suggest they should study the chullpas, as the stones are obviously intentionally hol-lowed out! There are many other burial chamber types at Sillustani. Some have only a few stones show-ing, and many probably have been destroyed completely or are buried or have had their stones re-used. Some look like small European-style passage graves. Most are round and a few are large square structures that may have been roofed. Some are "white towers" that had an original coating of white clay mixed with grass. Many have spectacular settings along the edge of the promontory. The tomb in Photo 6 looks out over the lake with Mesa Isla in view, which has had reports of UFO landings on it. Bandelier says "Permission to open ...one or more tombs...was unobtainable. The belief that valuable objects of metal are therein concealed is deeply rooted in the minds of the people, although there is no authentic recollection of the finding of any 'treasure' at Sillustani" (Ref. 1). Walking around Sillustani, one is struck by features that could just as easily be found in Dartmoor National Park in Cornwall or other sites in Europe. Photo 7 shows Rick McAllen with his hand on a large unmarked Standing Stone, a "men-hir," which, as usual, has no obvious purpose. South of it in a natural bowl is a stone circle (Photo 8), or at least most of one, with a fancy collar of surrounding stones. Above it on the hilltop is another circle (Photo 9), this one with a carved center-standing stone and a horizontal stone in the ring on the north side. Down the hill near the lake are standing stones in pairs (Photo 10). These appear to be set on a pointed hill in the distance to the north. This site needs some study by a researcher with astronomic expertise. Near the "camelones" farming area by the lake on the east side, there are several broken-shaped standing stones (Photo 11). They appear to be lying on their faces. They should be rolled over to see if anything interesting is carved into the faces of them. Two huge structures show up in Google Earth on the NW point (Photo 1), which I did not notice from the top of the Necropolis so are uninvestigated, but these are not on the 1905 map of Bandolier, so they may be something modern. An interesting stone carved in the shape of a condor head (Photo 12) can be found among the scattered stones on the highest ground. The condor ruled the upper world of the sky, the Puma ruled the surface, and the snake ruled the underworld in Tiwanaku mythology. These stone remains (the standing stones, the paired sight stones, the stone circles) reveal the presence of European megalithic culture, which for many years in prehistory was centered at Carnac on the coast of Brittany. We do not know exactly when they arrived here, or how many, but it appears that persons with Sumerian, Egyptian, and European backgrounds came here in prehistoric times. These "culture-bringers" had an impact that produced these unexpected cultural features in the necropolis. ∎

Photo 12: Possible condor head ruler of the upper world, the sky

1. Bandelier, Adolph F., "The Aboriginal Ruins at Sillustani, Peru", American Anthropologist, New Series Vol.7, No.1, Jan-Mar 1905, pp 49-68

2. Finlayson, Clive, The Humans Who Went Extinct, Oxford University Press, Oxford, 2009, ISBN 978-0-19-923919, pg 200

3. Mutic, A., Armstrong, K., Smith, P., Bolivia, Lonely Planet, 2011, pg 22.

4. Wakefield, J.S., de Jonge, R.M., How the SunGod Reached America c.2500 BC, A Guide to Megalithic Sites, MCS Inc., 2002, ISBN 0-917054-19-9, pgs 7-2, 7-3

5. Wakefield, J.S., de Jonge, R.M., Rocks & Rows, Sailing Routes across the Atlantic and the Copper Trade, MCS Inc., 2110, ISBN 0-917054-20-2

6. Sparavigna, Amelia C., "Landforms of Titicaca near Sillustani", Torino Italy, 2110 (internet)

7. Schaan, D., Parssinen, M., Ranzi, A., "Pre-Columbian Geometric Earthworks in the Upper Purus: a Complex Society in Western Amazonia", Antiquity, Vol.83, 322, 2009, P 1084-1095

8. "Ancient Amazon Earthworks Seen by Satellite", "http://www.westinstenv.org/sosf/2010/01/08/ancient-amazon-earthworks-seen-by-" www.westinstenv.org/sosf/2010/01/08/ancient-amazon-earthworks-seen-by-satellite/

9. "Prehispanic Earthworks of the Baures Region of the Bolivian Amazon", "http://www.sas.upenn.edu/~cerickso/baures/baures2.htm" http://www.sas.upenn.edu/~cerickso/baures/baures2.htm

10. Winters, Dr.C.A., "decipherment of the Cuneiform Writing on the Fuente Magna Bowl", "http://www.bibliotecapleyades.net/arqueologia/esp_boliviarosseta_5.htm" www.bibliotecapleyades.net/arqueologia/esp_boliviarosseta_5.htm

11. Winters, Dr.C.A., "The Pokotia Monument", "http://www.bibliotecapleyades.net/arqueologia/potokia01.htm" www.bibliotecapleyades.net/arqueologia/potokia01.htm

12. "Pokotia Monolith", "http://en.wikipedia.org/wiki/Pokotia_Monolith" http://en.wikipedia.org/wiki/Pokotia_Monolith

13. "Fuente Magna – Rosetta Stone of the Americas", HYPERLINK "http://www.world-"www.world-mysteries.com/sar_8.htm

14. Tiwanaku Guide, Museum of Tiwanaku, Tiwanaku, Bolivia

15. Wilkins, Harold T., Mysteries of Ancient South America, Citadel Press, 1956, pg 95.

16. Statnekov, Daniel, Animated Earth, North Atlantic Books, Berkley, 1987, P.41.

17. Corliss, W.H., Ancient Man: A Handbook of Puzzling Artifacts, 1978, ISBN 0-915554-03-8

18. Smith, J., Archaeology, "Listening to the Gods of Ancient Peru", July/Aug 2011, Pg 14.

19. Ossorio, Alejandro Vega, "http://www.troyanosargentina.com" www.troyanosargentina.com, 2/10/2011, "Trojans in Middle South –America/ All the Links for an Easy Search"

The Colonization of North and South America by the Beaker People

Jay S. Wakefield

An interesting question has been bothering my friends in Archaeology. The mounds of the Midwest of America have been found to contain many giant skeletons, up to eight feet tall, with huge limbs and enourmous skulls. They have been named the Adena People, the first potters, farmers, and mound builders in America. Who were these people? Where did they come from? I think we can now answer these questions.

Thirteen years ago (2002) I published *How the SunGod Reached America* (Ref.2). This book provides evidence that the megalithic Bronze Age monuments of Europe and America were intended to record and convey geographic information. The larger sites are walk-in stone maps, most often maps of the Atlantic Ocean. Also, thousands of small stone pendants made by the Bronze Age Beaker People of Iberia turned out to be stone maps of the ocean. Now, new artifacts have come to light (in this article) which strongly supplement this earlier material.

Photo 1

Five years ago (2010) I published a book entitled *Rocks & Rows* (Ref.3), which included an article "The Beaker People who Discovered America." That title was based on their pottery, found on both sides of the Atlantic, and their reputation for introducing copper to Britain. Photo 1, from this book, was taken in 1998 inside the Passage Grave of Fourknocks, Ireland. The photo shows my wife Suzy, with Reinoud De Jonge. You can see the repeating diamond pattern on the edge of a capstone, one of several examples of Beaker art on the huge stones in the chamber. These patterns are also seen on Beaker Pottery, such as the pot in Photo 2, which is a photo I took in the Devises Museum, in Devises, England, a small town just south of Avebury. These people were named for their pottery with elaborate zig-zag and diamond shaped geometric designs. The inset pot is an Adena pot, made in America about two thousand years later, also in a repeating diamond ("lozenge" motif (Ref.79). The pottery finds were concentrated in the fertile river valleys of Europe (Photo 3) (Ref.28).

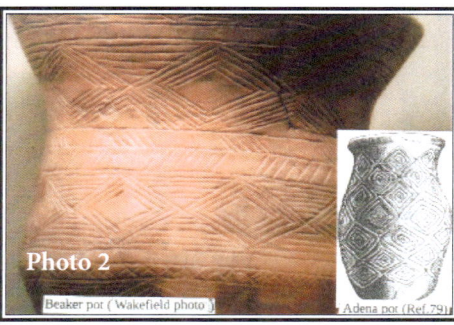
Photo 2
Beaker pot (Wakefield photo) — Adena pot (Ref.79)

These folks were the first farmers in Europe, the first potters, and used the first wristguards with archery. They raised livestock, barley and flax and brewed beer. Photo 4 shows a "typical round" Beaker skull (upper left), compared with a "typical long" skull (lower left) from Harrison's book *The Beaker Folk* (Ref.28). Harrison explains that early work suggested that "the men in particular were above average height, and more robust than was usual, and their skulls larger and rounder". The skulls on the right are Adena skulls, one found on a mound in Chilicothe, Ohio, the other in the famous Grave Creek Mound in West Virginia (Refs.4,13,33,62, and 78). They were clean-shaven, with long hair. They lived along rivers, and along the coasts of Europe, a culture that developed for several thousand years (c.3500 BC-1200 BC). They had metal technology and engraving techniques. They featured the wheel-cross motif we find so often on petroglyphs and artifacts in America (see one added to the corner of Photo 3). They dropped the neolithic "Long Barrows"

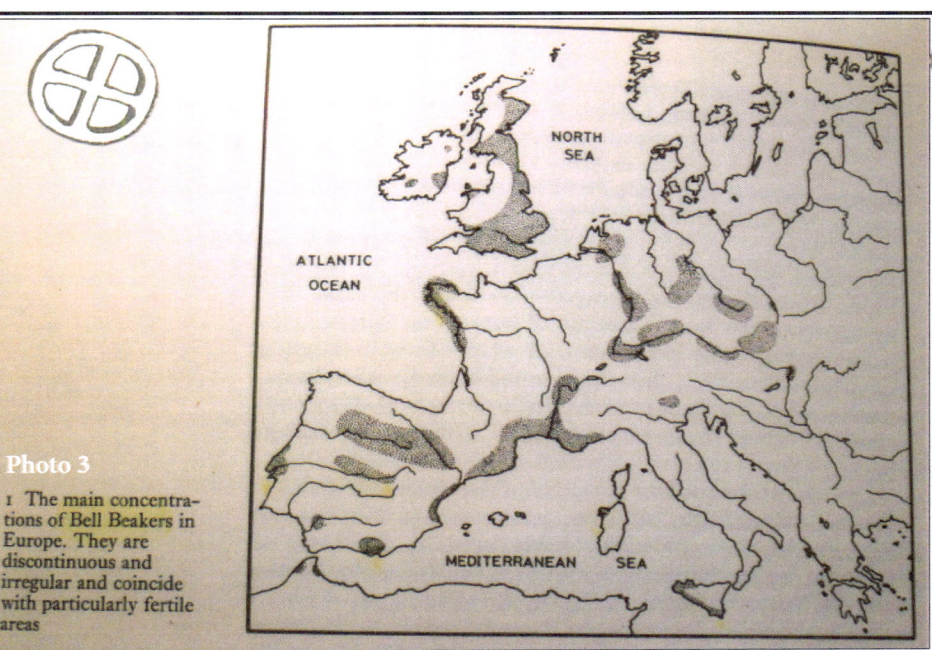
Photo 3
1 The main concentrations of Bell Beakers in Europe. They are discontinuous and irregular and coincide with particularly fertile areas

of multiple burials, and developed single burial mounds. They built Stonehenge, Avebury, and Silbury Hill. These people are known for being the seafaring folk who introduced copper and metals to the British Isles, starting in Cornwall, the south of England.

The clothing, too, leads us to think these Beaker People were American Mound Builders. Photo 5 shows Beaker clothing, in a huge new book *The Oxford Handbook of the European Bronze Age* published in 2013 (Ref.26). The book illustrates the woven woolen women's tunics and dresses of the Beaker People with pins and buttons. Adjacent to the four Beaker women, I have placed the dress and tunic images carved into the Wilmington Stone, found in an Ohio Adena mound called Spark's Mound. Unfortunately, the National Park Service paintings at mound sites show the mound builders to be loinclothed, ignoring this remarkable evidence. The blond and red-haired Urumc mummies found in northwestern China wear brilliantly colored well-made textiles, showing the extent of the Beaker People explorations to the Far East (Ref.73).

Jim Guthrie, a researcher with the NEARA group (Ref.43) states that "the Basques shared physical characteristics with the maritime Bell-Beaker people, who were larger than most others... It seems likely to me that the Adena had a significant Bell-Beaker component..." He is not the only one to suspect the Beaker People were the ancestors of the Adena. The wide variety of "reel-shaped gorgets" (Ref.79) would lead

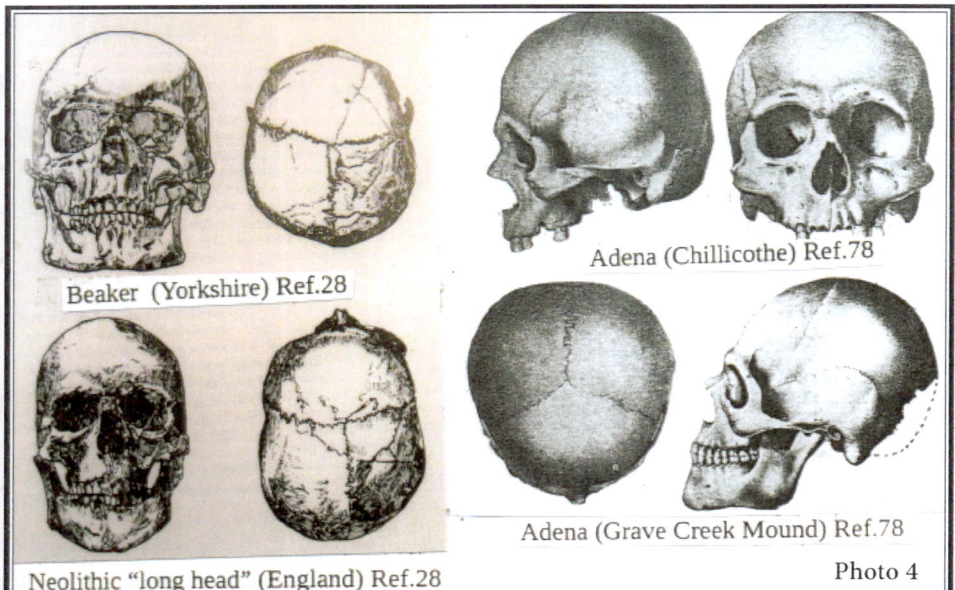

Photo 4: Beaker (Yorkshire) Ref.28; Adena (Chillicothe) Ref.78; Neolithic "long head" (England) Ref.28; Adena (Grave Creek Mound) Ref.78

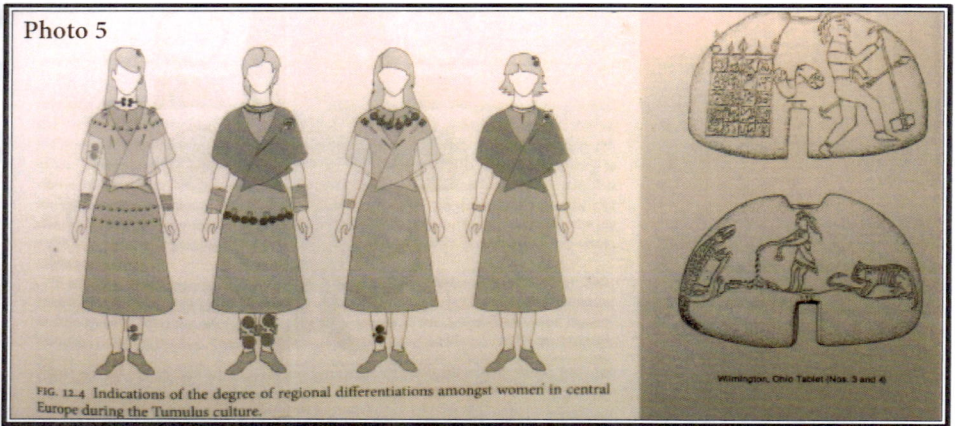

Photo 5: FIG. 12.4 Indications of the degree of regional differentiations amongst women in central Europe during the Tumulus culture. Wilmington, Ohio Tablet (Nos. 3 and 4)

anyone to suspect a relationship with the earlier copper oxhide ingots, which were similarly shaped. Researcher Zena Halpern recently sent me a copy of an unpublished 82 page paper by Archaeology Professor and Mexican expert, Robert Chadwick (1930-2014). His wife had saved his unpublished papers and has made them available at Tulane University. The title of his work "Toward a Theory of Trans-Atlantic Diffusion" (Ref.44) is based upon two ceramic vessel forms, the "shoe-shaped pot and the stirrup-spouted vessel." He concludes that there were at least two trans-Atlantic incursions … at 2000 BC and at 500 BC. We have shown that the Bell-Beaker cultures in the Old World are in some way ancestral...[to the Americas]."

We know from 25 years of studying Megalithic monuments of Europe, that these people were curious about what was on the backside of the Earth, and where the sun went each evening as it set. A jumping-off point for sailing explorations to the west was the base in the Orkney Islands (Refs.2,3). While exploring past Orkney, and then past the Faroes and Iceland, they found Greenland. Its south tip, Cape Farvel, was at 60 degrees north. They celebrated this discovery by building the 60-stone Ring of Brodgar, on Mainland, the large island in the Orkneys. The site was on a neck of land that narrowed between two lakes, simulating Greenland's southern Cape which narrows between two seas, so the site is another Megalithic "walk-in map."

Photo 6, Photo 7

Recent excavations on the Ness (neck) of Brodgar have revealed a walled building complex. Archaeologists have found it surprising that no bronze artifacts have been found in the excavations. However, we know that the copper of Michigan had not been discovered yet, so these Beaker People, (known for introducing copper to Britain) did not have the metal yet. Archaeologists were also surprised to find the "bones of 600 cows, all eaten in a great feast, and after it, the people moved on" (Refs.63,64,69). When new land, the home of the SunGod was discovered west of Greenland (by explorers sailing west at 67 degrees) there must have been a celebration, and a great stocking up of dried meat for their ships. One can imagine the excited farmers and sailors, closing up their farms, and loading their ships for the voyage to the new lands.

Photo 6 shows one of the petroglyphs in the passage grave of La Pierrre's Plates, which is located at the mouth of the Gulf of Morbihan, on the coast of Brittany, France. The petroglyph on the inside of the passage wall stone is four feet tall. On the petroglyph there are four pairs of descending rings., described in the literature as "breasts". In their explorations westward, trying to see what might be on the backside of the Earth, they had discovered that the ocean to their west contained offshore islands. As explained in the Introduction of How the SunGod Reached America (Ref.2), the top circle on the right side of the petroglyph represents Iceland, the next, the Azores (open to the west, not explored there yet), the next, the Canary Islands (continuing to the East), and below, the Cape Verde Islands. The glyph has distance lines on both sides (from both coasts), and the usual southern tip of Greenland, coming down in the Ocean at the top of the glyph. They had not yet been to the backside of the Earth, but thought it reasonable to suppose there were also offshore islands there, so they show imaginary islands there in the left half of the petroglyph. This later turned out to be a good guess.

Photo 7 shows a Portuguese pendant, described as a "female plaque" when it was offered to me, sight unseen, by email. I was sure it would have multiple sets of engraved circles before I saw it, as it does. The pendant also shows descending island images, with their concentric distance lines. It is clear that the graphics of these two carvings are similar in concept and style, so are probably similar in age, making this "female plaque" a very early pendant. It is additional evidence that the peoples all along the Atlantic Coast of Europe shared a common "Atlantic Seafaring Culture" as claimed by Barry Cunliffe, the head of archaeology at Oxford University, in his book about the Beaker People, entitled Facing the Ocean (Ref.29).

I have recently been able to acquire an unusually long and narrow Beaker People Iberian pendant from a "Manhattan collection." I have noted an explanation of its features beside the stone in Photo 8. All of the pendants are unique, highly stylized, "one-offs." They are found in Passage Graves, accompanying the dead. This anthropomorphized pendant, with eyes of the Sungod, has the ocean wave motif. Like most of the thousands of pendants, the width of the Ocean is shown by three big triangles with half triangles at the sides, and its six vertical divisions show the 60 degrees from the equator to southern Greenland at 60 degrees north. This pendant is unusual in having three big upright "vees", which I think represent the three known best routes across the Ocean. As noted by Professor Lillios in her book *Heraldry for the Dead* (Ref.22), "the plaques all follow a rigorous set of rules, probably differentiate those who traveled, and were a medium for record-keeping and memorializing." These pendants warranted to the Sungod that the bearer deserved a hero's status, as they had braved the waters to the Underworld on the backside of the Earth.

The beautiful bone ocean pendant, Photo 9, which is called an "Idolos Oculados", an idol with eyes. This pendant was found with other bone amulets in an archaeological cave dig "in about 1977" near the river Turia, at Gandia, inland of Valencia, Spain. On this Mediterranean coast of Spain, there were not the outcroppings of slate, but obviously sailors from there were making pendants on bone, in a similar style to the slate pendants of western Iberia. The rays around the eyes are 12 and 11 in number, totaling 23. This is the declination, or tilt, of the Earth in its orbit. This tilt causes the summer/winter change of seasons. This number is described by Mixter (Ref.55), in his textbook on *Navigation*, as the "most important number in navigation." We find it very often in megalithic monuments and petroglyphs, including Stonehenge. This important latitude was clearly part of the scientific knowledge at the time.

Below the eyes (Photo 9), are carved four boats, and below them, are three rows of divided triangles. Three is very common in "megalithic art." In our books, we have shown many examples which lead us to conclude that these refer to the three island groups of the Azores, out in the Atlantic. In another article, I will illustrate the stone pyramids, trackways, balanced stones, stone structures, and petropots that remain of the Bronze Age colonies there. Note that if you count the spaces (= distances) in the triangles, you find 13+13+13 for a total of 39. This is the latitude of Corvo, of the important West Azores, the first islands you reach when sailing east from North America at the 39 degree latitude line. This is, by the way, the sailing instruction given to modern sailors sailing to Europe from America. These numbers are not "plowmarks" or accidental. They were carefully carved by a sailor or navigator.

Photo 10 shows the most sophisticated, most carefully crafted, Bronze Age pendant I have ever seen. I call it "crossing pendant". It is a box-latitude sailing chart. It comes from the same cave dig near Valencia as the pendant discussed above. The eyes are carefully carved, with 32 rays from each eye. These ocean dimensions are not only shown by the 32dl, but again in the three triangles, and again by the four rows of 27 small boxes below of one degree of distance each direction in each box. (The earliest chart of the Atlantic, in latitude boxes, draped like a fishnet over a huge stone, is in the chamber of the Kercado Passage Grave in Brittany c.2200 BC (Ref.2).)

The three triangles at the bottom are divided into segments of 8, 6 and 9, totaling 23, the declination of the Earth. Of course the width of the Ocean varies by the latitude where it is measured. The 32 Egyptian moira (degrees) of the eyes are reasonable, for a normal crossing, declaring that the residence of the SunGod is 32 moira west. However, the horizontal boxes were very finely carved, I think by a sailing captain or navigator. He or she is stating that with a two-ship voyage, he found a route that was only 27 moira. There are 60 nautical miles in each degree (one degree = one megalithic Egyptian moira), so this is equal to 60 x 27, or 1,620 nautical miles. This is the shortest distance across the Atlantic, from the Cape Verde Islands to the coast of Brazil, as shown in Photo 11. This route is straight downwind. A coconut in the water will always follow this route. The big red triangles of Photo 11 and the map's vertical longitude lines with with ten degree spacing, show the features found upon many petroglyphs and pendants. The three center triangles show the "open ocean" distance. The dotted triangles at each

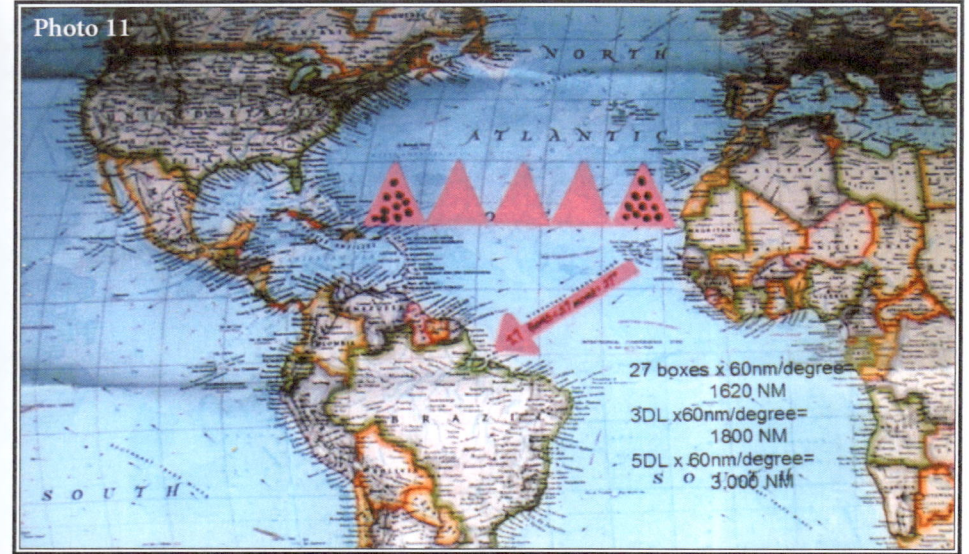

Photo 11

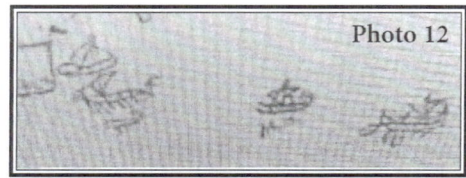

Photo 12

side are often shown partially, on the edges, showing portions of the Ocean that contain islands, or showing extensions into the Carribbean, European coast, or the Mediterranean Sea. The red arrow shows the length of the 27 dl crossing accomplishment.

Photo 12 shows a Spanish cave painting of the Beaker People, associated with the Idolos Oculudos (pendant images). The paintings are located in the Cueva de Laja Alta, a cave near Cadiz, in southern Spain. The panel in red and black ochre "is a naval scene of seven ships, considered one of the most valued historical documents of 1,000 BC" (Cadiz net.com). The Beaker People had not only the motive (find the home of the SunGod), but also the means (sailboats) and the ability (accurate navigational knowledge) to sail the oceans.

The use of latitudes in Central America at early dates is illustrated by the gold figurines in the book *Atlantis in America* by Costa Rican Professor Ivaar Zapp (Ref.57). These little gold figurines have knotted cords and small rectangles held in their mouths, illustrating the "Kamal," a term given by later Arab users of this instrument used to determine latitude. "These figurines have been found throughout the Diquis Delta region of Costa Rica," the area where most of the huge stone balls have been found. I have seen these balls also in the courtyard of the Departmental Museum in Quimper, and the ouside yard of the Prehistoric Museum of Penmarch. both in Brittany, the homeland of the Beaker People. I have seen them also in Bosnia, another place reachable by the culture of the Beaker People. The gold figurines in Costa Rica, and probably all the balls, are a vestige of the navigational traditions of the culture which made the figurines and carved the balls. Researcher Jim Bailey said in his book *Sailing to Paradise* (Ref.56), that "according to the Greek historian Diodorus Siculus, the Atlas People (Bronze Age) were famous for teaching the "Doctrine of the Spheres." Remember that 1300 stone circles were constructed in the British Isles from 2500 to 1200 BC. The Adena are known for their "sacred circles" of "paired post-molds," some 95 feet in diameter, found in many Adena sites. Authors Webb and Snow (Ref.78) thought these were "generically related" to the circular structures in England.

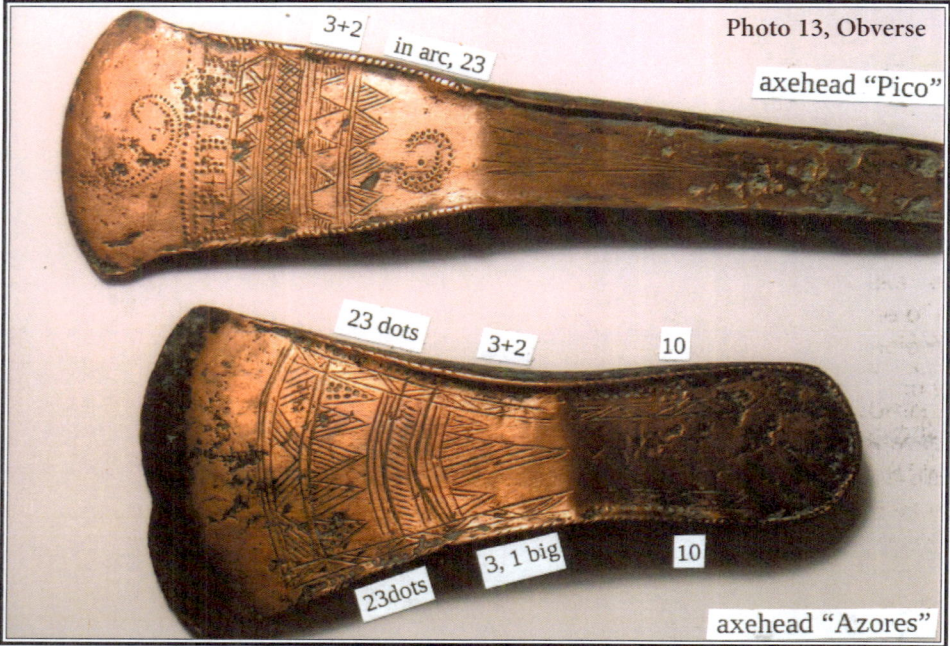

Photo 13, Obverse — axehead "Pico" / axehead "Azores"

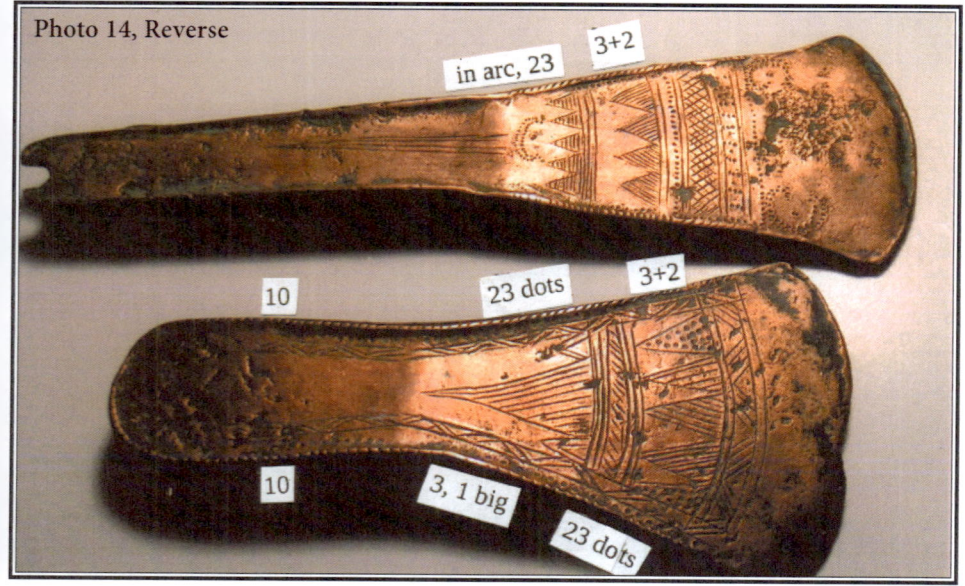

Photo 14, Reverse

Photos 13 and 14 show two remarkable copper or bronze axeheads of the Bronze Age. They are from the collection of Dr. Moog, in southern Germany. They were almost totally black before I recently polished them so they could be accurately studied. The detailed information on these Beaker axes is astonishing. The shorter one is nearly identical on its two sides. The longer one has two arcs of 23 dots on its backside and one oval glyph of 23 dots on the front. The "handle" end of the shorter axehead has exactly ten dots on each side, on both the front and back. Following arrival on the coast of South America, and turning to starboard up the coast, one would need to sail north ten degrees to enter the Carribbean Sea between Venezuela and the Windwards. The four tens, added to the four 23s, give 33, the latitude of Madeira four times.

The reverse side of the short axehead has 23 dots in its sides. Both sides have 3 prominent triangles, with the center one much larger. I think this reflects the importance of the colonies they had in the Central Azores (article in preparation). Note the three triangles below, with the dotted triangles on each side, and compare this with the triangles of Photo 11. These axes were made with much care and casting expertise. They carry the same data as the pendants of Iberia. They were exquisite posessions of the Beaker elite, and carry some of the navigational knowledge of their civilization.

Photo 15 shows both sides of another axehead from the collection of Dr. Frederich Moog, named "Atlantic." Again, it is thought he acquired it from an older southern German collection. The blade has a beautifully wide semicircular shape, with different patterns. By cleaning off the hard black patina, I could see the details well enough to count them accurately. Let us call the blade side with the three center dots the "front," and the side with the four center dots the "backside." To start, from 20 years of studying petroglyphs, I suspect the 3 dots on the "front" probably represent the three island groups of the Azores, because we have seen this so often. There are small lines between these dots. We have learned from other megalithic glyphs that they have a convention of using the spaces between the lines to represent open distances. The lines only divide the water into a number of distances, usually the distance of one moira, the Egyptian distance of one degree. In all, there are 34 lines, which give a distance of 38 spaces, or 38 degrees. This is the important latitude of the colonies in the Central Azores, on Pico and Terciera. So it seems the suspicion that the 3 dots were the Azores was correct. The large dots on the inside of the edges, total 16 on one side, and 17 on the other, so total 33, the latitude of the island of Madeira, stepping-stone to the Azores. The dots along the ridges total 17 and 19, totaling the latitude of their homeport of Tartessos, near the entrance to the Mediterranean.

The "backside" is even more interesting. The outer ridge dots are again 17 and 19, so total 36, confirming Tartessos again. The inner horseshoe of large dots only total 22. I suppose this was intended to be 23, the

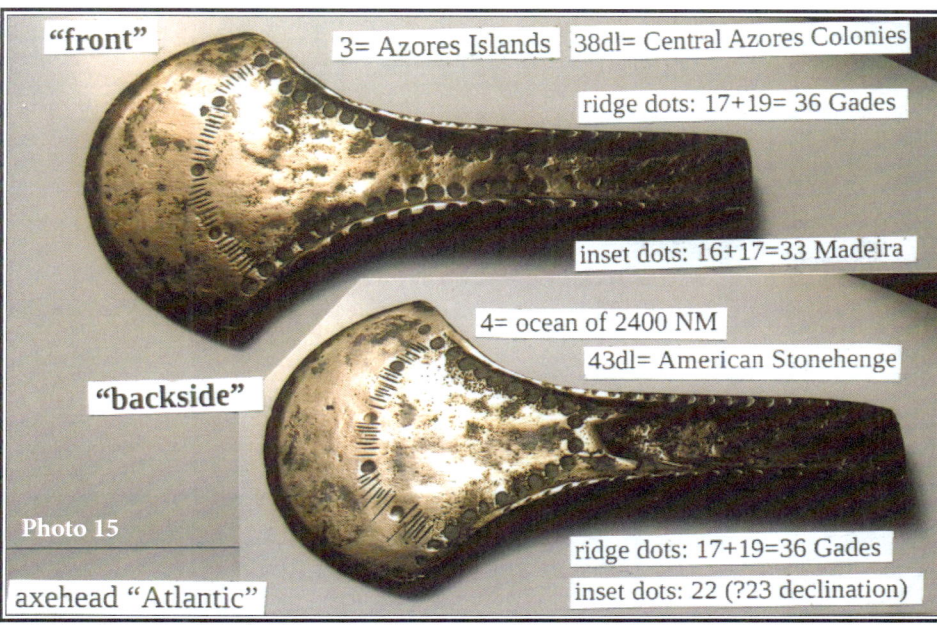

Photo 15 axehead "Atlantic"

"front" — 3= Azores Islands — 38dl= Central Azores Colonies
ridge dots: 17+19= 36 Gades
inset dots: 16+17=33 Madeira

"backside" — 4= ocean of 2400 NM — 43dl= American Stonehenge
ridge dots: 17+19=36 Gades
inset dots: 22 (?23 declination)

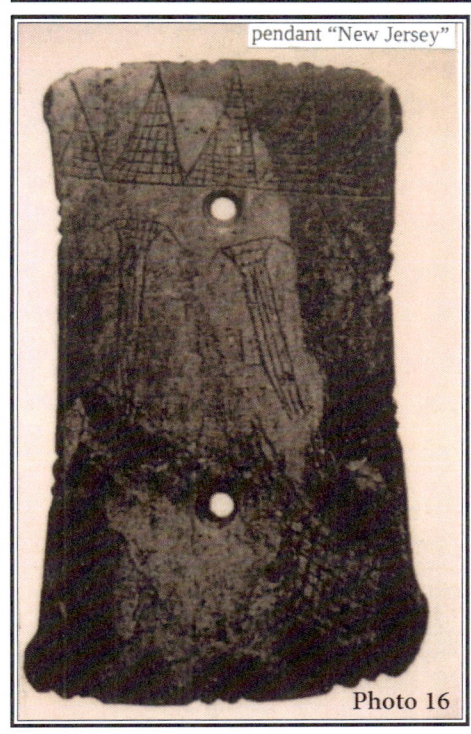

pendant "New Jersey"

Photo 16

declination. There are four blade dots, maybe the width of the Atlantic Ocean in DL (big dl) of ten degrees each. This would produce an Ocean width of 4 x10 x 60 NM/degree, equal to 2400 Nautical Miles. Between these dots are 38 lines, making 43 spaces. At 43 degrees north is located the monument of American Stonehenge, built at about the same time as Stonehenge in England, for the teaching of navigation (Ref.2). Sailing to Europe in the Bronze Age required traveling to 43 degrees north on the American coast to American Stonehenge, making your sacrifices there, then sailing east to the West Azores, to be found at the latitude of 39 degrees north, with their colonies at 38 degrees north. So this "decorated" axehead shows knowledge of the sailing route back across the Atlantic from west to east, from American Stonehenge to the Azores, Madeira, and Gades. Some of the data is duplicated on both sides, as we have also seen on the bone pendants. This is the most detailed and accurate navigational information ever found on a Bronze Age artifact.

The Beaker People actually left a colony of people called the "Guanaches" in the Canary Islands archipelago that was living in harmony when first visited by the Portuguese (Ref.21). The Guanches were "robust" big fair-haired blue-eyed white people, who decorated burial caves filled with mummies of their forebears. You can Google their cave art, and see the Beaker-style geometric patterns in it, though the panels have been recently "reconditioned" with bright paint. Their pyramid complex on Tenerife is now part of the "Piramides de Guimar Ethnographic Park", established by Thor Heyerdahl and his friends. Unfortunately, the Guanaches were the first people to be wiped out by the Portuguese slave traders. The pyramids on Pico, in the Azores, remain from a similar colony. This does illustrate, though, a path of the Beaker People in the Ocean, during their nearly two thousand years of explorations.

We are now going to look at some American artifacts that show the presence of the Beaker People. Photo 16 shows a "bannerstone" pendant found in New Jersey with good provenance, having been described by archaeologist W.K. Moorhead, in 1917. Note the three central, and two edge triangles, the same pattern as on many Iberian pendants. Who was carrying this pendant in New Jersey? Where had they been, to carve classical stone columns on the pendant? Egypt probably.

Photo 17 is a "personal find" by Chris Peters, shown in the beautiful relic magazine *Prehistoric American*. Found in a Missouri streambed in the spring of 2014, it

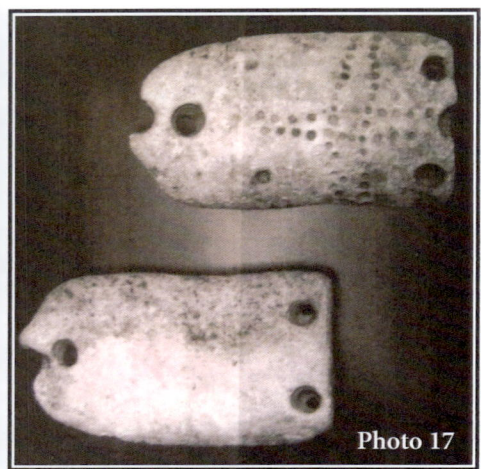

Photo 17

is described as a "stone gorget." It appears to be very worn, broken and re-drilled at the top. It is actually a Bronze Age digital latitude sailing chart, using the same methodology previously seen on the bronze German axes. The mouth of the Mississippi river is shown at the bottom (the slate pendants always have north at the top), with twelve dots representing degrees of latitude running up the river to Chicago (30 degrees at the river mouth, to 42 at Chicago). The ships carrying copper from Isle Royale could sail directly from the Great Lakes down the Chicago River during the Bronze Age (until 1200 BC) according to Dr. James Scherz, Ph.D (The Ship Petroglyph Ref.47).

The Olmec cities were being built at the same time as the mounds at Poverty Point, Louisiana, around 1500 BC. They were located between the Bay of Campeche (18 degrees N - the upper horizontal row of 18 dots), and the Gulf of Tehuantepec (16 degrees N - the lower horizontal row of 16 dots). This pendant shows the location of the Olmec cities, and the length of the copper route up and down the Mississippi (two rows). This was created using the same methodology of one dot or one rock, for a distance at sea of one degree of latitude. This methodology had been used for at least a thousand years in Europe. The rows of Carnac, or the Lagatjar rows (both in Brittany), and many other sites use this methodology. It is the same methodology we have seen on the German bronze axes, and the Iberian pendants. So this pendant was made in the megalithic tradition, probably by a sailor of the Beaker Culture. It was lost, or intermittently saved as an interesting relic, before being lost again and being saved as an interesting relic by Mr. Peters.

Photo 18 is a slate plaque found in 1908 at a site called "Spanish Hill" in Pennsylvania (Ref.20). Called the "7-hole pendant", has the usual 3+ wavy horizontal line ocean wave motif (which means "water" in Egyptian heiroglyphics), with three spaces between four vertical longitude lines, showing the correct 30 degree width of the open Ocean, tapering to the top to Greenland. There is a diamond in the middle, common on pendants and petroglyphs, showing the mid-ocean islands (Azores). The site is a large flat-topped glacial mound near the Susquehanna river on the New York / Pennsylvania border. The place was named "because of the fortifications found at this ceremonial hilltop enclosure." While clearly related to the Iberic pendants, this item alone does not prove Spanish Hill was an Iberian (Beaker) colony, but this is a piece of hard evidence that it might have been.

It should be mentioned that the later Adena (1000 BC) are noted for their intricate patterned tablets, which are about the size of the Iberian pendants. This hilltop enclosure of ten acres inside 7-8 foot earthen walls with a palisade atop (surveyed in 1878) was located on a major waterway connection between the mounds of the Ohio valley, and the stone chambers/colonies of the Hudson River valley. Other artifacts and petroglyphs have shown this to be a highly trafficked area, and perhaps thickly populated (Ref.2).

The long-term presence of the Beaker People in America is indicated by their pots as well as their pendants and the physical size and bone structure of their descendants. One exhibit in the museum of Poverty Point (Louisiana) is a pot that is a near-copy of one I photographed in England, as shown in Rocks&Rows (Ref.3). Mind you, Poverty Point is regarded as a pre-pottery "archaic" site. Pottery is regarded as a characteristic of "woodland" cultures, along with mounds and agriculture (which are also all Beaker Culture characteristics). The later local "indians" in the Poverty Point area, called the Caddo, made many pots with Beaker designs, shown beautifully in *The Art of the Caddo* (Ref.51). Surely, the Beaker People were seeking metals, and were miners of Michigan copper, along with the Minoans. The Minoan presence has been documented by copper oxhide ingots and molds at the Smithsonian dig at Clinch River, Tennessee, and other evidence including bronze axes, pendants, and petroglyphs. The extent and location of the Beaker settlements during the thousand years of mining is still unclear. Myron Payne directed me to an internet article on the "Petaga Point Archaeological Site in Minnesota, where replicas of big Beaker pots are on display and the original shards under study (Ref. 65). The Lake Kegonsa 15-acre "Prehistoric Fort" was brought to my attention by Bob List. It is 7 miles south of Madison, Wisconsin. It is reported to have a village site outside its walls, with large skeletons, gorgets of slate, stone lined ovens, round molds, and various ores (Ref.72). Undoubtedly there are other sites.

The copper mining in Michigan ended during the 1200 BC 50-100 year period of cataclysms thought to have been caused by impactors from the breakup of comet Enecke. We still see remnant showers of it each Fall. This period is called the "Plenard period" by climatologists. All the reigning civilizations on Earth fell, including the

Photo 18

pendant "Spanish Hill"

Shang, the Hittite (Turkey), the Babylonian, the Egyptian, the Indus (India), the Trojan, and the Mycenaean. All these cultures and their economies suddenly ceased to exist. The Plenard Period was followed in North America by the "Adena," with giants among their elite, and in South America by the "Regional Classical" (to be discussed). I am proposing that the Beaker People were ancestral to both cultures. Bailey (Ref.56) correctly states "they provided a small ruling class to each society they took over."

Now we will look for evidence for Beaker People in South America. In her book *Heraldry for the Dead* (Refs.1 & 22), University of Iowa Professor Katina Lillios says that Argentine paleontologist Florentino Ameghino (1854-1911) included a discussion of the Portuguese plaques in his study of the history of La Plata, Argentina. He "saw clear parallels between the engravings on the Portuguese plaques and those on stone plaques from the Rio Negro region of Patagonia." "We find these signs to be absolutely identical to those found on some slate plaques of Portugal that the distinguished Portuguese geologist don Carlos Ribeiro has informed us about" (Ameghino, 1880; 273). Professor Lillios, who speaks Portuguese, emailed me that she has been unable to locate this report, or photos of the Argentine plaques. They might provide some hard evidence for a Beaker People transoceanic Bronze Age tin trade. Sailing south from their landfalls on the South American coast would have been a natural thing to do. The winds would have been favorable to Rio de La Plata. A big "stonehenge" is located north of the mouth of the Amazon, and fields of standing stones

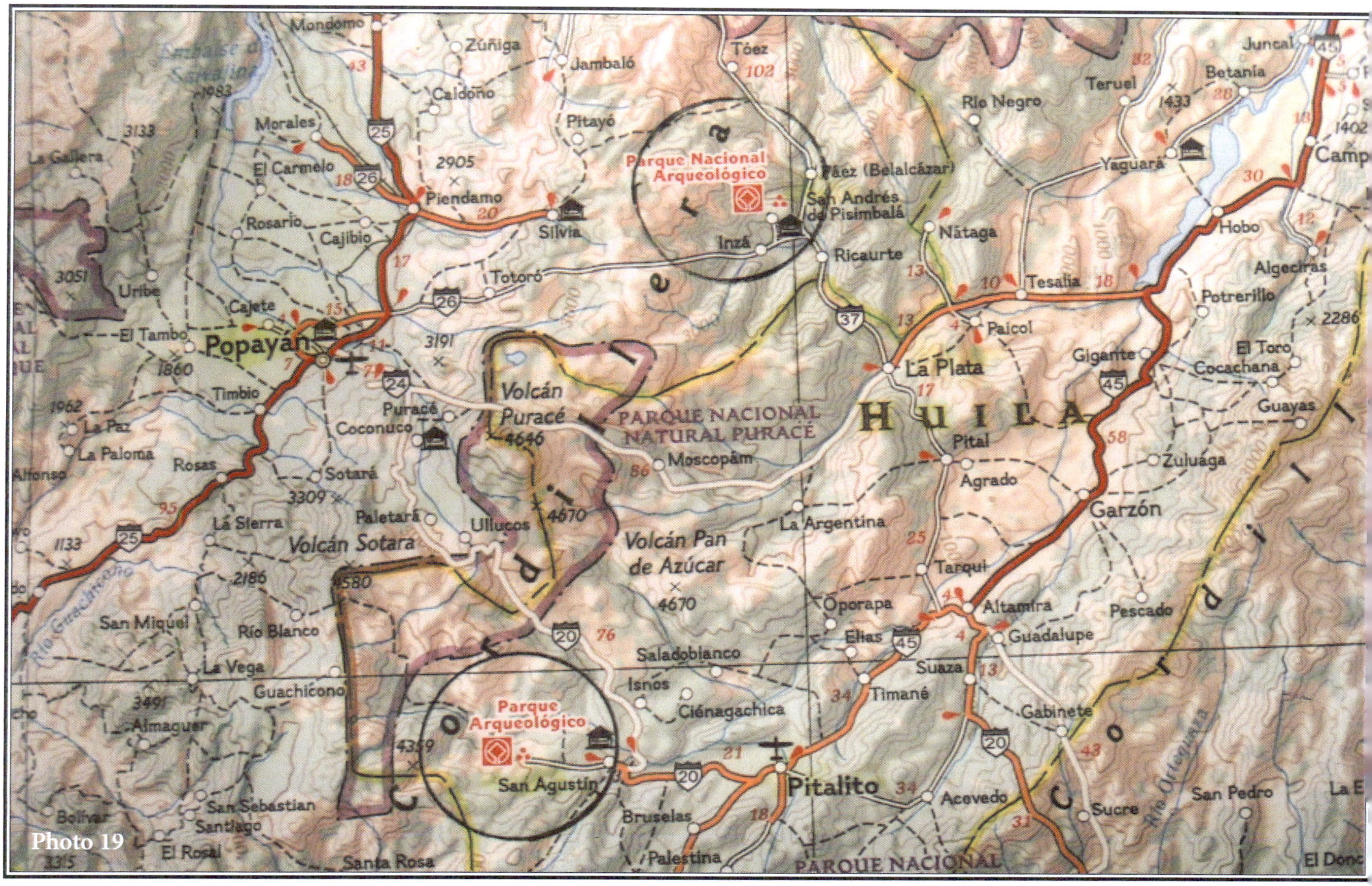

Photo 20

Photo 21

Photo 22

can be seen in a number of locations (Refs. 11,81). Much evidence is still being unearthed at Tiahuanaco (Bolivia). The site now includes pyramids, Sumerian cuneiform writing, turbanned heads, and so on. This needs more research.

The huge Rio Magdalena drains a big basin of northern Colombia between two ranges of the Cordillera of the Andes. It enters the Carribbean Sea near the city of Barranquilla, Colombia. Across a huge bay, in the foothills of the Sierra Nevada, are the mysterious ancient cities of Ciudad Antigua, and Ciudad Perdida. These sites, with huge staircases, and platforms in the jungle, take several days hiking to reach, but have been used in some movies. They were considered ancient by the Spanish Conquistadores. Like the Mississippi, this large Rio Magdalena would have attracted early boaters, who themselves lived along rivers in their homelands. Paddling upriver would have been easy through the myriad lowland lakes and swamps of the lower Magdalena. The river course gradually rises into a huge highland valley in the Andes at just two degrees south.

At the headwaters of the Rio Magdalena are "archaeologic sites for 60 miles along the river," and sprawling over 2000 square kilometers, considered the largest pre-Columbian site, and oldest cultural site in South America. Though near the equator, the climate is described as "eternal spring." The Parque Arqueologico of San Agustin and Parque Nacional Arqueologico of Tierradentro (Photo 19) are United Nations World Heritage Sites, with "500 statues" and tombs, including passage graves and hypogea. These passage graves with huge coversyones (Photos 20, 21, 22) would look at home on the coast of Europe, and are clearly the work of the Beaker People.

Archaeologists have defined an "archaic period" from 3300 BC to 600 BC. The first adventurers up the river found a beautiful and fruitful place to settle, and lived there a thousand years. The area has remained populated through cultural changes, for over 5300 years. Today the stone tombs of the early culture bringers survive at the lowest levels of these sites, with new sarcophagi, and huge statuary added inside and above the passage graves. The first colonizers of South America are officially "unknown," although those of us who have studied passage graves in Europe, like Hugh

95

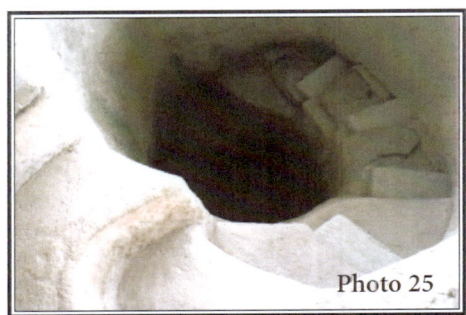

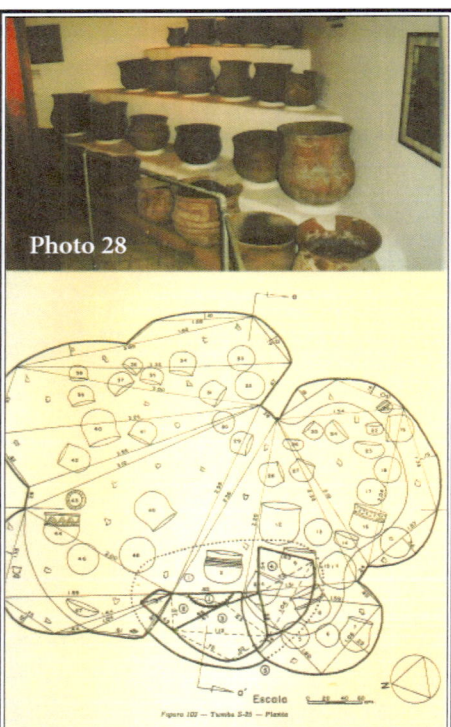
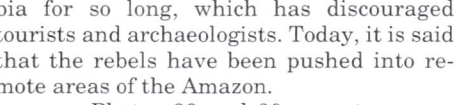

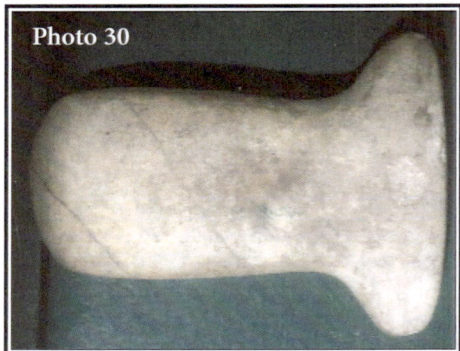

Newman (Ref.23) can see the Beaker People here.

Photo 23 shows what it is like to descend into one of the hypogea, or underground carved-out tombs of Tierradentro. In Photo 24, another tomb, note the scale of the stairs. To us, a normal step is six inches. The tallest step I saw was 32 inches. In Photo 25 you can see that the local park service has added small square intermediate steps to help the tourists. These hypogea were carved out, with all the rock hauled up the stairs. It appears we have found evidence for giants! Indeed, in the works of Wilkins (Ref. 15,16), it is reported that native legends tell of "giants" arriving from overseas, and reports of cave sites where giant skeletons have been found. Inca legends say that the god Viracocha created a race of giants, and the giants built Tiahuanaco (Ref.61).

Photos 26 shows the interior of the burial chamber at Alto del Aguacate, one of the Tierradentro Archaeological Park hypogea sites, and Photo 27 shows another. Note the repeating diamond patterns of the Beaker People. Photo 28 shows the Beaker pots found in one tomb. Many of the ridgetops in this mountainous area have these "Mesita" (man-flattened tops), with tombs on them, though those found outside the park, are said to have been looted. It is said that much of this culture remains to be found, "10% excavated." The reason given for so little archaeology is because of the rebels and violence that has plagued Colombia for so long, which has discouraged tourists and archaeologists. Today, it is said that the rebels have been pushed into remote areas of the Amazon.

Photos 29 and 30, are stone axeheads in the San Agustin museums. They are similar to the pre-dynastic axes of Egypt, and the three found on Isle Royale in Michigan, as discussed in *Ancient American* magazine recently (Ref.9). Another one was in a display case in the Convento Santa Cruz de la Popa in Cartagena. It was found when the

Spanish conquistadores were having the foundations of a convent dug in the sand. I have seen many of these axeheads on exhibit in the Gold Museum in Lima, Peru, an enormous collection and museum funded by an aristocrat there. I have also seen one in the Prehistoric Museum in Gdansk, Poland, among a Beaker exhibit that inclued beautiful Beaker pots. Since three of these axeheads were found on Isle Royale, it appears the Beaker People may have been the miners on Isle Royale (Ref.9).

The art and the technology of the Bronze Age Beaker People is found on their pottery, their stone circles, their hero pendants, and their tombs on both sides of the Atlantic Ocean, and in both North and South America. Their huge physical size is found in Europe, Asia, the Canaries, Columbia, Michigan, and in the Adena elite. Clearly the Beaker People, a subset of the megalithic people, were a lot more than European potters, but exploring the world, gathering its resources, and colonizing it for thousands of years. Their navigational technology was up to the task. They deserve recognition for the important role they have played in history. ∎

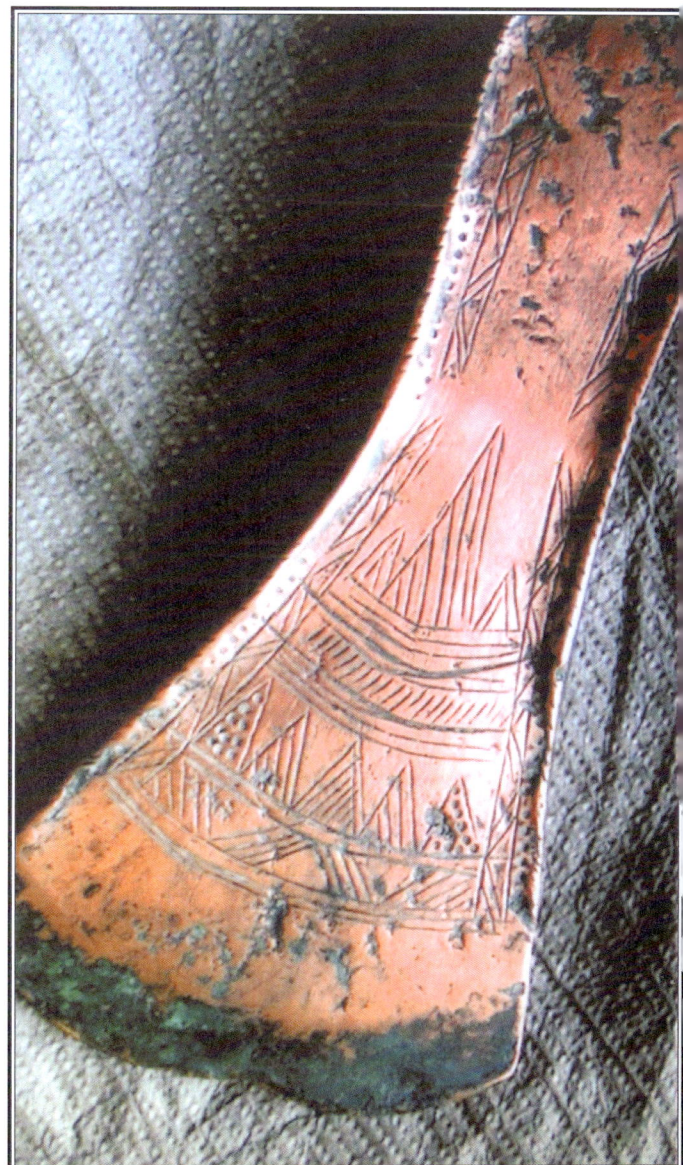

The Use of Latitudes in Bronze Age Sailing

by Jay S Wakefield

By sheer dumb luck I have been able to acquire eight different rare copper/bronze axeheads, from the Moog Collection in Southern Germany. I have not seen these axes in museums, books, or on the internet. It is thought that perhaps Dr. Moog had assembled the only collection of these decorated axes, but the records of archaeology in Germany suffered greatly through the destruction of two world wars so we do not know. Hopefully there are more of these decorated axes for study in museum basements or other collections.

I suspected that the "decorations" on these axeheads might be important, though they could not be clearly seen through the thick black patination. After cleaning them, the notches, vees, and dots in these castings showed important latitudes in the Atlantic. This data corroborates what we have learned about the use of latitudes in Bronze Age sailing over the last twenty years.

In How the SunGod Reached America (2002), the use of latitudes was shown to be common in megalithic monuments, so the monuments were shown to be geographic as well as astronomic. Then, as now, latitudes run from 0 degrees at the equator, to 90 degrees at the pole, following a system of 360 degrees in a circle, long used in antiquity.

Measurements of latitude have always been taken by observing the maximum height of the sun above the horizon. As one travels north, the angle of the sun in the sky at noon becomes lower, while as one travels south, it becomes higher. This could be measured by simple devices, precursors to the modern sextant.

Encoded latitudes are seen in megalithic monuments in the number of stones, and often, in the angles between stones. For example, the monument of Gavrinis (3600 BC), on the coast of France (Figure 1), is a cairn made of 39 immense stones, with an axis pointing to 38 degrees north, indicating something important to the builders at 38 and 39 degrees north. Thirty nine degrees north is the latitude of the West Azores, and thirty eight degrees north is the latitude of the Central Azores, where the good harbors are located. These islands were important in eastward Atlantic crossings, for copper shipping in the Bronze Age, the galleons of the Spanish, and are still important stopovers for yachts sailing to Europe today.

The most important number in navigation is 23. This is the tilt of the Earth's axis, or "declination" of the Earth. This is the farthest north the latitude of the noon sun at midsummer, before it

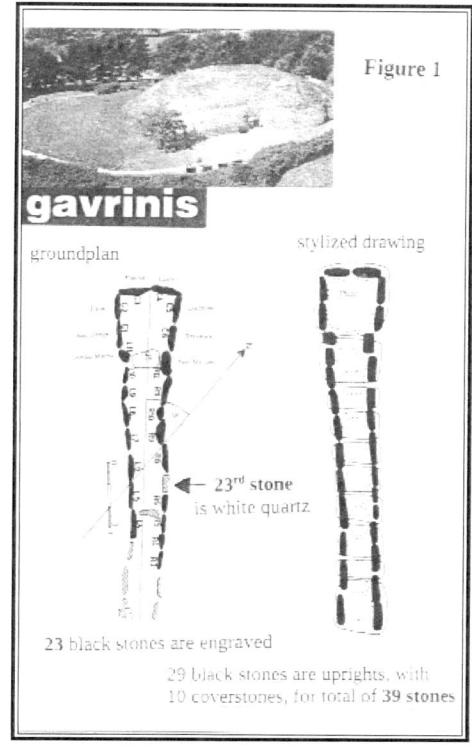

Figure 1

goes south, changing summer to Fall. This number can be found in nearly all megalithic monuments. In Gavrinis, for example, there are 23 decorated stones. The 23rd stone, which is undecorated, is white quartz. It was the use of latitudes that enabled megalithic peoples to navigate the oceans of the Earth. It was the frequent finding of 23 on Iberic pendants and the decorated axeheads that first showed me that the artifacts contained navigational information.

At Stonehenge in England, on the earthen ring once stood four Station Stones, which formed a rectangle, as shown in Figure 2. Each of the four stones stood out from the center at an angle of 23 degrees. The short sides of the rectangle were parallel with the axis of the monument, facing the most northerly rise of the midsummer sun. The long sides of the rectangle faced the furthest southerly rise of the full moon. The 90-degree angle of the lower left corner of the rectangle was thus determined by two astronomical events that each occurred once each year at this latitude of 51 degrees north.

Why was a 90 degree corner angle useful to the builders? Looking at Figure 3 with a protractor, you can see that the first stone placed at the other side of the ring is at an angle of 23 degrees while the next stone is at the site latitude of 51 degrees. The placement of these two stones is enough to confirm the knowledge of and use of latitudes by the builders of Stonehenge.

With continued use of a protractor on Figure 3, look at the stones anciently placed at the entrance of the monument, the "heelstone", the "slaughter stone", and so on. The angles of these stones are 59 degrees (Orkneys), 62 degrees (Faroe Islands), 64 degrees (So. Iceland), 66 degrees (NW Iceland), and 67 degrees (Greenland). This is the pathway of the discoveries across the North Atlantic. At the time this portion of Stonehenge was built, Greenland was the most westerly known land on Earth, and so the western home of the SunGod. Due to the fearsome summertime fogs and icebergs west of Greenland, there would not be a crossing further west for at least 800 years. These discoveries were recorded

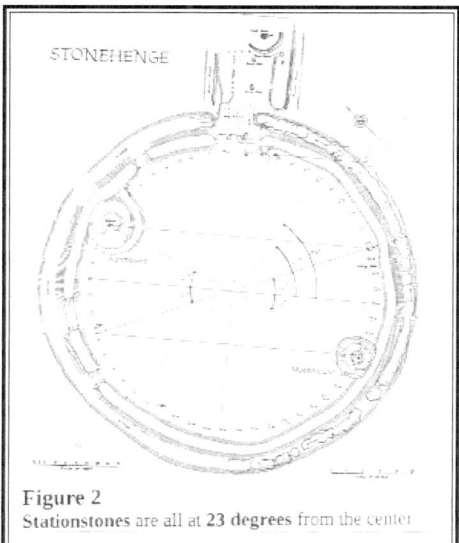

Figure 2
Stationstones are all at **23 degrees** from the center

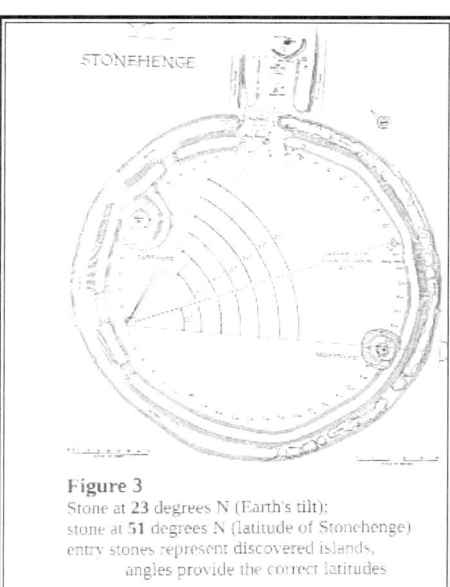

Figure 3
Stone at 23 degrees N (Earth's tilt);
stone at 51 degrees N (latitude of Stonehenge)
entry stones represent discovered islands,
angles provide the correct latitudes

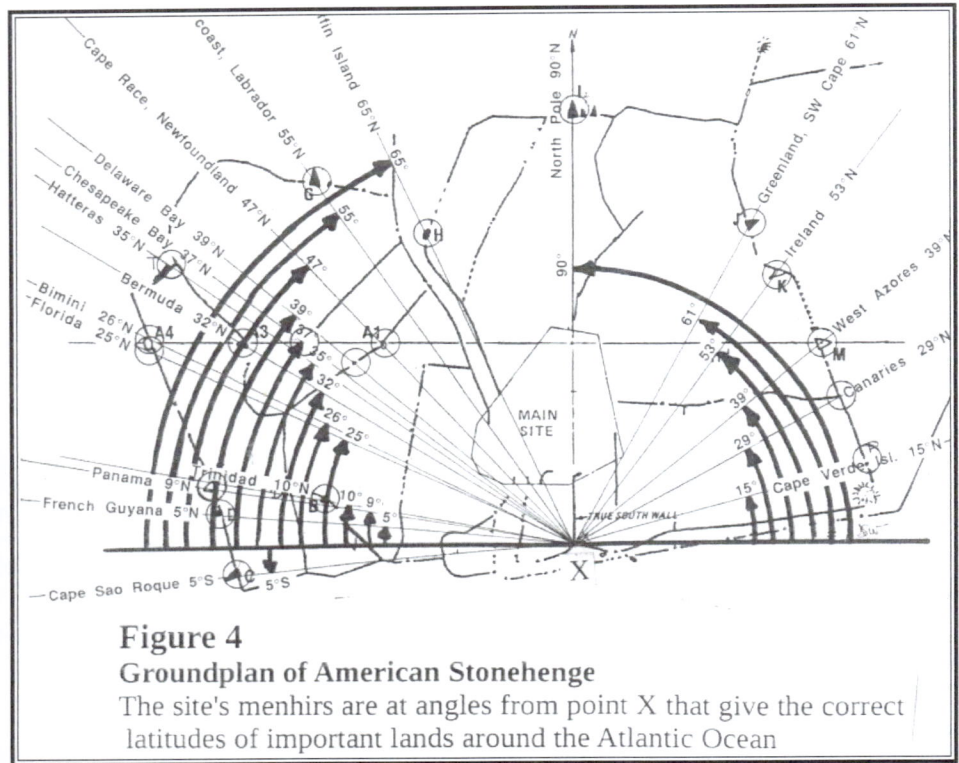

Figure 4
Groundplan of American Stonehenge
The site's menhirs are at angles from point X that give the correct latitudes of important lands around the Atlantic Ocean

and commemorated by the construction of Stonehenge Phase 1, 3000 BC.

Forty-five hundred years ago American Stonehenge, formerly called "Mystery Hill", was above a bay near the New Hampshire / Massachusetts border. Numerous carbon dates indicate the monument was built about the same time as the third and last phase of Stonehenge in England (2,000 BC). Figure 4 (www.howthesungod.com) shows the site to be a walk-in-map of the Atlantic Ocean laid out in big rocks. As seen from a point X, the angles give the latitudes of all the important lands on both sides of the Atlantic. The site taught sailors how to safely cross the Ocean, and was the place to make sacrifices to ensure a safe voyage. For a few hours in July of 2002, we explained the details of the monument to its former owner, founder of NEARA, Robert Stone, who thanked us, and said "I finally understand my site".

The Four axehead photos show both sides of two of the bronze axeheads. The flat sides have been polished so the inscriptions in the castings can be counted accurately. In some spots, the corrosion has eaten away the metal, so a missing dot or two must be inferred from the spacing pattern. However, I doubt this is making much difference in the results. Since these objects were made by a metals artisan, most likely not a sailing captain or navigator, there are plenty of possible sources of error. Also, there are encodings I cannot explain. Hopefully, others will study these, and more will be understood. We are lucky that they recorded data onto an object as durable as a bronze axehead,

side the side ridges. On the side marked "front, the vees are 14 and 19, totaling 33, which is the latitude of the Madeira Islands. The line of dots total 53, the latitude of Dublin or Galway, Ireland, and 62, which is the latitude of the Faroe Islands (also the latitude of the inhabitable West Fjords of Southwestern Greenland).

On the side marked "back" (Fig.6), the vees total 12 and 14, totaling 26, probably the latitude of the lost ancient seaport city thought to have been near Cape Boudajour, Africa, south of the Canaries. When you combine all the vees on both sides (26 and 33), you find the 59 degree latitude of the Orkney Islands, where some of the largest stone monuments in the world were built, including the enormous 60-menhir Brodgar Stone Circle. The line of dots on this side total 49, the latitude of the NW Cape of Brittany. Nine of the 49 stand a bit alone, so might also represent the nine islands of the Azores. The 60 dots along the other inside edge show the latitude of Cape Farvel, South Greenland, and the Brodgar monument celebrating its discovery. These numbers are places important in north Atlantic sailing.

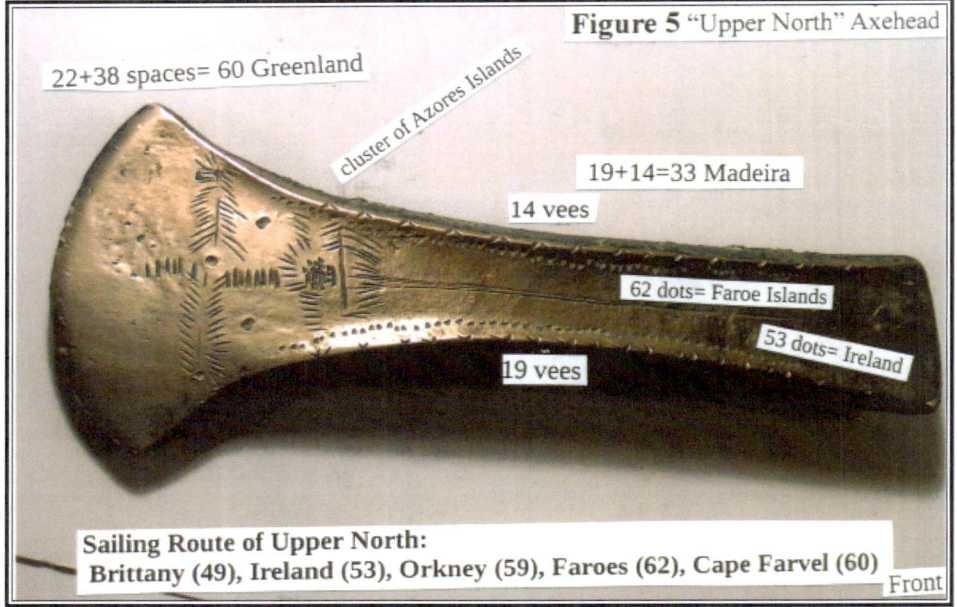

as most of their records on more perishable materials are obviously lost. As they explored the sea to the west, looking for what was on the backside of the Earth, where the sun went every evening, they found islands. Over time, they colonized some of these islands, so sailing to them was frequent. While both sides of the axes show data, like many of the Iberic pendants, some are also anthropomorphic, showing "Happy Faces" of the SunGod.

The four ridges on the sides of the "Upper North" axehead (Fig.5) have "vee" shaped markings on the ridges in the casting, and "dots" running along in-

On the front side (Fig.5) is seen a clump of islands (the "mouth" of the SunGod figure), while on the backside (Fig.6) we find three segments of a line of 3 island groups, with three marks for the islands in each group. The nine islands of the Azores are customarily shown as three groups of three in megalithic petroglyphs. Both sides of this axehead show a "ladder" of distance lines from the Azores up to the Sailing Route of the Upper North of 17 to 20 degrees between Cape Farvel and the Azores islands showing they had explored north of the Azores.

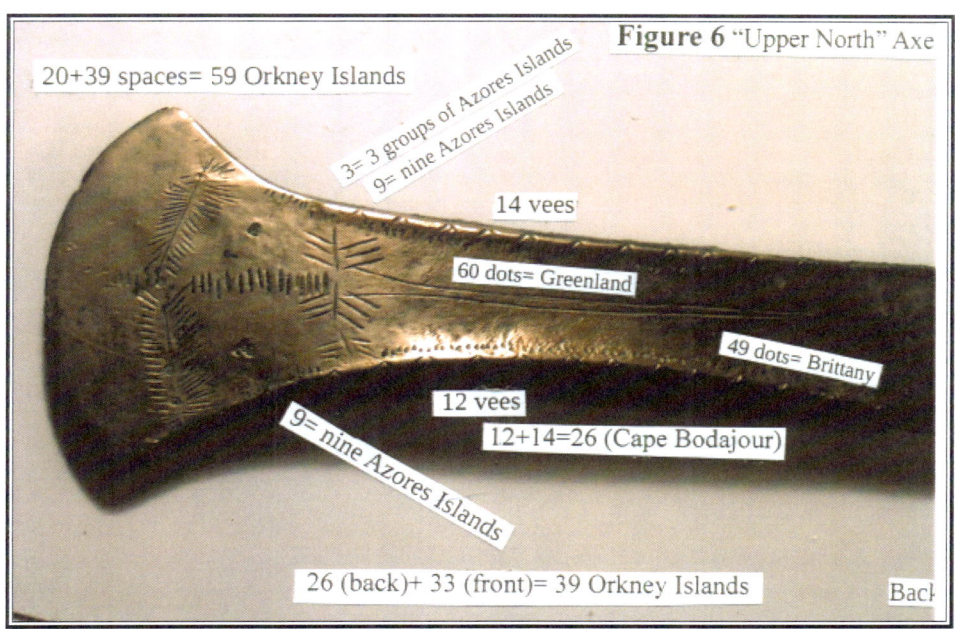

Figure 6 "Upper North" Axe
- 20+39 spaces= 59 Orkney Islands
- 3= 3 groups of Azores Islands
- 9= nine Azores Islands
- 14 vees
- 60 dots= Greenland
- 49 dots= Brittany
- 12 vees
- 12+14=26 (Cape Bodajour)
- 9= nine Azores Islands
- 26 (back)+ 33 (front)= 39 Orkney Islands

The detailed distances, perhaps sketched in, as shown across the hairline of the figure, are more difficult due to the curvature of the Earth. I think Iceland is in the center at the top on both sides of the axe. The distances shown of 12 degrees between Orkney & Shetland to Iceland and 12 degrees from Iceland to Greenland & West Fjords, are roughly correct.

The dots on this axe are not accidental or plowmarks, but were put there by the mind of man. They show amazing numbers. The latitudes encoded are 49 (Brittany), 53 (Ireland), 59 (Orkney Islands), 62 (Faroe Islands), and 60 (Cape Farvel, Greenland). These are the same latitudes of the Upper North Sailing route (Fig.7). These places are encoded in angles at Stonehenge and in petroglyphs Cairn T at Loughcrew, Ireland (www.howthesungod.com, www.rocksandrows.com).

Figure 7

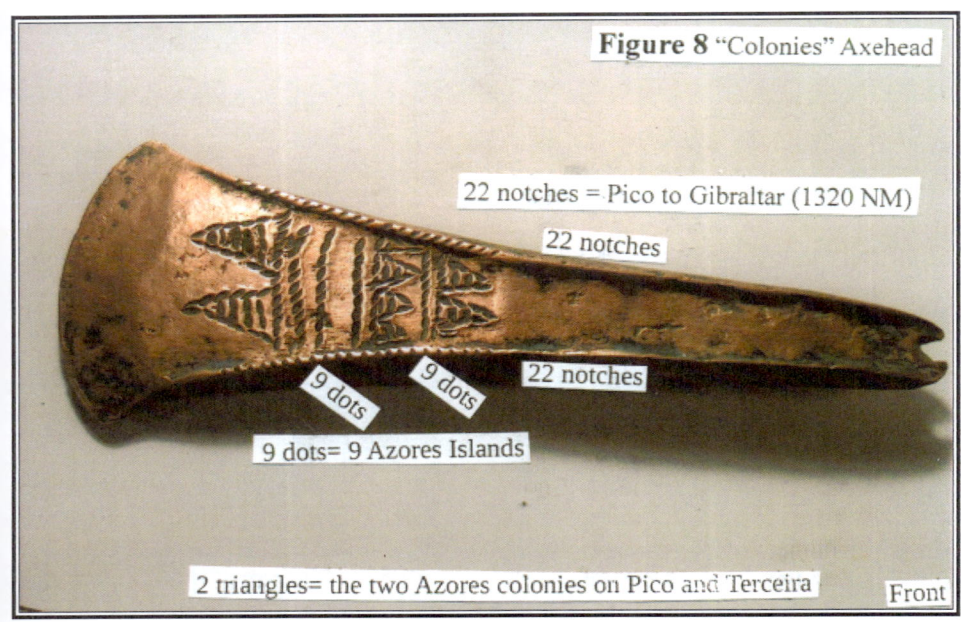

Figure 8 "Colonies" Axehead
- 22 notches = Pico to Gibraltar (1320 NM)
- 22 notches
- 22 notches
- 9 dots
- 9 dots
- 9 dots= 9 Azores Islands
- 2 triangles= the two Azores colonies on Pico and Terceira
- Front

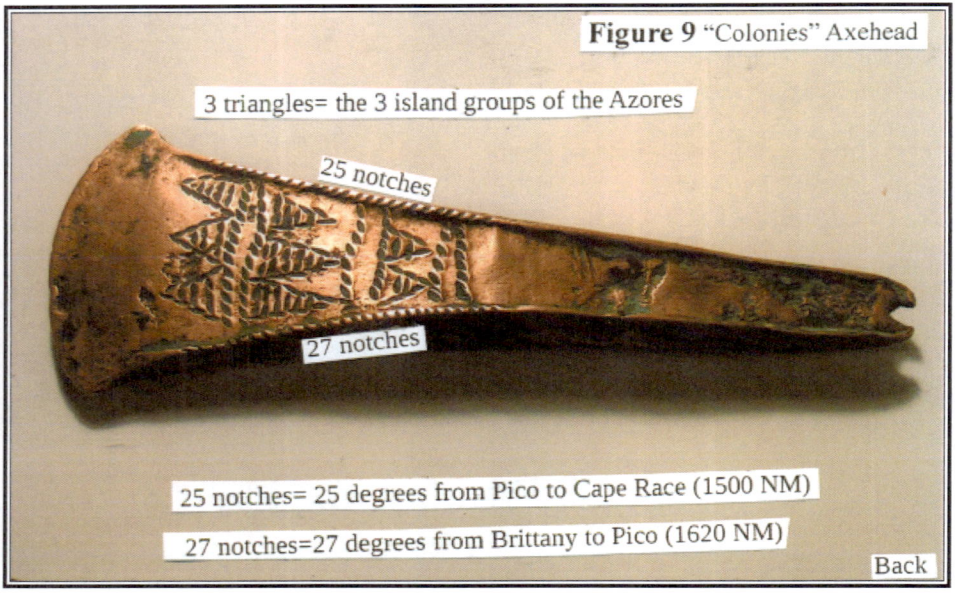

Figure 9 "Colonies" Axehead
- 3 triangles= the 3 island groups of the Azores
- 25 notches
- 27 notches
- 25 notches= 25 degrees from Pico to Cape Race (1500 NM)
- 27 notches=27 degrees from Brittany to Pico (1620 NM)
- Back

Clearly navigational data was lifesaving to these people, who were putting their lives on the line in sailing boats.

The axehead with the triangles on both sides shows the usual three triangles, for the three island groups of the Azores Archipelago. Where two triangles are shown, the two most important islands are being illustrated, because of their importance. These were the islands they had colonies on: Pico and Terceira (article in preparation). Pico is a huge volcanic cone, visible many miles at sea. Terceira had a natural harbor used later by Spanish galleons, and both the islands have harbors that are still in use today. The design shows several rows of nine dots, again confirming the Azores Islands. The axe edges (Fig.8) are notched, with two rows of 22 (22+22= 44, the latitude of NW Iberia), and rows of 25 and 27 (Fig.9) (25+27= 53, the latitude of Dublin, Ireland a huge natural harbor & river mouth). The distance from Pico to Cape Race is a distance of 25 degrees (1500 Nautical Miles). The distance back to Carnac, in France, is 27 degrees (1620 NM). This axehead may be detailing knowledge that the Azores are nearly in the center of the Atlantic, as illustrated commonly on their slate and bone pendants, where a chain of diamonds run down the center of ocean maps.

Were these axes pneumonic devices used by navigators, or were they copies of commonly used sailing data onto tokens of the elite? In any case, the confirmation of how oceanic sailing was accomplished, moves forward our understanding of the accomplishments of man in the Bronze Age. ∎

The Southern Crossing:
New Evidence on Bronze-Age Axeheads
by Jay S. Wakefield

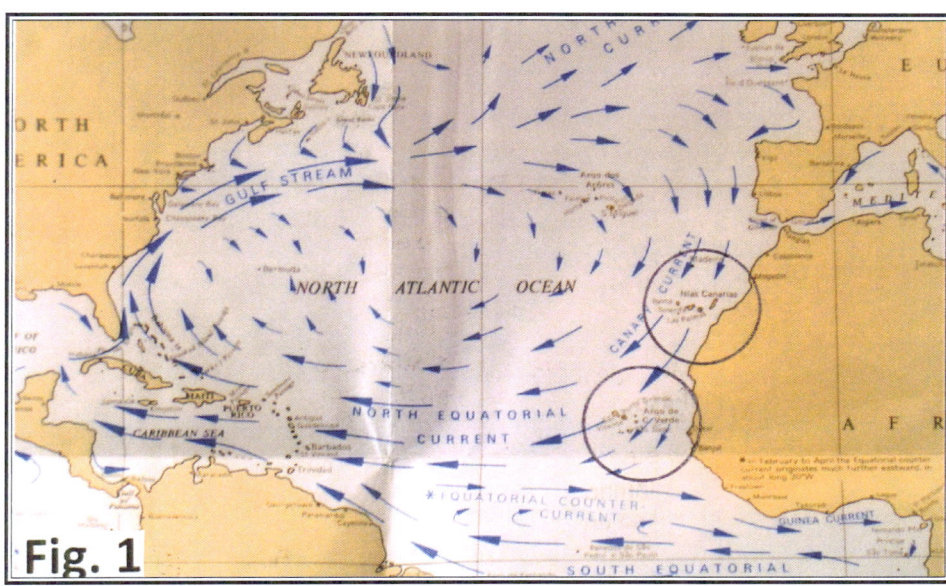
Fig. 1

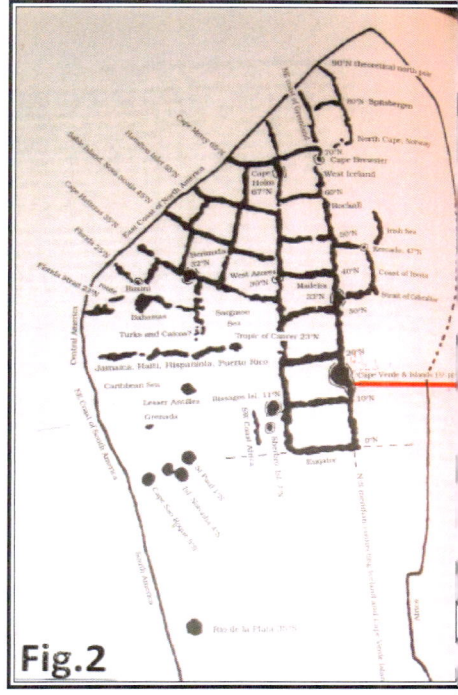
Fig.2

In *How the SunGod Reached America*, (www.howthesungod.com), eight petroglyphs are shown which illustrate the Southern Crossing. Now, fourteen years after publication of this book in 2002, new information has been found which confirms these petroglyphs. While it is most doubtful that the markings on these cast axes could be random, the likelihood that the markings are intentional encodings is increased by the duplication of similar encodings on both sides of most of the axes, and the appearance of latitude data important to navigation.

First, the ocean pendants of Iberia were noted during our travels in Portugal, published in 2010 (www.rocksandrows.com.). Then, decorated copper/bronze axes were obtained from the collection of Dr. Moog of Germany. The first three decorated axeheads were presented in Ancient American Magazine, Vol. 19, #109, the December issue of 2015. Two more were shown in the March, 2016 issue, and three more are in this article. Like the Iberian pendants, they are each unique "one offs", probably used for personal adornment or ceremonial purposes.

The Current Chart (Fig.#1) shows currents in blue arrows (from *Oceans of the World*). On the copied portion I have circled the Canaries (upper circle) and the Cape Verde Islands (lower circle). Figure #2 reproduces the oldest known full chart of the Atlantic Ocean, on stone C-1 of the passage grave of Kercado in Brittany, (from www.howthesungod.com).

Note the big dark dot at the lower right, that is the Cape Verde Islands, at 15 degrees North, while the big dots at the left are islands off the South American coast, at the other end of the Southern Crossing. A modern map of these islands and their latitudes is shown as Figure #3.

The axehead Labeled "Cape Verde Islands" (Fig. #4, front and back) has pronounced dots on it, six on the front, and four on the backside. These are the ten islands of the Cape Verdes, which have six northern islands, and four southern islands. The little modern chart (Fig

Fig.3

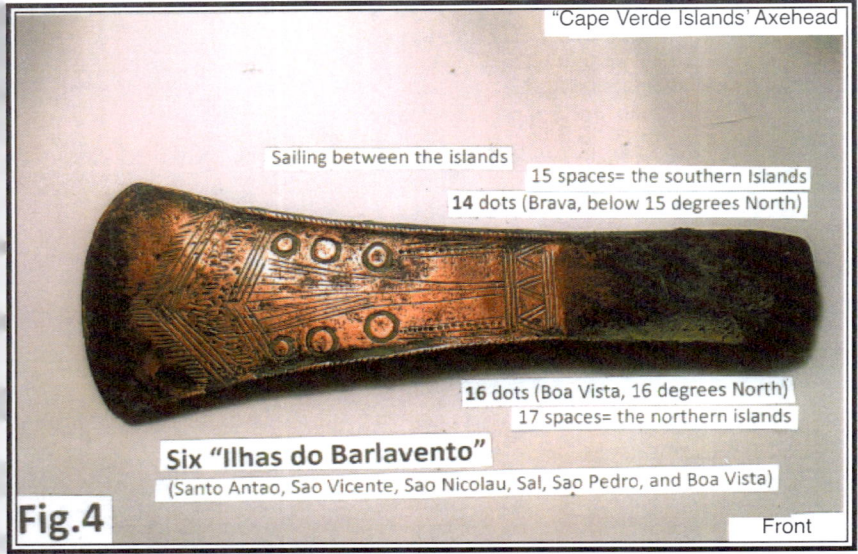

Fig. 4 — "Cape Verde Islands' Axehead" (Front)
- Sailing between the islands
- 15 spaces = the southern Islands
- 14 dots (Brava, below 15 degrees North)
- 16 dots (Boa Vista, 16 degrees North)
- 17 spaces = the northern islands
- Six "Ilhas do Barlavento" (Santo Antao, Sao Vicente, Sao Nicolau, Sal, Sao Pedro, and Boa Vista)

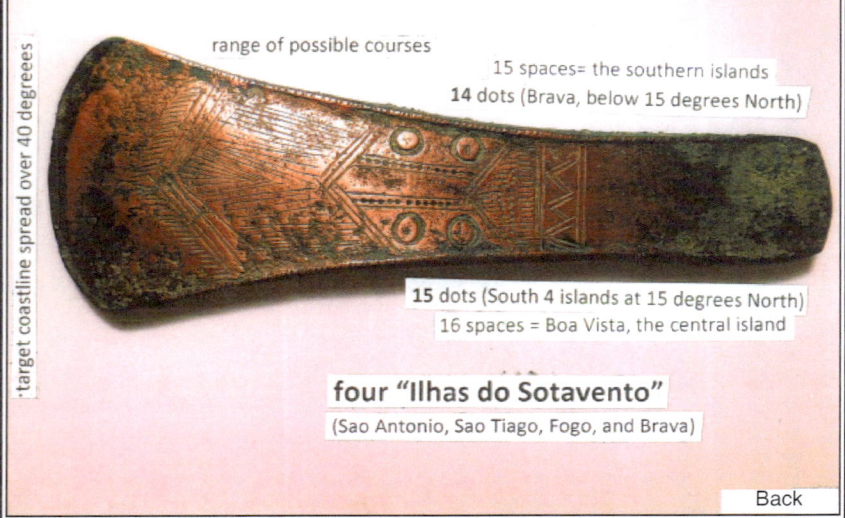

(Back)
- range of possible courses
- target coastline spread over 40 degrees
- 15 spaces = the southern islands
- 14 dots (Brava, below 15 degrees North)
- 15 dots (South 4 islands at 15 degrees North)
- 16 spaces = Boa Vista, the central island
- four "Ilhas do Sotavento" (Sao Antonio, Sao Tiago, Fogo, and Brava)

Fig. 5

#5) shows how these are named the "Islas do Barlavento" (the northern group) and the "Islas Sotavento" (the southern group), as they are illustrated on the axehead.

The tail ends and the sides of the thick (1/4") axe were not cleaned of the thick black patina, because no traces of inscriptions were showing. The zigzag Beaker Culture Atlantic Ocean motif starts the markings on both sides. The backside has an enclosed area, with 23 dots between 23 lines below, and 23 above, all within the enclosed area. This number 23, the tilt of the Earth's axis, is responsible for the change of seasons from summer to winter, was well known among bronze-age people. It appears on so many bone and slate pendants, and in so many megalithic monuments, it seems like a "holy number" of the sun-religion. It is called the Tropic of Cancer on nautical charts, a terminology that must be of ancient origin related to the zodiac.

The lines of "dots" are very clear on the axe, and correctly identify the latitudes of the Cape Verde Islands. It is no accident that they are indicated similarly on both sides. The six northern islands on the front side are shown with sailing routes between them, while the southern islands show a wide range of possible downwind courses, with a forty-degree spread as the target on the South American coastline, which is correct. We have learned that in the Bronze Age the ocean was divided by lines or dots, segmenting the ocean. When one counts spaces rather than dots, the totals are one larger number, so the 14 turns 15, the 15 to 16 and the 16 to 17. These are the correct latitudes of the northern, central, and southern Cape Verde Islands, as shown in Figure 5.

Figure #6 shows another copper/bronze axehead "Islands", this one very heavy, 7½" long, and also decorated on both sides. Innumerable notches and dots run on the edges and inside the edges on both sides from end to end, and seem to be decorative. On the front side, the two rows of intentional dots total 17 and 16, the latitudes of the northern Cape Verde Islands, but together, add to 33, the latitude of Madeira. Since the Spanish and Portuguese later found white-skinned "human stock" which they sold into slavery on Madeira, as they did in the Canaries, there may have been a bronze-age colony on Madeira (or the small adjacint island of Porto Santo) also.

Moving toward the blade, the spaces between the next set of groove lines (which divide the ocean into distances of one degree) show the Tropic of Cancer, 23, the route of the Sun God. The next set cannot be determined accurately on one side, so skip this set. The next set of 13 and 15 spaces add to 28, the latitude of the Canaries. The most distal set, which rise to a counterpoint, show 21 and 18 spaces, totaling latitude of 39, the latitude of the West Azores.

On the backside, the dots total 14, and spaces 15, seen on another axe as the latitude of Brava, the southern Cape Verde Island, the departure point for the Southern Crossing. The next lines (not the spaces!) total 23 again. Going toward the blade, we find 17 spaces, and 11 spaces, totaling 28, the latitude of the Canaries (Fig. #7). The forward sets of marks show 21 spaces and 17 spaces, for a total of 38, the latitude of the Central Azores, where colonies were located on Pico and Terceira (article in

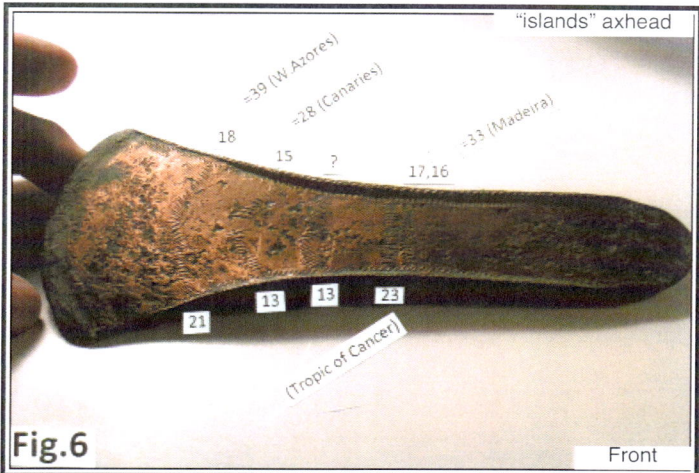

Fig.6 "islands" axhead — Front

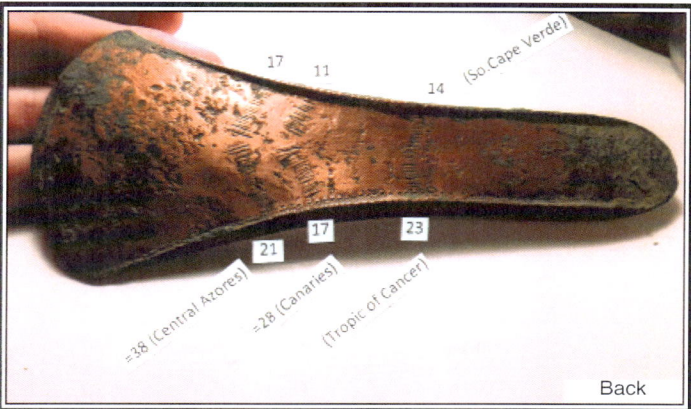

Back

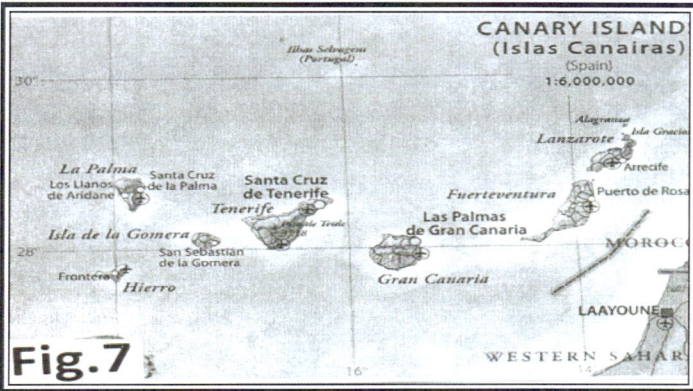

Fig.7 CANARY ISLAND (Islas Canairas)

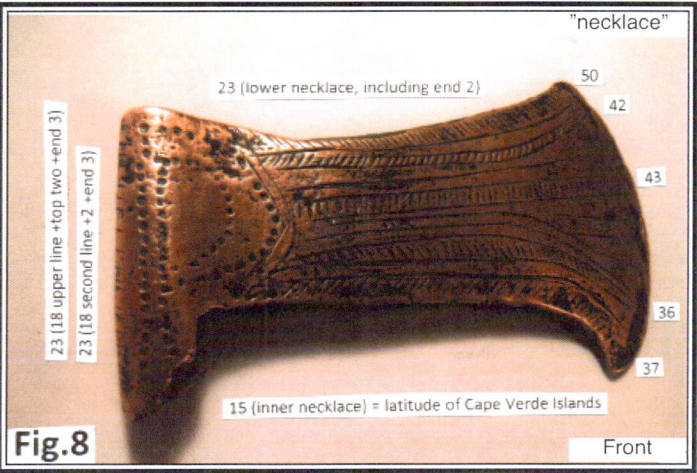

Fig.8 "necklace" — Front

preparation). This axehead seems to record or celebrate the Bronze Age colonies that had been established in the western ocean.

A third little axe "Necklace" is presented (Fig.#8). It is only 3¼" long. It is bent on the back end, so it could hang on a string or a necklace. Three rows of dots in the casting can reasonably each total 23, including the lower "necklace". This again is the Tropic of Cancer, the tilt of the Earth's axis. The inner necklace of 15 dots encodes the Cape Verde Islands again, the gateway to the Southern Crossing.

The central column, coming down the blade, shows 43 marked intervals, perhaps recording the bronze-age site of American Stonehenge at 43 degrees North. On each side, the columns provide totals of 36, the latitude of Gibraltar, and 42, the latitude of Oporto, a seaport on the Iberian coast. The edge marks total 37, the latitude of the East Azores, and 50, the latitude of Land's End, England. On the backside are markings that appear to be merely artistic, added to the casting without much effort or accuracy, though perhaps echoing the route dispersal shown on the other side.

The Southern Crossing is an easy downwind route to the West that replaced the Northern Crossing across the Faroe Islands, Iceland, and Greenland. It became the principal route West during the copper trade of the later Bronze Age (2,000 - 1,200 BC). After the 1,200 BC cataclysm, with its collapse of the copper trade, the route was inherited by the Phoenicians, and then used by the Carthaginians until Carthage was defeated and burned to the ground by the Romans. The route was found again during the "Age of Discovery". ∎

Sailing to America: Latitude data for the Copper Trail to Isle Royale and Egypt recorded on Bronze Age Axeheads

Jay Stuart Wakefield

These "decorated" axeheads are from the collection of Dr. Frederich Moog, in Rhineland-Palatinate, west southwest Germany. He acquired large antiquities collections which had been collected much earlier. Dr. Moog died leaving no heirs. In 1996 the part of his collections upstairs went to local museums. My friend was asked to sell what remained. "The larger portion of his collection had been stored in the cellar, which was untouched, but damaged from flooding and covered with mold. From the various materials, the shapes, and a few pieces with labels or writing on them, it is probable these axes had been collected in south and southwestern Germany, and maybe border regions that were once part of Germany."

I have examined bronze axe collections in the museums of Brittany, Spain, Portugal, London, Vienna, Budapest, Bratislava, Hallstat, and others, and have never seen a decorated axe like these on exhibit. Hopefully some will soon be found in museum basements or in private collections, to add to our knowledge. The remarkable Natural History Museum of Vienna has a huge bronze axe covered with decorative art, collected by a Hapsburg Emperor, who was a collector of antiquities, but not a smaller decorated axe like these.

I have bought twenty of the decorated axes of Dr. Moog, because upon cleaning the first one, I found four rows of 23 notches on the four sides. In study of megalithic monuments, the number 23 has come up many times. For example, at the Gavrinis passage grave on the coast of France, there are 23 highly decorated standing stones in the passage, while the 23rd stone is white quartz. At Stonehenge, England, the 4 station stones each lie at 23° from the center. In Bruce Cathie's 1997 book, he reports on his study of 3,000 stone circles and standing stones. He concludes that "every one is aligned to neighbors up to 20 miles away at an angle of 23 1/2° or a multiple of this angle". This is the Tropic of Cancer, the latitude the Sun reaches (overhead at noon) before it returns south again, turning Summer to Fall and then Winter. Clearly the axes had navigational data recorded on them in latitudes

No wooden Bronze Age vessels have been found intact, except two entombed in pieces next to the Great Pyramid in Cairo. PHOTO 1a shows a replica

PHOTO 1a: Uluburun was first discovered in 1982 by Mehmed Çakir, a local sponge diver, on a steep rocky slope at a depth of 44 to 52 metres, with artifacts scattered down to 61 metres. Excavating it was a mammoth task, and required eleven consecutive campaigns of three to four months, conducted by the Institute of Nautical Archaeology, totalling 22,413 dives between 1984 and 1992.
The ship itself was 15 metres long and is the earliest known example of a ship constructed using the advanced mortise and tenon technique, where planks were joined by flat tongues of wood inserted into slots cut into the planks. The wood is Lebanese cedar, indigenous to the mountains of Lebanon, southern Turkey, and central Cyprus. The featured image is an accurate replica wreck of the Uluburun, showing how the ship would have once appeared. 12 AUGUST, 2014 - APRILHOLLOWAY, used with permission. http://www.ancient-origins.net/ancient-places-asia/uluburun-one-oldest-and-wealthiest-shipwrecks-ever-discovered-001962

of the Ulu Burun shipwreck of 1300 BC as it would have appeared just after it sank. PHOTO 1b is a museum model of the Uluburun. PHOTO 2 is the actual wreck site. PHOTOS 3 a & b show an elegant axe "AS43", that is decorated, and now polished, on only one side. Its blade is damaged, indicating some hard use. Between the water symbols on the side are 42 marks. Counting the spaces, which represent the water, where the markings only divide the water, we have 43, or 43°. This axe records and celebrates the location of the largest and most important megalithic monument in the Americas, American Stonehenge, now in New Hampshire at 43°N. La Coruna, near Cape Finisterre (Spain), is at 43°N also. This axe connects the two sides of the ocean, both important in the megalithic culture.

PHOTOS 4 a & b are the front and back sides of another decorated axehead from

PHOTO 1b: Museum model depicting the Uluburun ship

Dr. Moog's collection. I call it "Azores rows" because of its similarity to the world's largest megalithic monument, the

Rows of Menec and Kermario in Carnac, Brittany, France. That monument is all about sailing to and from the Azores, with each of hundreds, if not thousands, of boulders representing each degree of latitude (www.rocksandrows.com). Looking at this 8 ½ inch axe from the handle end of the front side, we see lines extending to rows of dots. On the front side, there are four rows of these dots, extending across three sections to the blade of the axe. On the backside, there are five rows, extending in five complicated sections to the blade. Like the Carnac monument, this axe is designed around 4 & 5 = 9 rows. Note that in the second segment there is a column of nine dots, again the number of the Azores Islands.

    The four notched edges of 39 are difficult to count accurately. Perhaps they were made too carelessly, or have suffered corrosion damage. Though some or all of the 39 counts are arguably off a digit or two, four 39s make sense, as this is the important latitude of the West Azores. This latitude had to be used to find the islands when sailing from the west along the routes illustrated on the axe. This lat-

PHOTO 2: Top left; Some of the Cypriot ceramics and copper ingots found on the Uluburun (credit Image Source). The wreck site as viewed from the deeper end showing displaced anchors originally stowed near the bow (credit: INA).

PHOTO 3a: "Axe AS43" decorated only on one side, damage on the blade

PHOTO 3b: Side view, showing water symbols, and 43 spaces across the waters. This connects American Stonehenge at 43 degrees N, with La Coruna in Iberia, also at 43 degrees N.

PHOTO 4a: Four of 9 Azores rows, notched edges of 39, the latitude of the West Azores at 39°N. The first two sections hold 7 dots, the Central and E Azores. The blade has route data.

PHOTO 4b: Five of the 9 Azores rows, notched edges of 39, the latitude of the West Azores. The first two sections hold 7 dots, the Central and East Azores. Blade with route data of the American Coast around American Stonehenge.

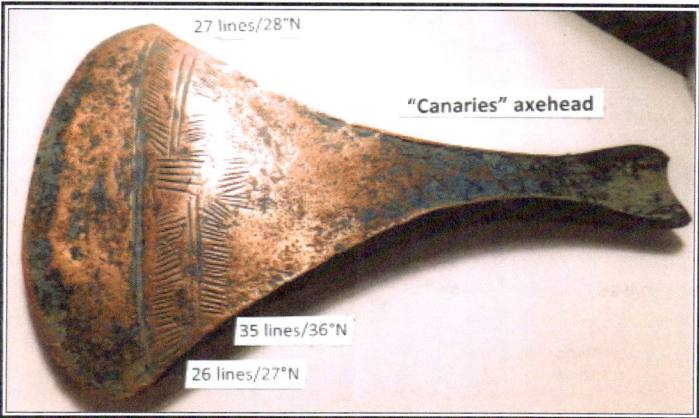

PHOTO 5: The "Canaries" axehead. The 5 Central, and 7 Canary Islands, with their latitudes of 28°N and 27°N, and the latitude of Gibraltar at 36°N.

There are rows extending to the blade. These numbers probably represent distances thought to have been sailed from various places to reach the Azores, starting with Cape Race, Newfoundland. On the backside, the first two sections of dots also hold 7 dots, this time clearly the 5 central and 2 eastern islands. The distance across these islands is also about 7 degrees. Approaching the blade, combining the row data with the 31 dots in the first box provides origination latitudes of 40, 41, 43, and 44. This especially makes sense for 43, the site of American Stonehenge, where teaching navigation of the Atlantic Ocean was the purpose of the monument (www.howthesungod.com).

PHOTO 5 is the front of another decorated axehead from the Moog collection I call "Canaries". The center of the front side has five big strokes and two small ones, for the five large and two small Canary Islands. The upper left column of 27 marks provides the 28°N latitude of the northern Canaries. The lower left column of 26 marks provides the 27°N latitude of the southern Canaries. The long wiggly line of 35 marks provides the 36°N latitude of Gibraltar. The upper groups of 12 marks and 7 marks may provide distances from Iberia to Madeira and the Canaries. The back has too much corrosion to be read.

itude is celebrated in the huge 3600 BC monument of Gavrinis, on the coast of France, made of 39 enormous blocks of stone.

On the front side, the two sections of dots hold rows of 7 dots, for the seven central and eastern Azores islands.

PHOTOS 6a & b are the front and back of another Moog decorated axehead, the "Island Groups" axehead. On the front, the axe seems to be focused on locating the landmark Pico volcano, on the Island of Pico in the Central Azores (the tall peak on the axehead). In the peak are 8 marks, the 9 spaces of the nine Azores. The left side of the axe shows 37 marks, 38 spaces, the correct latitude of PICO at 38°N. The back shows a count of 36 dots across the blade, the 37°N latitude of the East Azores. The 27 dots below the triangle show the 28°N latitude of the Canaries,

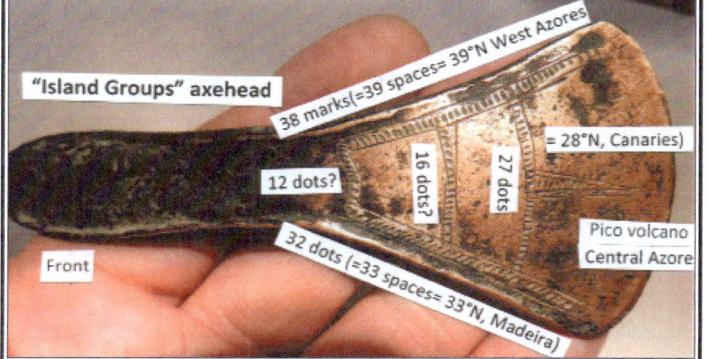

PHOTO 6a: The front side of this "Island Groups" axehead shows a tall central triangle volcano of Pico in the Central Azores, with nine spaces of the 9 Azores in the triangle. The upper side shows 38 marks, or 39 spaces, for the 39°N latitude of Corvo and Flores. The lower edge marks total 32, so 33 spaces=33°N, Madeira. 16=Cape Verde Island, 12=Latitude of Magdelena River Approach.

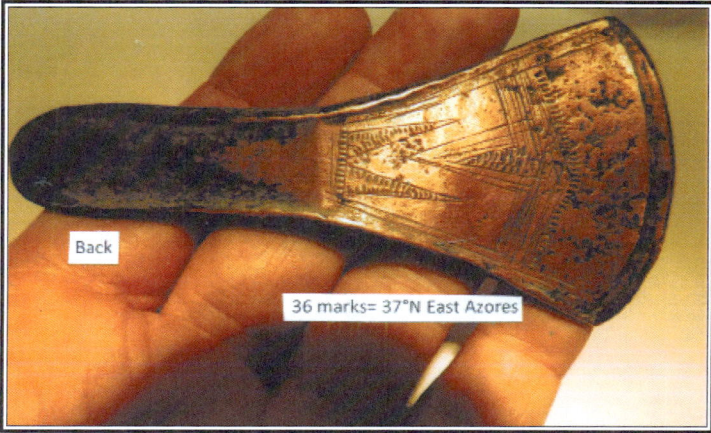

PHOTO 6b: The backside has 36 dots across the blade, the 37°N latitude of the East Azores.

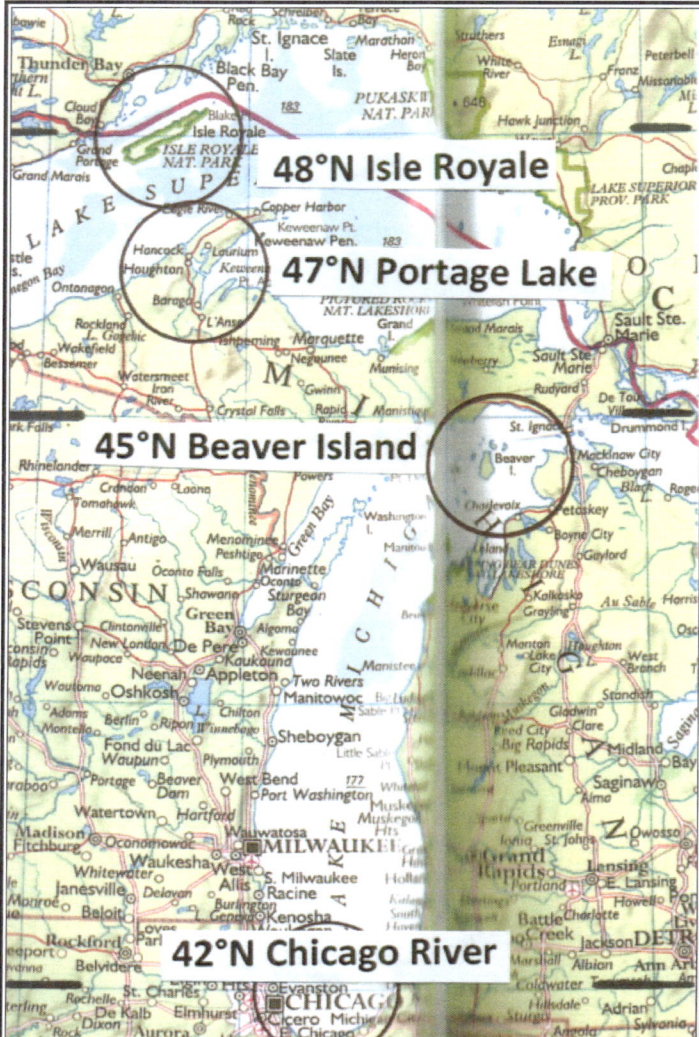

PHOTO 7: "Traveler" necklace pendant, showing the bearer had traveled many routes in his life. Right: Shipping routes map

further south and east, off the coast of Morocco. Two of the three lower triangles show totals of 23, the holy number of the Sun-God's route across the ocean at 23°N, even further south. PHOTO 7 shows a "Traveler's" necklace pendant, showing that the bearer had traveled many routes during his life, and is proud of it. PHOTOS 8, Front and Back show the 21cm "Copper Trail" axehead of 2000-1700 BC. We first notice the "wave" zigzag patterns of the Bronze Age ocean motif, across both sides of the blade. The front pattern records a correct Atlantic Ocean width of 4 triangles, plus two partial triangles (=4DL = 40 Egyptian moira of one degree= 2,400 NM + 2 sides, so =5DL = 3,000 NM, with 60 Nautical Miles in one degree). The backside shows a smaller wave pattern, consisting of 23 bars (in the 11 ½ triangles), encoding the important Tropic of Cancer.

The powerful and unique features of this axe are in the mid-section of the front side of the axehead. There are four very clear counts of 30, two along each side of the the feather-shape in the center, and two along the rims beside the feather down each side. When repeated so much, something important is involved. To ancient people, thirty was a magic number in geography. It was the latitude of the mouth of the Nile, the center of the most important civilization on Earth, and also the latitude of the mouth of the huge Mississippi River, in the Western home of the SunGod. This was the location of Poverty Point, and Cedarland and Claiborne, the places where copper oxhides were made and obtained for shipment abroad. Pointing to the blade edge are approximately thirty long marks, again emphasizing the importance of the copper source and the customer in Egypt, both at 30°N.

Along the sides of the front side of the blade are dots that are a bit hard to read, but total seventeen on each side. When combined with 30, this encodes the important source of copper at 47°N, Portage Lake on the Keweenaw Peninsula. Big boatload storage pits containing the corrosion products of ancient copper have been found along the shoreline of Portage Lake. Twenty-five dots stretch across the blade, inside the arrowpoint line. Given that the shipping of copper ingots across the Atlantic was a major undertaking, I suggest that rounding the peninsula of Florida at 25°N was of prime importance, and a landmark to be remembered.

On the backside, near the edge of the blade, there is emphasis shown about finding the volcanic peak of Pico in the 5 (five spaces in the peak) Central Azores Islands, where their colonies lay on the homebound route. The nine dots on each side

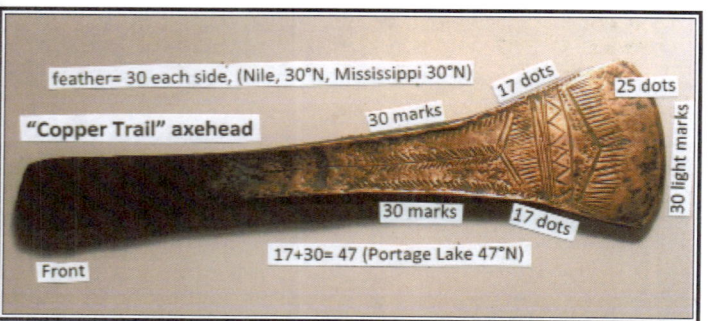

PHOTO 8 Front & Back: I call this the "Copper Trail" axehead, as it clearly records 30°N four times. This is the latitude of the Nile River and the Mississippi River, which is the latitude of the source of the copper oxhides, and the latitude of the most important customer, the Egyptians. Also recorded is the 17 + 30 = 47°N latitude of the source of the copper at Portage Lake, on the Keweenaw Peninsula, the 48°latitude of Isle Royale, and the latitude of the Chicago River at 42°N.

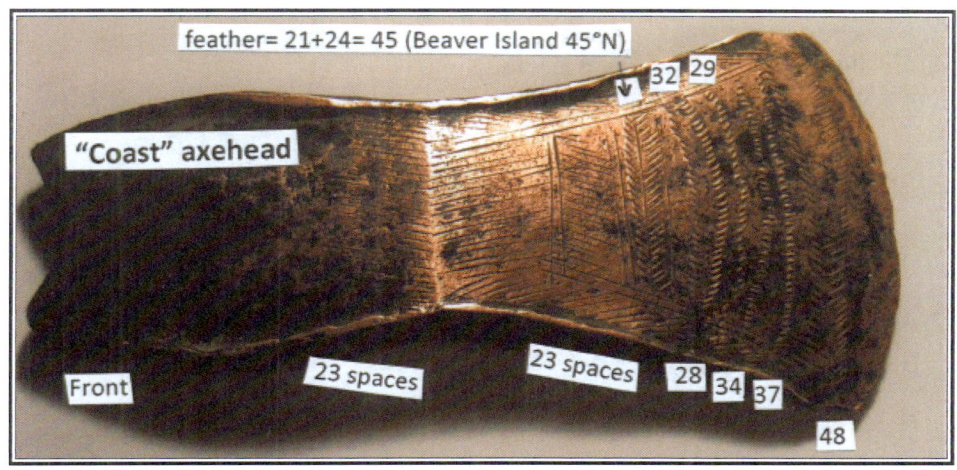

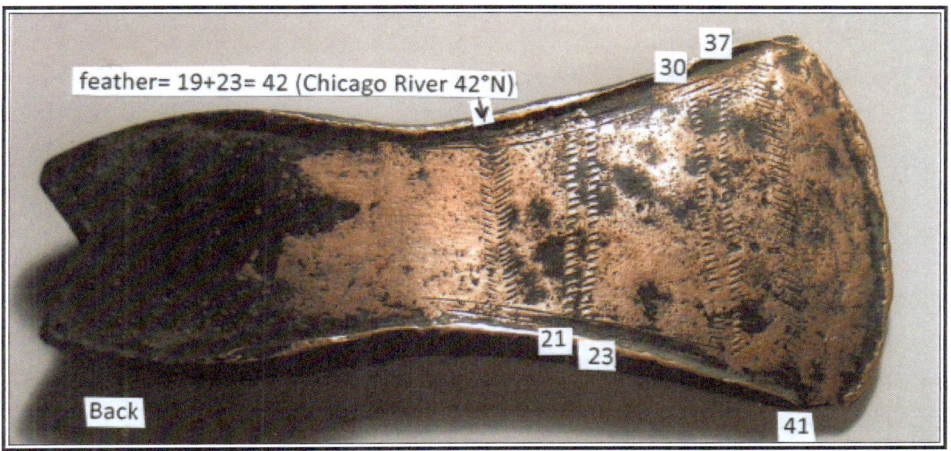

PHOTO 9 Front & Back: this small "Coast" axehead, apparently has a number of mid-latitudes recorded, probably important coastal sailing harbors. The "feather" glyphs show encoding of the likely colony on Beaver Island, and the entry to the Great Lakes at Chicago, where the Chicago river drained out of Lake Michigan during the Bronze Age.

twice repeat the nine islands of the Azores, a common motif. The central "feather" glyph has marks of 12 and 18, again totaling 30. Combining 12 plus 30 provides the latitude of the entry to the Great Lakes at 42°N, and 18+30 provides the latitude of Isle Royale at 48°N. These numbers are not plowmarks or accidents, but designed by the mind of man and very carefully crafted into the casting.

Photos 9, Front and Back show the small (10 ½ cm) enigmatic "Coast" axehead. On the Frontside, a bump is at the thicker center. There are a lot of thin faint lines. On the tail side of the bump, there are 23 spaces, and there are probably 23 spaces in the first box, toward the blade. It is not surprising to find repetition of this most popular number in Beaker Culture iconography, and most important number in navigation. The "feather" glyph has 21 and 24 marks, totaling 45, recording the latitude of the probable colony at Beaver Island at 45°N. There are six columns of small marks (28, 32, 29, 34, and 37) across the blade, and a column of 48 thin lines near the blade edge. On the backside, there is another "feather" with 19 marks on one side, and 23 marks on the other. These total 19+23= the latitude of the entry to the Great Lakes again at the latitude of the Chicago River, at 42°N. Note the two pairs of columns (21,23,30, &37), followed by 41 marks near the blade edge. I can only guess that these represent important places up the American coast that were important to them, such as the mouth of Chesapeake Bay (37°N), the mouth of the Hudson River (41°N), and perhaps American Stonehenge at 43°N, or the crossings of the Upper North route on both sides of Greenland at 67°N. I do not know if these decorated axes were just prestige items of the elite or actual tools, or neumonic devices. I do not know if the artisans carving the plugs for these castings were copying from important fragile master records, or recording commonly known information. In either case, we now know more about Bronze Age capabilities and achievements. I hope there are others who will want to study these artifacts. ∎

The SunGod Religion and Sailing Routes to Colonies in the Americas
by Jay Stuart Wakefield

I have had the lucky opportunity to obtain twenty-two highly patinated Bronze Age cast bronze axes from the estate of Dr. Moog, in southern Germany. He was a collector of older collections, prior to the two world wars that ravaged the country. Through the patination, in some places triangles or "Christmas Trees" could be faintly seen. Upon cleaning the first one, twenty-three deeply incised marks were found on the four edges of the axehead. I have cleaned all of them now. Some of them have only a few lines, but some contain many lines of recorded data. Some of the data patterns are easily decipherable, some are not. Obviously, this is a situation where more study by others will bring new insights.

PHOTO 1a: "Pathway" axehead, front side. The middle route, "hatched", is the SunGod's route west at 23° each night

A great deal is known about the Sun Religion of the Egyptians because of their plethora of funerary monuments, mummies, and *Book of the Dead* texts. They had an obsession with "life after death", which involved following the SunGod Ra to the west, on his daily journey in his "solar boat". It could be seen at midsummer that he went west at the 23 degree latitude "Tropic of Cancer", and it was thought that sailors might find the western home of the SunGod, and the backside of the Earth by following this 23° latitude line to the west.

PHOTOS 1a and 1b are the front and back sides of a decorated axehead that is probably a religious ceremonial artifact containing a geographic design and latitude data. I call it the "Pathways" axe, as it has a hatched pathway cast into both sides.

The marks are little impressions in the casting. They are easier to count when rotating the axe under a desk light, rather than looking at photos. The accuracy of some of my counts can be reasonably argued, though I have tried to be accurate. The number 23 has shown up on many of these axeheads, as well as in megalithic monuments (www.howthesungod.com), so we know the number was very important in Bronze Age times. This 23° tilt of the Earth's axis is a latitude known as the Tropic of Cancer in the northern hemi-

PHOTO 1b: "Pathway" axehead, back side. The SunGod's route to the west

sphere, where the sun appears to turn around and head south, changing Summer to Fall. The repeated appearance of the number 23 is how I could see that I was looking at recorded navigational data on these axeheads.

Because of the frequent use of 23, we say it was a "sacred number" of the SunGod religion of the Bronze Age.

Counting the dots of each row on the front side of the axehead reveals the numbers of 25, 24, 22, 21, and 19 that are labeled in PHOTO 1a. You can see that the hatched pathway in the center is the unlabeled 23 path. We think they were trying to discover what was on the backside of the Earth, where the sun traveled each night, only to reappear

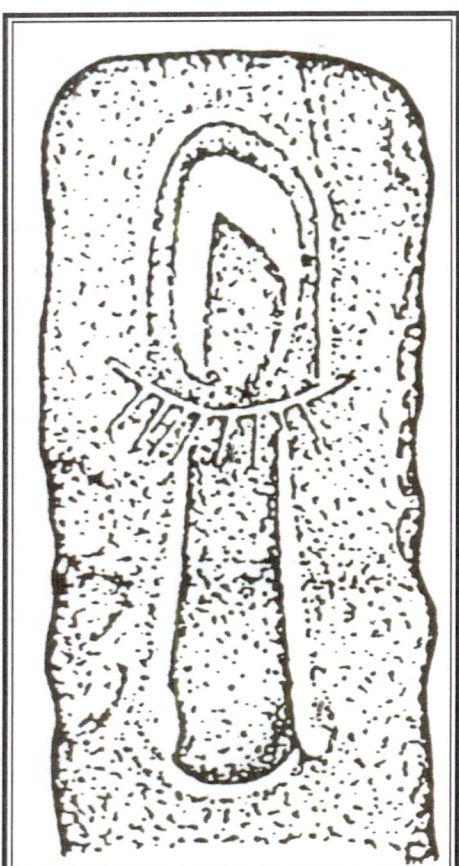

PHOTO 2: Petroglyph at Gavrinis monument showing a 9-stroke sailing vessel on the ocean, with a long shadow at sunset, or setting out on the Holy Pathway at 23°

PHOTO 3a: Front of the "Egypt" axehead, with 23 twice, and the Nile Delta across the blade at 31°N

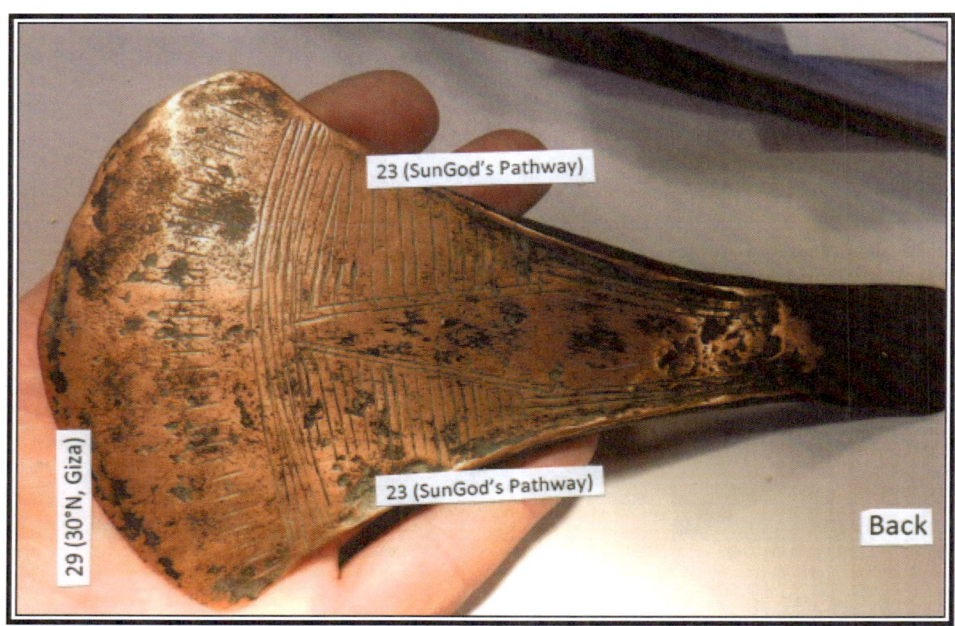

PHOTO 3b: Back of the "Egypt" axehead, with 23 again twice, and the latitude of Giza, 30°N across the blade, the center of Bronze Age civilization, and the location of the largest SunGod monuments on Earth

every morning. Probably a lot of heroes died sailing the 23°path. They did not yet know the tradewind patterns of the Earth, and were actually sailing into the "horse latitudes", where there was little wind. At this latitude "Age of Discovery" (15thC-18thC) sailors were becalmed so long they ran out of food and water and had to eat their horses. Some of the Bronze Age sailors apparently paddled north, maybe following a breeze, or birds, and discovered the Azores Islands. The Azores then became the westernmost known land in the world, and therefore the western home of the SunGod for nearly a thousand years. Colonies developed there ("Bronze Age Colonies with pyramids in the Azores and Canaries", Ancient American, Vol. 112, September, 2016).

The discovery of the Azores was celebrated and commemorated by the construction of the monument of Gavrinis on the coast of Brittany (France) (www.rocksandrows.com). It was made of 39 huge stones, and its axis is set at 38°N, the latitudes of the western and central Azores. It has 23 passage stones decorated from floor to ceiling with petroglyphs, and a 23rd stone, which is undecorated white quartz. Archaeologists have dated the Gavrinis monument to 3600 BC. At Gavrinis, one of the petroglyphs (PHOTO 2) is this carving of a sailboat sailing into the sunset. The boat has 8 oars in the water, and a hull, so is drawn with 9 strokes, showing the 9 islands of the Azores archipelago. This may be the oldest image of a sailboat on the ocean. The shadow of its sail, or the pathway of the sunset in the sea, is consistent with the pathway image on the axehead. This petroglyph at Gavrinis may be commemorating the heroes who ventured out on the pathway shown on the axehead, and discovered the Azores.

PHOTO 3 (a&b) shows another decorated Bronze Age SunGod axehead from the Moog collection. The columnar lines in the triangular areas on both sides, which look like the headdress of an Egyptian Pharoah (see inset) total 23 in all four locations (as noted on the photos), so we know the axe is about the Tropic of Cancer, the SunGod's

European petroglyphs, and are very similar to bone and slate artifacts of the Beaker People from Iberia. On the side (PHOTO 4b) are the 7 islands of the eastern and central Azores, shown as horizontal marks, with the important two western Azores (Corvo and Flores) placed as two vertical marks, for 9 islands total of the Azores. The other side shown adjacent, shows 3 marks, for the 3 island groups of the Azores. The boxy pattern on the front contains 5 horizontal and 5 vertical lines, the five islands in the Central Azores, where their colonies were located on Pico and Terciera. Above it, the boxed 13 marks might record the distance from Madeira. The six horizontal lines with bulbs at the ends of each line may show the distance of 6° across the Island groups.

PHOTO 5 is an Anglo-Saxon pendant of later date, but again with 23 sundots on one side, and 23 below the necklace hole on the other.

PHOTO 6 shows the eyes of the SunGod on an uncleaned anthropomorphized ceremonial Bronze Age axehead photographed on the internet. In this condition, analysis of data is problematic. It is, though, a beautiful example of the sunGod motif.

PHOTOS 7a & 7b. This recently acquired "Holy Route" axehead illustrates again the SunGod's 23° Holy Pathway as shown on PHOTO 1.

ABOVE. PHOTO 4a: The front and back sides of the "SunGod" axehead. The encodings appear to relate to the five Central Azores islands, where colonies were located. The eyes are very similar in style and appearance to many bone and slate artifacts from Iberia.

RIGHT. PHOTO 4b: The sides of the "SunGod" axehead, one side showing the 3 island groups, the other, with the 9 islands, showing the important western two set apart.

route to the west. The shorter marks across the blade edge on each side total 29 and 30, and so the spaces between the marks provide the latitudes 30°N and 31°N. These are the latitudes of the Nile Delta and of Giza in Egypt, the biggest civilization then on Earth, and home of the sun religion. So this axehead illustrates Egypt and its sun religion, and the pathway to the west at 23°N.

PHOTO 4a shows both sides of a heavy hollow casting with eyes of the SunGod. The eyes are similar to some

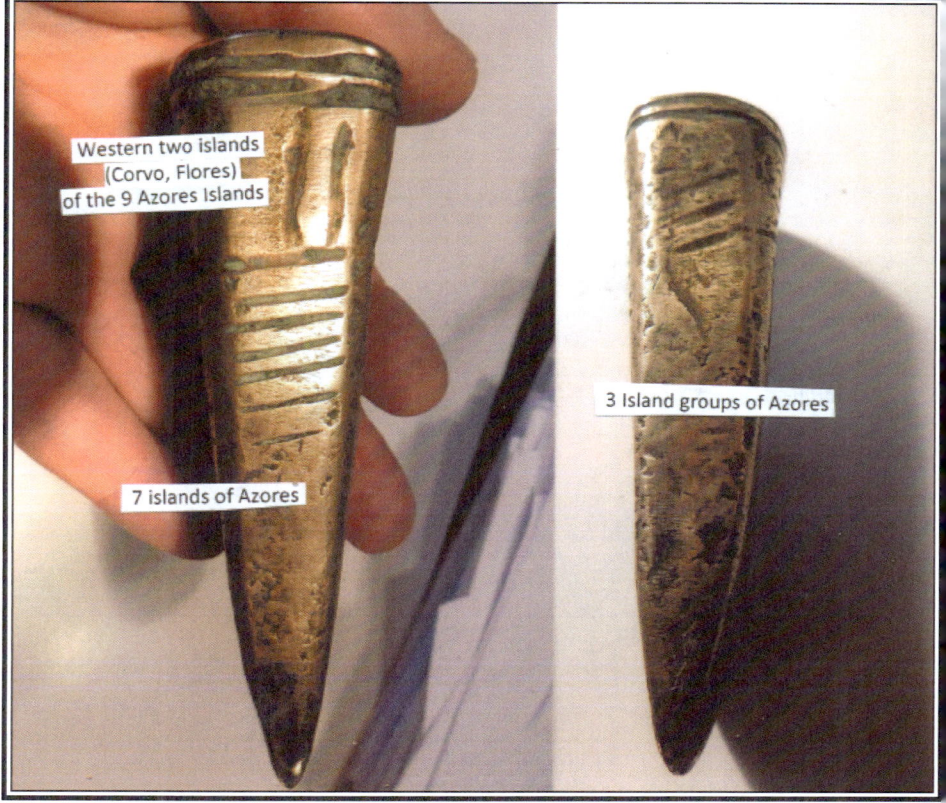

PHOTO 5: An Anglo-Saxon pendant with 23 SunGod sun symbols (Egyptian hieroglyphic symbol for Ra or Re). the count includes the hang hole on one side, not on the other.

PHOTO 6 shows the eyes of the SunGod on an uncleaned anthropomorphized ceremonial Bronze Age axehead that is not cleaned. In this condition, analysis of data is problematic.

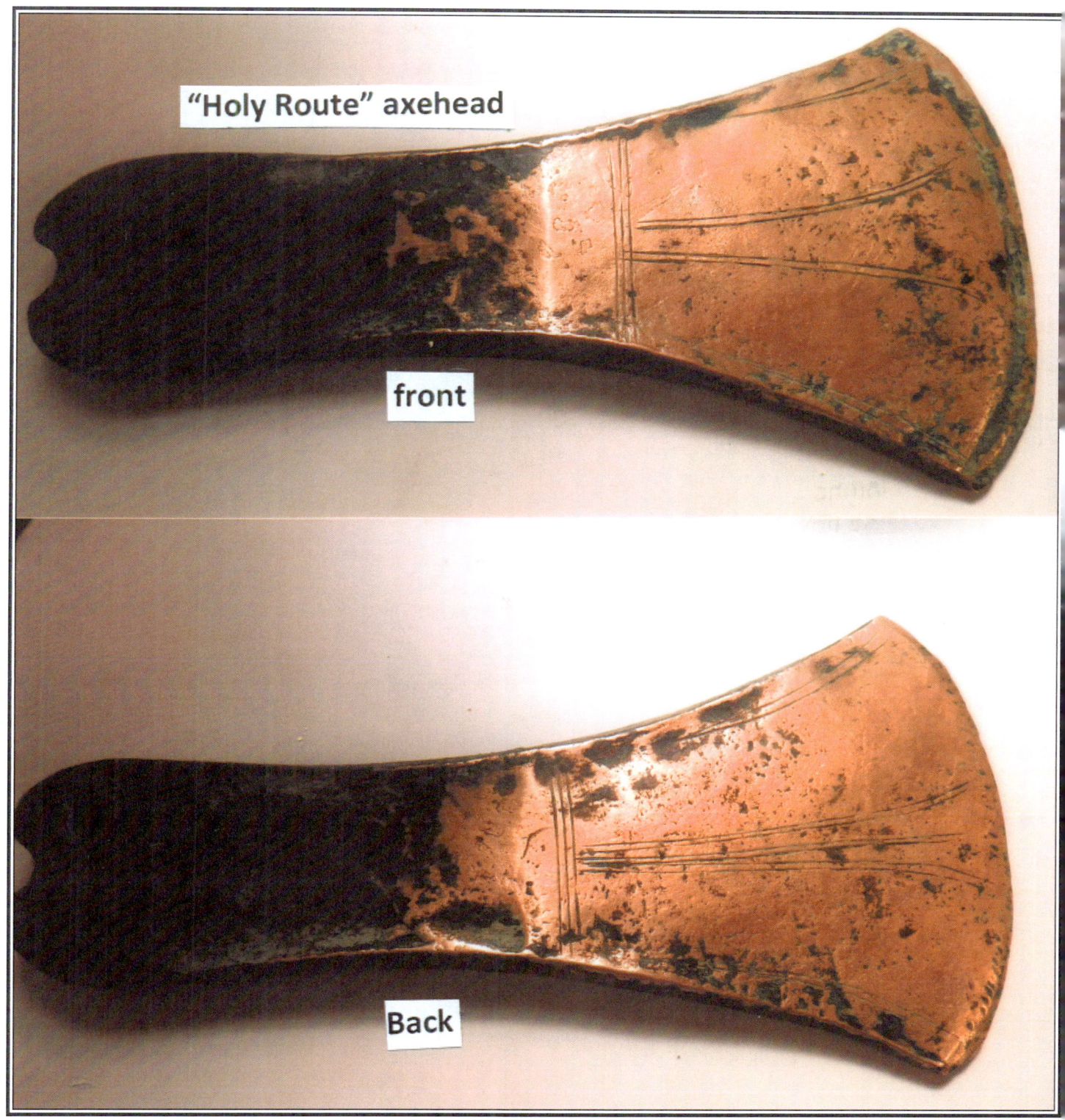

PHOTOS 7a & 7b: This axehead illustrates the SunGod's Holy Pathway across the Atlantic Ocean to the west at sunset. On the back of the axe, the preferred route is shown down the middle of this small chart

The "Caribbean" Axehead (PHOTOS 8a & 8b) shows similar "SunGod Pathways" (rows down the center toward the blade) on both sides of the axe. The central path of dashes on the "front" is composed of 11 and 12 marks, totaling the usual 23 of the SunGod. The 11 and 12 are the latitudes of the mouth of the Magdalena River, the great river of Columbia. As shown in Ancient American #109 ("The Colonization of North and South America by the Beaker People"), the upper reaches of this river, between two of the Cordillera of the Andes at 0°N, was the site of the earliest and largest civilization of South America, colonies of the Beaker People. These are the people who made these Bronze Age axes. It is reasonable that they would record the latitude of their colonies, and how to get there.

Also prominent on the front side of this axe are two triangles, which

117

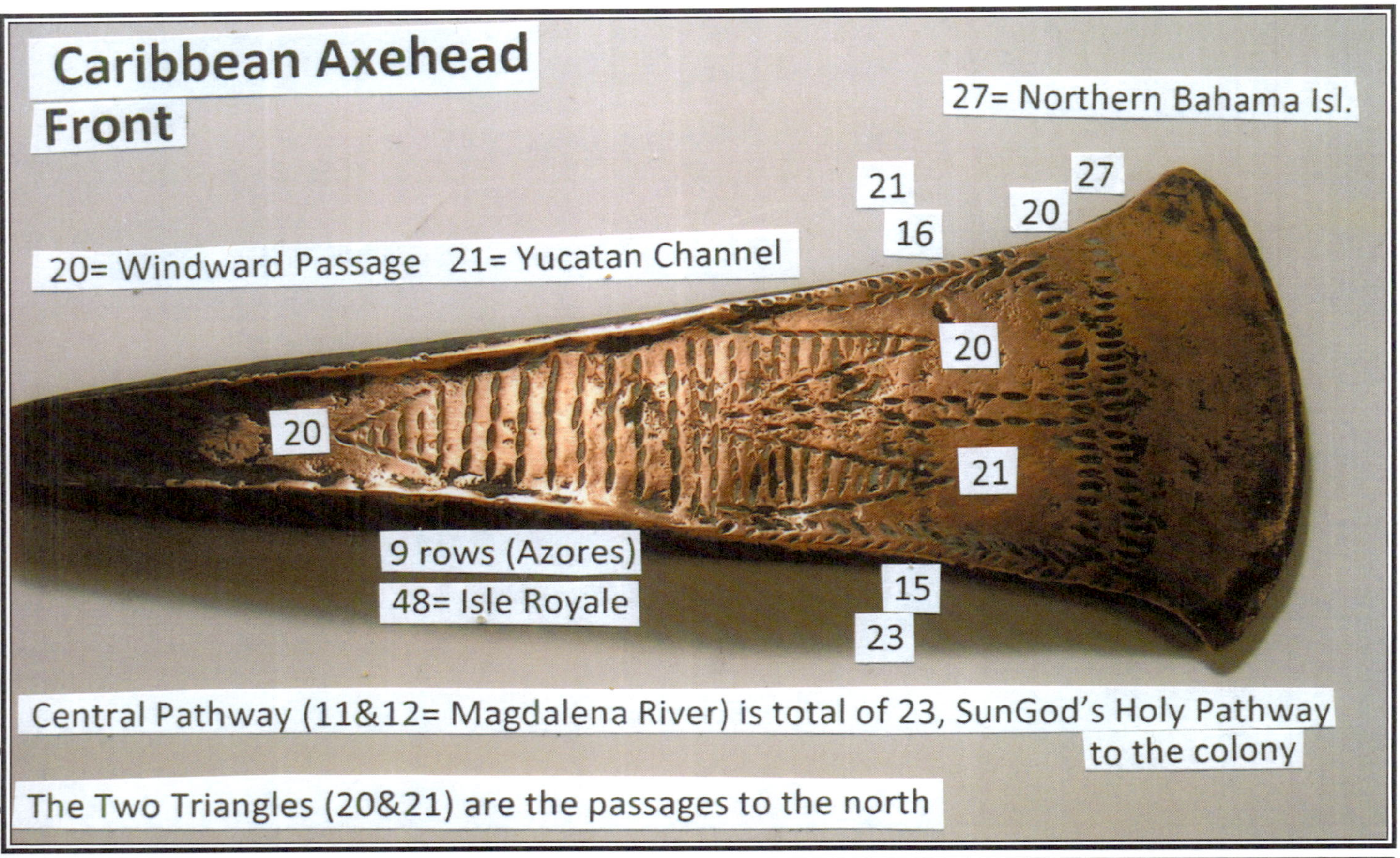

Caribbean Axehead Front

27 = Northern Bahama Isl.

20 = Windward Passage   21 = Yucatan Channel

- 21
- 16
- 27
- 20
- 20
- 20
- 21

9 rows (Azores)
48 = Isle Royale

- 15
- 23

Central Pathway (11 & 12 = Magdalena River) is total of 23, SunGod's Holy Pathway to the colony

The Two Triangles (20 & 21) are the passages to the north

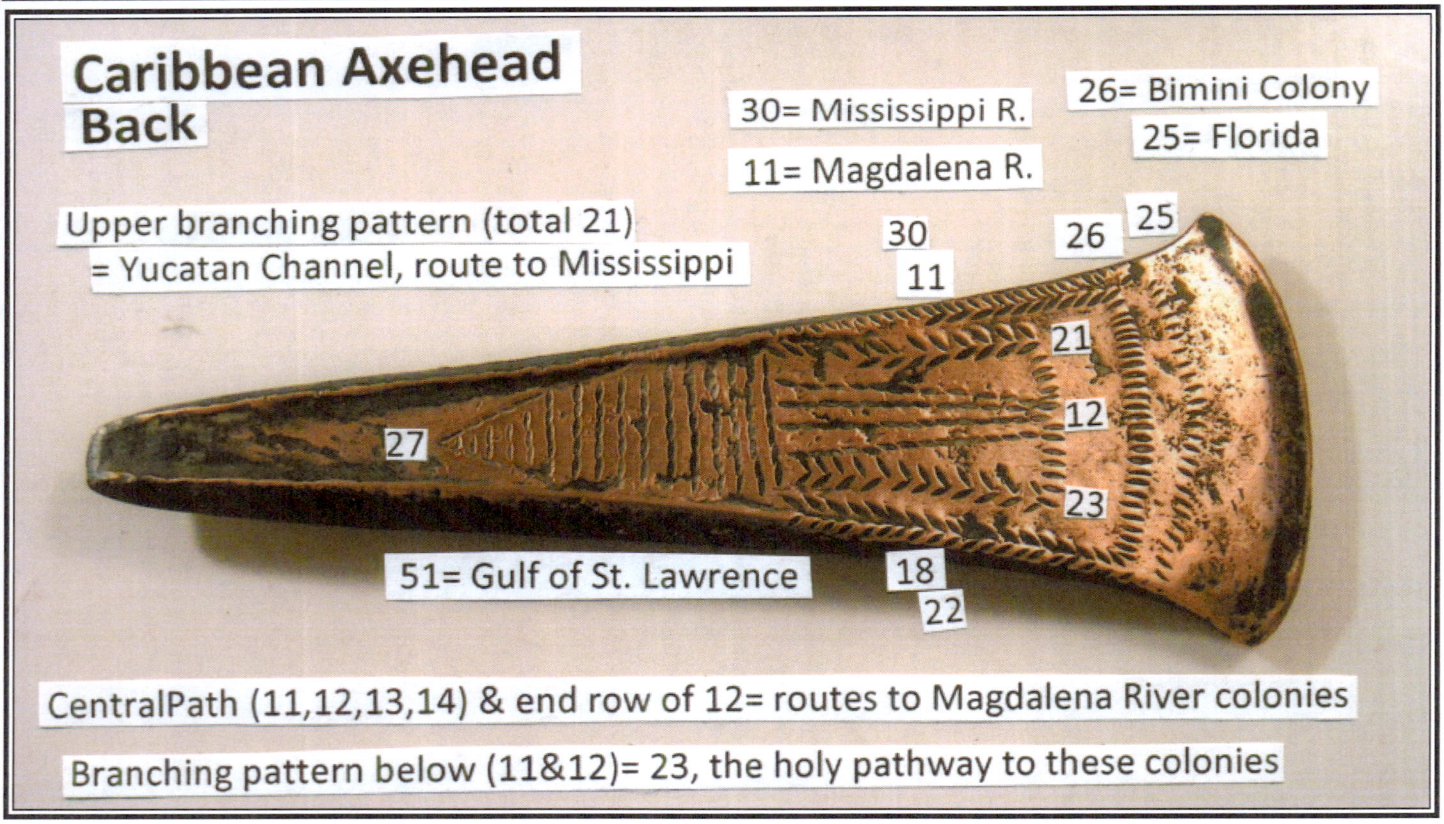

Caribbean Axehead Back

30 = Mississippi R.
26 = Bimini Colony
11 = Magdalena R.
25 = Florida

Upper branching pattern (total 21) = Yucatan Channel, route to Mississippi

- 30
- 11
- 26
- 25
- 27
- 21
- 12
- 23

51 = Gulf of St. Lawrence
- 18
- 22

CentralPath (11,12,13,14) & end row of 12 = routes to Magdalena River colonies

Branching pattern below (11 & 12) = 23, the holy pathway to these colonies

PHOTOS 8a & 8b: this "Caribbean" axehead encodes the holy pathways to the Beaker Colonies in North and South America: up the Magdalena River, in Yucatan, Cuba (?), Bimini, and at the mouth of the Mississippi. It also records how to sail north through passes past Cuba to the Gulf of Mexico.

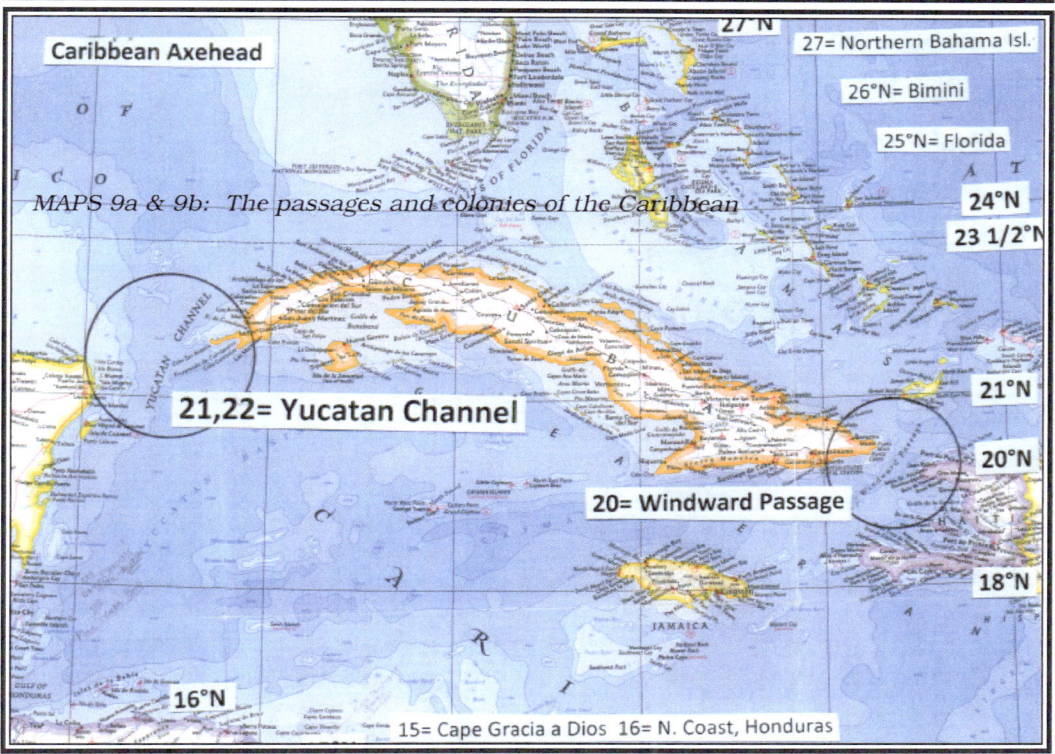

MAPS 9a & 9b: The passages and colonies of the Caribbean

I think point to the important passages for going into the Gulf of Mexico, through the Yucatan Channel, between Yucatan and Cuba at 21 and 22°N, and through the Windward Passage at the eastern end of Cuba at 20°N. I suppose the Yucatan Channel was much preferred as passage there would usually have the wind and current at your back, while the Windward Passage is famous for rough seas, and strong northeasterly winds. It makes sense then, to see 15°N and 16°N recorded, the important Cape Gracia a Dios and the north coast of Honduras, important on the approach to the Yucatan Channel. It is interesting that the furthest row toward the blade provides 27, the latitude of the most northern Abaco Islands of the Bahamas. The number nine shows in a few places on the axe, reminding us of their important colonies in the Azores. The nine central rows are made of 48 marks, the latitude of Isle Royale, the source of the copper which provided wealth to these people for more than a thousand years (2500 BC to 1200 BC).

On the backside, the four lines of marks in the center of the casting (11,12,13, and 14 marks) point to a line of 12 marks. These also locate the routes on the South American coast to the Magdalena river, and its colonies (mouth near Barranquilla on the small map). The branching pattern below (11 and 12 marks), again locate the Magdalena, and total 23, showing that the route is also a holy route of the SunGod. The row of marks below (18) gives the latitude of the ("Olmec") city of La Venta. This row connects with the vertical row (26), locating the colony on Bimini at 26°N. The upper branching pattern has a total of 21 marks, the latitude of the Yucatan Channel.

Above, is a row of marks (30) that give the location of the copper oxhide factories at Cedarland and Claiborne at the mouths of the Pearl River and Mississippi River. The 22 marks at the bottom of the axe may encode a colony now deep underwater off the west end of Cuba. In summary, there is a horse-shoe pattern on this axe which encodes the latitudes of Bronze Age colonies in the Caribbean and Gulf of Mexico.

    Photos 10a and 10b show the front and back of the "Ocean Pathways" Axehead, my 22nd acquisition. This is another Beaker People's "decorated axe", and it also shows pathways across the ocean to the west. In the midsections are 3 +1/2s and 4 triangles, with most of them divided into 9 spaces, encoding the nine Azores Islands. These triangles are slashed

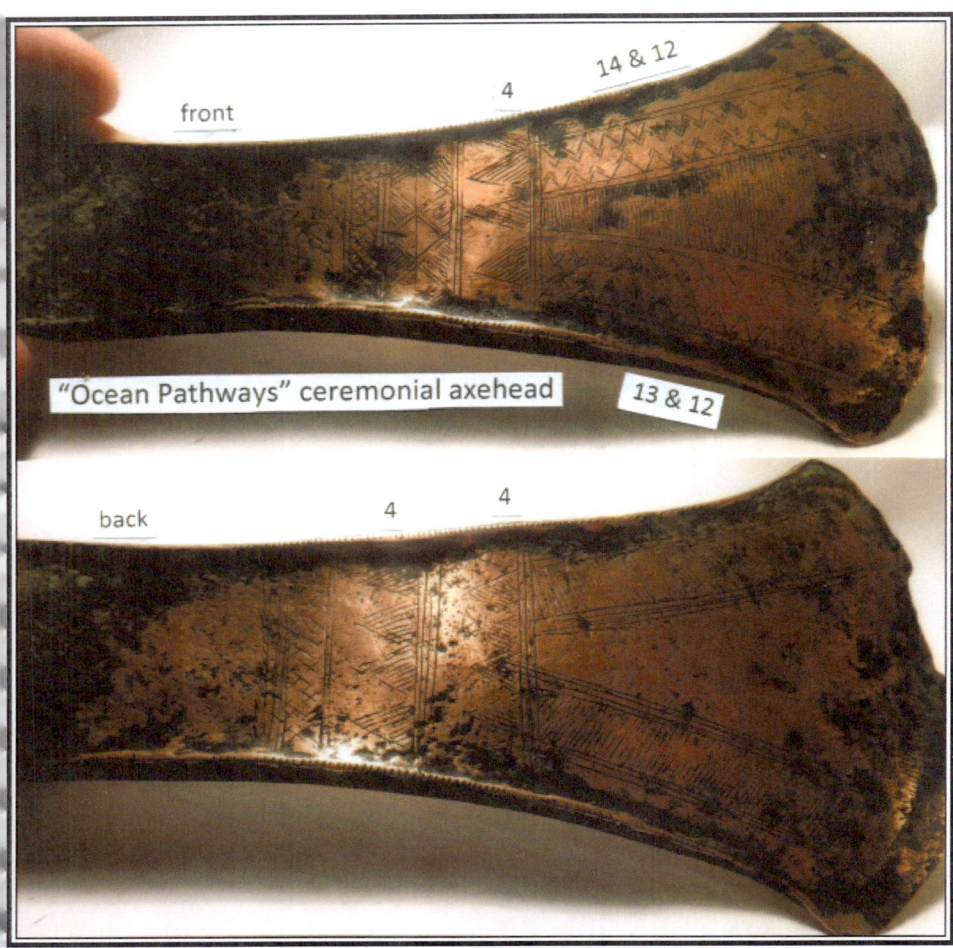

PHOTOS 9a & 9b: Beaker People's "decorated axe" showing pathway across the ocean to the west.
Ocean width of 4 trianges = 40 moira, (Egyptian degrees); k 60 NM/degree=2,400 NM.

diagonally, in exactly the same manner as the bone pendant "Crossing" from Valencia, Iberia, and the Moog axehead "Azores", both illustrated in the prior chapter entitled "The Colonization of North and South America by the Beaker People". The ocean width of 4 triangles equal 40 moira (Egyptian degrees). Forty multiplied by 60 nautical miles per degree = 2400 NM a correct distance. The triangle rows in the blade pathways of 14 and 12 and 13 or 14 and 12, are encoding the latitudes of their destinations in the Caribbean. In the Lesser Antilles, Curacao at 12°N has a deep natural protected harbor at Willemstad, with a Shell refinery in it. I was there recently on a Panama Canal cruise. The Spanish fortifications at the harbor entrance have been later used by the Dutch. This still is a very important harbor, not far from the South American coast. I am not surprised it is indicated to be a colony during the Bronze Age. The island of St. Lucia, at 14°N, in the lower Windwards, has beautiful small harbors on its SW coast, near the remarkable tall volcanic cones called the "Pitons". These are visible quite a way at sea, and are unique in the Caribbean. St Lucia would have been a good choice for a safe stopover location or probably a small colony enjoying life in a spot as beautiful as it gets in the Tropics.

I have been studying Bronze Age Sun Religion and Atlantic sailing routes for 25 years, using information derived from petroglyphs and megalithic ruins on both sides of the ocean. It is amazing that now these sailing routes are corroborated by cast bronze artifacts that were not known to exist until now. ∎

A 2500-2200 BC Date for the Arrival of Michigan Copper in Europe

(Los Millares, Andalucia, Spain, c.3,200-2,200 BC)
J.S. Wakefield, jayswakefield@yahoo.com

Los Millares is a ruin of a Chalcolithic (Copper Age) town protected by several rings of fortified walls. It was an important smelting center, 12 miles from the coastal city Almeria on the SE corner of Spain. The site sits on a flat point of land, with dramatic cliffs down to now-dry rivers on both sides. Obviously the climate has dried up, from when the town was functioning. In back, the land rises to hilltops, with 13 trenched and walled ancient forts on them. The site was discovered in 1891. Recent excavations since 1978 have been supervised by Professor Arribas and Molina of the Department of Prehistory and Archaeology of the University of Granada. One of these archaeologists reportedly has spent his career convincing his profession that this was a megalithic copper smelting center, occupied for a millennium. We could see no green rock in the surrounding area, so we think rock for smelting must have been brought down the rivers from mine sites in the Sierra Nevada Mountains. On the hillside above the walls of the settlement, the site is known for "over 100" circular, chambered corbel-roofed tombs, called tholoi, some of which were found to have paint on the walls. They say there was a pottery factory, as there are quite a few pot shards scattered about.

Photo 1: What remains of one line of the defensive walls of the town of Los Millares. (Photo taken looking south, town to the left, tombs to the right. May, 2008)

The attached photos we took in 2007 show the remains of the town wall, and a smelting center. The site signs advise that the site was abandoned in c.2,200 BC. Our work on megalithic sites for the last 15 years has taught us that round-trip routes to and from America were found possible in 2500 BC (Ref.: How the Sun God Reached America, c.2500 BC). It is reasonable to suppose that by 200 or 300 years after the discovery, that the slabs of "float copper" flushed from their lava beds by the huge glaciers in Michigan could have been discovered, mined, and shipped. Michigan float copper is 99.9% pure crystallized copper, but has some lumps of silver crystallized in it, called "halfbreed" copper. The vast quantity of float copper was unique in the world, and of extreme value. When the old miners' pits were deeply mined in the late 1800's, the copper was used to electrify America. Shiploads of Michigan float copper in the nearby harbor of Almeria would have changed the copper market, which we guess caused the closing of this smelting center.

Corroborating evidence is also coming from England. "In the English Lake District, stone axe factories date from 3650 BC. Stone axes continued to be made for 1500 years, but at 2500 BC with the introduction of bronze axes, production declined sharply, and ceased altogether by c. 2300 BC." (Bradley & Edmonds, Interpreting the Axe Trade, Production and Exchange in Neolithic Britain, Cambridge R. press, 1993).

When you are in the British Museum, read the placards on their beautiful Bronze Age axhead collection. One of them says, "the use of Bronze, previously found around the Mediterranean, suddenly exploded all over Europe after c.2500 BC."
In the Late Copper Age (2450 to 2250 BC) the first bell beakers appeared, a form of pottery that was produced henceforth on a large scale in the settlement. The site appears to have been finally abandoned around 2200 BC. ∎

Photo 2: Remains of copper smelting building at Los Millares (Photo by authors, May, 2008)

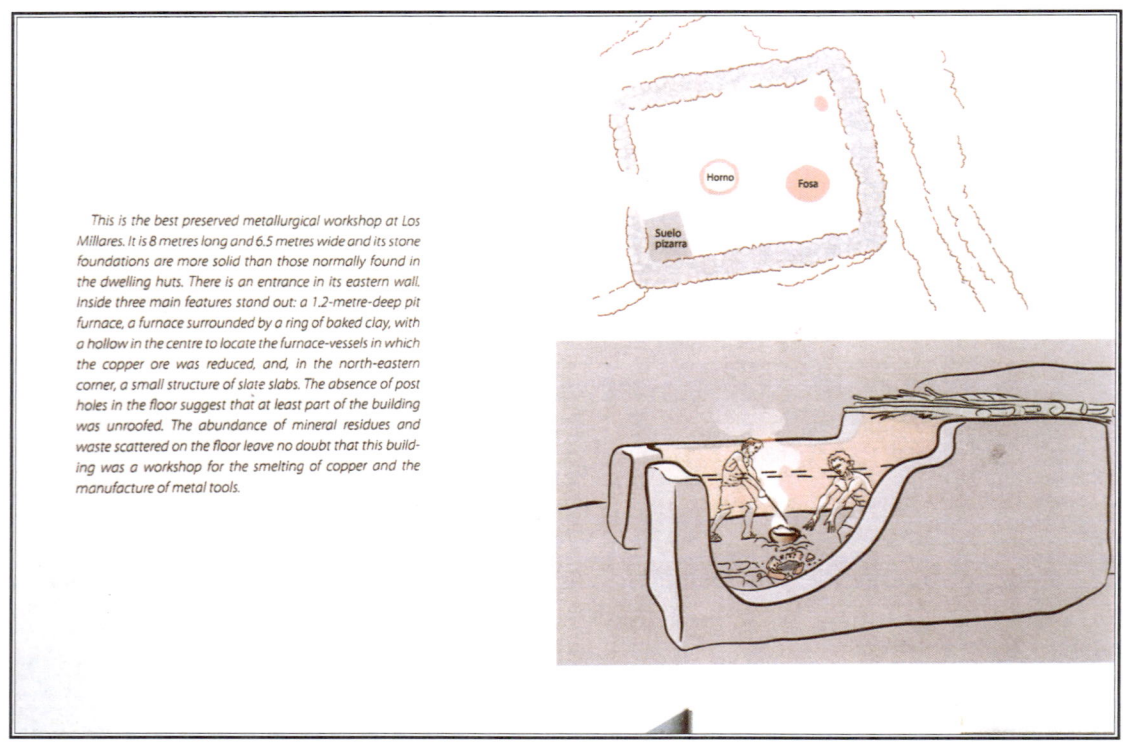

Photo 3: Close-up of the smelting sign (Photo by authors, May, 2008)

A Culture Terminated by the Michigan Copper Trade — Understanding Bronze Age Malta

Jay S Wakefield

Upon arrival September 19, 2016, the Maltese Islands were found to be hot and humid, while dusty and dry. "It last rained last November" I was told. Close to Africa, the islands receive winds from the hot south. Surrounded by a salty sea, they are humid, but not high enough to hold rain clouds, like volcanic islands are. The islands are made of uplifted limestone sea bed, some of it hard, some of it very soft. The Mnajdra temple has an obsidian glass "snake" in the entry door sill, with nearby glass associated with a half-inch tubeworm fossil, the results of "hot smoker" volcanism on the ancient seafloor. Since the south shore of both the larger islands is beaten by rough seas. Both islands have a long face of spectacularly tall and steep cliffs, often beyond vertical.

The soft stone is used to build everything, most of the houses 2 or 3 stories tall, with stone balconies and ballustrades (posts under the railings) turned of the pink stone. There is a lot of construction going on, and old buildings being torn down, so there is a lot of fine light grey/pink sandy dust. There is apparently one farming season, after it rains. Fields everywhere were tilled, waiting for the rain. It did not appear that farming is any longer a prosperous occupation.

The construction is focused on new

Photo 1: Cart Ruts, Clapham Junction, Malta

apartments or condos along the waterfront of Valletta, and other waterfront cities and towns. The marinas and bays were filled with yachts, some of them huge. A sleek dark blue sailboat with four masts and five spreader sets, and a five story black & white power yacht "from India" caught my eye. It dawned on me that I was observing a tax haven in operation, and my guess is that the new buildings going up are also tax haven condos for the rich of the world. A sharp gal in a tourist information office at a Heritage Malta site confirmed that "none of it belongs to Maltese".

The city is ancient, and it has obviously been difficult to build a 4 lane highway through the buildings and narow alleyways. So driving around Valletta is not only a left-side of the road challenge leftover from the British, but you need to negotiate tunnels, construction projects, and complex unlabeled offramps. Thank god for the innumerable traffic circles, an innovation that helps a great deal, though we got lost a number of times in spite of a GPS. In lots of places, however, there is not room to build a real traffic circle, so they have painted a blue dot, maybe five feet in diameter at complex intersections of the multiple one-lane streeets in the center of towns, to show you that you are supposed to drive as though there were a

Photo 2: Temple of Hagar Quim, prior to installation of tarp roof by European Union

traffic circle there. It mostly works. The locals are fast and aggressive, but do not honk much. Coming out of a torturus underground parking garage, a fast truck in the street swiped the dust off our front bumper. The car rental guy laughed and said "that's Malta!" Malta is famous for its many cart-ruts. They appear all over the island, wherever the topsoil is eroded away. Similar ruts have been found in the Azores, France, Turkey, and other places, but nowhere are there so many as on Malta and Gozo. If one envisions Neolithic man living on a forested land, with sandy topsoil, one can begin to see the mud or sandy grit being ground into the soft stone, wearing it away, below the wheels or travois legs. So the tracks come and go, like potholes in the ancient forest floor. Some tracks lead into the sea, some under ancient walls, others off cliffs, so we know they are old. Photo 1 shows some of the deepest ruts, at a famous place called "Clapham Junction", at Buskett, after a busy junction in London. The strange thing about the ruts is that usually, when a cart is pulled by an ox, the hooves have carved a pathway between the wheel tracks, but in these, center bumps are often high, and a center path has not been observed.

Photo 2 shows an aerial view of the Hagar Qim temple before it was roofed by UNESCO. There were originally 23 known temple sites, but now there are four major sites that are bring preserved, Gantija, on Gozo, and three roofed sites on Malta: Tarxien, Hagar Quim and Mnajdra. These temples built of big stones started small, and grew in size and complexity for twenty-five hundred years, from 5000 BC to 2500 BC. Note that these structures contain trilithons, megalithic stone chambers once roofed, and menhirs. Fourteen freestanding dolmen have been found, and large freestanding menhirs were erected. We found one big menhir between two houses, but another is private, seen only in a photograph, while another at the airport was moved to an inner garden there. A pile of well-made slingstones is in a museum exhibit, just like the ones in the Canaries and the Baleric Islands. Remember that Hannibal had a whole division of "Baleric "slingers" in his over-the-Alps army. The Canary Islanders slung stones at the arriving Portuguese to keep them from landing on the beach. So that while the Neolithic Maltese developed a unique Temple culture and artistic style, it was by many measures, a part of the greater megalithic culture. It is thought that the first people arrived from Sicily, with knowledge of how to make pottery. There is a clay layer on the island, between the sandstone layers, which has provided pottery material, and a water barrier, so pumping can retrieve old rainfall trapped in the sandstone above the clay layer. A wide variety of pottery types have been indentified with time zones within the temple building period. The pottery decoration "after 2500 BC is immediately distinguishable from Temple Period wares. This decoration is now strictly rectilinear, with bands of parallel heavily-incised lines, horizontal or forming deep zigzags. The resulting triangles are hatched." An example is **Photo 3**. Note that these two small cups are joined together. There were three examples of this in the museum cases, one with the bottoms broken. I have not seen this design before, though there is a lot of ancient joined pottery in Mexico and Peru.

Within the temples, and the Hypogea (bones of 7,000 individuals in it), large statues and and all the way down to small statuettes of obese women have been found. **Photo 4** shows some of them from a museum collection, and **Photo 5** shows the bottom remains of a large one in the Tarxien temple. These figures, and the temple and hypogea walls, have remaining coats of red ochre, thought to have been traded by sea from volcanic islands, like Lipari, off Italy. Most all of these figures are missing their heads. Fragments of the most finely-carved meter-high statue, with elaborate pleated skirt were found scattered, intentionally smashed, and scattered over the large burial pits at Xaghra Circle. This appears to be deliberate mutilation of the Temple's sacred icons, out of desires to eradicate the memory of the previous regime. The late Temple, Mnajdra, features Or-

Photo 3: Bronze Age pot, Archaeological Museum in the Castello, Victoria, Gozo

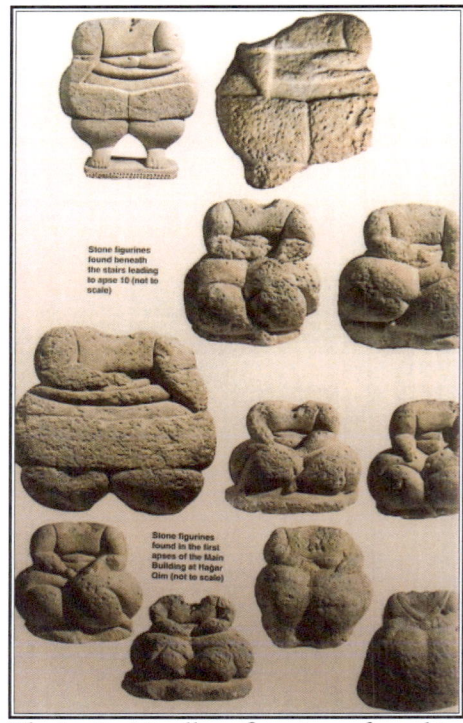

Photo 4: Headless figurines, found in Hagar Quim temple, Malta

Photo 5: Remaining portion of 2m statue in first apse of South temple, Tarxien, Malta

Photo 6: Seven cm male clay figurine with shell jabbed into the clay prior to firing, Tarxien temple

acle holes, "which imply a priesthood". Were its power and exactions resented by the rest of the population? "We have deduced hints of increasing exclusivity of the priesthood from Temple plans, particularly the walling off of inner apses and presence of oracle holes. Could there have been increasing demands and a progressively more recalcitrant populace?" One small clay figure found at Tarxien **(Photo 6)** found has balls, and "splinters of shell jammed into the clay body before firing". Is this the dark side of a male-female conflict?

The historians who have written all the guidebooks to the Malta Temple sites all agree that there was a sudden and complete collapse and social change at 2500 BC that brought in bronze axes "imported from abroad" **(Photo 7)**, a different people with different skills and principles, and new pottery styles. Also described is a "mysterious disappearance of the temple people ... and repopulation with new people who disposed of their dead by cremation and used bronze tools and weapons". A large eroded stone half covered with ship "graffiti" was found at Tarxien. The curved ship hulls have high prows and sterns, but the experts cannot determine whether they should be dated to the early Bronze Age or at the 2500 BC juncture, when it is known that ships appeared. "The sophisticated temple culture suddenly collapsed.. At Skorba at least it could be seen that great chips had been knocked out of the temple structure... Tarxien was turned into a cemetery, and Skorba and Borg-in-Nadur were taken over by squatters". All the temples were abandoned." "It is as if the islands were abandoned utterly". "In other parts of the world, the introduction of what must have always have been expensive metal is almost invariable accompanied by the appearance of sharp divisions within society... it is probable that strong leaders arose".

After 2500 BC, the beautiful artwork of the temples **(Photo 8** here as preserved in the National Museum of Archaeology in Valetta) is to be found on Bronze Age Minoan vases **(Photo 9**, taken in the Heraklion Museum in Crete). The art of Malta is also found on the entrance Stone at Newgrange, Ireland **(Photo 10)**. The big Boyne Valley site is at latitude of 54°N, because it is the reciprocal of the important 36°N latitude of Malta, due to the then-holy science of the spheres (54+36= 90, which is ¼ of the 360°shpere of the Earth). The Minoan involvement in the trans-Atlantic trade in copper, starting at 2500 BC brought them past Malta with boatloads of copper ingots. We know these were sold in Sardinia, Egypt, and elsewhere by the Minoans. It appears the actual cast bronze axes found on Malta were manufactured on Crete or Sardinia, and brought to Malta by traders. ■

Photo 7: Bronze axes found in Malta, "imported from abroad"

Photo 8: Temple blocks with repeat spiral pattern art, Tarxien temple, now located in the National Museum of Archaeology, Valletta, Malta

Photo 9: Bronze Age Minoan amphora with Maltese pattern art, in the Heraklion Museum, Crete

Photo 10: Bronze Age Newgrange Entrance Stone with Maltese pattern art, at 54°N

References:

Trump, David H., Malta, Prehistory and temples, Midsea Books, undated, Malta, ISBN 99909-93-94-7. sales@midseabooks.com

Trump, David H., Cart-Ruts and their impact on the Maltese Landscape, Heritage Books, 2008, Malta, ISBN 978-99932-7-209-0

Caruana, Daphne M. S., GGantija Temples and Heritage Park, Xaghra, Gozo, Heritage Books, Malta, 2015, ISBN 978-99932-7-526-8

Stroud, Katya, Hagar Quim & Mnajdra Prehistoric Temples, Heritage Books, Malta, 2015, ISBN 987-99932-7-317-2

Vella, Nicholas C., The Prehistoric Temples at Kordin III, Heritage Books, for Cambridge University, TEMPER project, 2004, ISBN 99932-39-87-9

Pace, Anthony, The Tarxien Temples, Heritage Books, Heritage Malta, 2006, ISBN 99932-7-078-4

Pace, Anthony, The Hal Saflieni Hypogeum, Heritage Books, Heritage Malta, 2004, ISBN 99932-39-93-3

Sultana, Sharon, The National Museum of Archaeology, The Neolithic Period, Heritage Books, Heritage Malta, 2006, ISBN 99932-7-076-8

Conti, Emmanuel M., The Malta Maritime Museum, Vittoriosa, Heritage Books, Heritage Malta, 2006, ISBN 99932-7-075-X

Cassha, Kevin, Malta, Its Archaeology and History, Plurigraf, Miller Guides, Malta, 2000, ISBN 978-88-7280-704-0

Bonanno, Anthony, Malta, An Archaeological Paradise, M.J. Publications. Ltd., 1991

Giorgio, Cynthia de, St John's Cathedral, Valletta, Malta, Heritage Books 2007, ISBN 97899932-7-171-0

End of the Bronze Age

The Bronze Age copper trade ended at 1200 BC with a worldwide catastrophe. The catastrophe is thought to have been caused by impacts of segments of exploded comet Enecke which rained down over the world during a 50-100 year period. All the cities in the Eastern Mediterranean burned without apparent explanation. All the high civilizations of the Earth collapsed in chaos and famine, including the Egyptian New Kingdom, the Shang Dynasty of China, the Indus Civilization, the Hittites, and the Mycenaean Civilization. Climatologists call this the "Plenard Period".

It took humanity many centuries to recover. The Phoenicians (later as Carthaginians) inherited the secrets of the old sailing routes. The "mound-building cultures" developed in central North America. Some Alexandrian Egyptians, Jews, Africans, and others excaped capture by Roman Legions by sailing away from a southern Mauritanian Atlantic Port in the Mauritanian fleet. They developed a colony on the Wabash River on the Illinois/Indiana border that lasted about 500 years (0-500AD). This information comes from stone carvings found in a funerary cave used by the colony, not yet known to the public.

Since there is great interest in studying these stones, I reproduce a sampling of some of the better ones, and particularly "mapstones". These mapstones have never been photographed professionally before now, and many have not been seen by more than a half dozen people. I hope that making these photographs available, most in their actual size, will facilitate analysis and academic research.

Two thousand year-old Mapstones

The following section shows photos of mapstones taken from a limestone cave by Russell Burrows and sold to his acquaintances, many of whom are now deceased. The stones are reproduced here close to their actual sizes, some reduced, some enlarged a bit. Despite their enormous historic importance, most of these mapstones have never been seen by more than a few persons until now. Though the cave remains unopened, and there is controversy regarding its location, it is reported to contain funerary crypts of refugees from Roman tyranny, who sailed from Alexandria and then from the West African coast of Mauritania.

The cave contents are thought to date roughly from 0 AD to 500 AD, when the colony nearby ended and the cave was closed. Portraits carved into stones in the cave include Jews, Alexandrian Egyptian priests, armored soldiers, Africans, American natives, and important historical figures, such as Julius Caesar and Jesus. We think the leader of the colony to have been a royal personage represented by the symbol AII on many portraits. We think this person was Alexander Helios (sun), Cleopatra's son by Antony, who "disappeared from history", after his half-brother Caesarion, fathered by Caesar, was put to death by Octavian. Helios sailed away with the help of his sister Selene (moon) and her husband King Juba II of Mauritania, who had a fleet of ships, which also disappeared from history. It is thought they may have secreted away, in the holds of the ships, the most important treasures of Egypt, including perhaps the not-yet-found remains of Alexander the Great.

Although you will find extensive claims on the Internet that these stones are fakes, you can see from studying the details that they are not. Most of those claims are made by people who have not seen them. When you carefully study the stones, you find they contain details that would not be familiar to someone trying to make fakes, such as the correct location of Poverty Point in 100 AD. Some of the stones have texts in four languages, mostly Celt-Iberian, some Ogham, and others including early Etruscan. Progress has been made in the decipherment of them, and this will be an exciting subject of study and controversy for quite some time. So far, decipherments claim to include the biology of whales, UFO sightings, and religious/political themes.

It is hoped that all these stones will be donated to a new museum of Pre-Columbian American artifacts, and so be on exhibit for public study.

References:

The Mystery Cave of Many Faces: A History of Burrows Cave, Russell Burrows and Fred Rydholm, Superior Heartland Inc., 1991

The Lost Treasure of King Juba: The Evidence of Africans in America before Columbus, Frank Joseph, Bear & Co., 2003, ISBN 1-59143-006-2

The Mystery Cave of Many Faces, Russell Burrows, and James P. Scherz, PhD, Superior Heartland Inc., 1992

Ancient Mariners in America, Beverly Moseley Jr., (CD), Midwest Epigraphic Society, 2006

Ancient Mediterranean Treasures in North America, Harry Hubbard, 1993-1995, Alexander Helios Inc., ISBN 0-9638190-0-3

Tomb Chronicles Part II: The Curse of Alexander's Tomb, 1995-1997, recorded by Harry Hubbard for Alexander Helios Inc., Lazeria Publishing Co., ISBN 0-9638190-2-x-13

Midwestern Epigraphic Journal, Vol.10, No.1, 1996

Ancient American, Vol.3, Issue 16

Seventeen "Burrows Cave" Mapstones

This collection of mapstone photos, is intended to help researchers by making available some of the material in private collections. It is hoped the original stones can soon be donated to a public museum focused upon exhibition of pre-Columbian American artifacts. After mapstone 17, I have added some photographs of other stones from Burrows Cave. One stone shows a ship, others show portraits of people. One remarkable stone shows the myth of Adonis losing his leg to a boar. The beautiful two-sided seal stone shows a ship on the ocean.

Amazingly, as can be seen in the four mapstones of the Great Lakes, routes to the copper on Isle Royale and the Keweenaw Peninsula, were important 1500 years after the end of the Bronze Age. The copper routes had been changing with lake levels, but were obviously in use for at least 3000 years.
The cities that now cover these trails are less than 200 years old.

1. Inverted Waters Mapstone
2. Basic Mississippi River Mapstone
3. Beverly Mosely Gift Mississippi River Mapstone
4. High Center Mississippi River Mapstone
5. Seven Circle-Cross Mississippi River Mapstone
6. Buffalo and Ogham Mississippi Mapstone
7. Ogham Column Mississippi Mapstone
8. Poverty Point Mississippi Mapstone
9. Poverty Point on East Side of Mississippi Mapstone
10. Pointed Mound Mississippi Mapstone
11. Round Mound Mississippi Mapstone
12. Allegheny Mountains Mississippi Mapstone
13. Ohio River and East Coast Mississippi Mapstone
14. Great Lakes Mapstone
15. Great Lakes with Ships Mapstone
16. Great Lakes and Routes Mapstone
17. Copper Trails Mapstone

1. Inverted Waters Mapstone

2. Basic Mississippi River Mapstone

3. Beverly Mosely Gift Mississippi River Mapstone

4. High Center Mississippi River Mapstone

133

5. Seven Circle-Cross Mississippi River Mapstone

6. Buffalo and Ogham Mississippi Mapstone

7. Ogham Column Mississippi Mapstone

8. Poverty Point Mississippi Mapstone

9. Poverty Point on East Side of Mississippi Mapstone

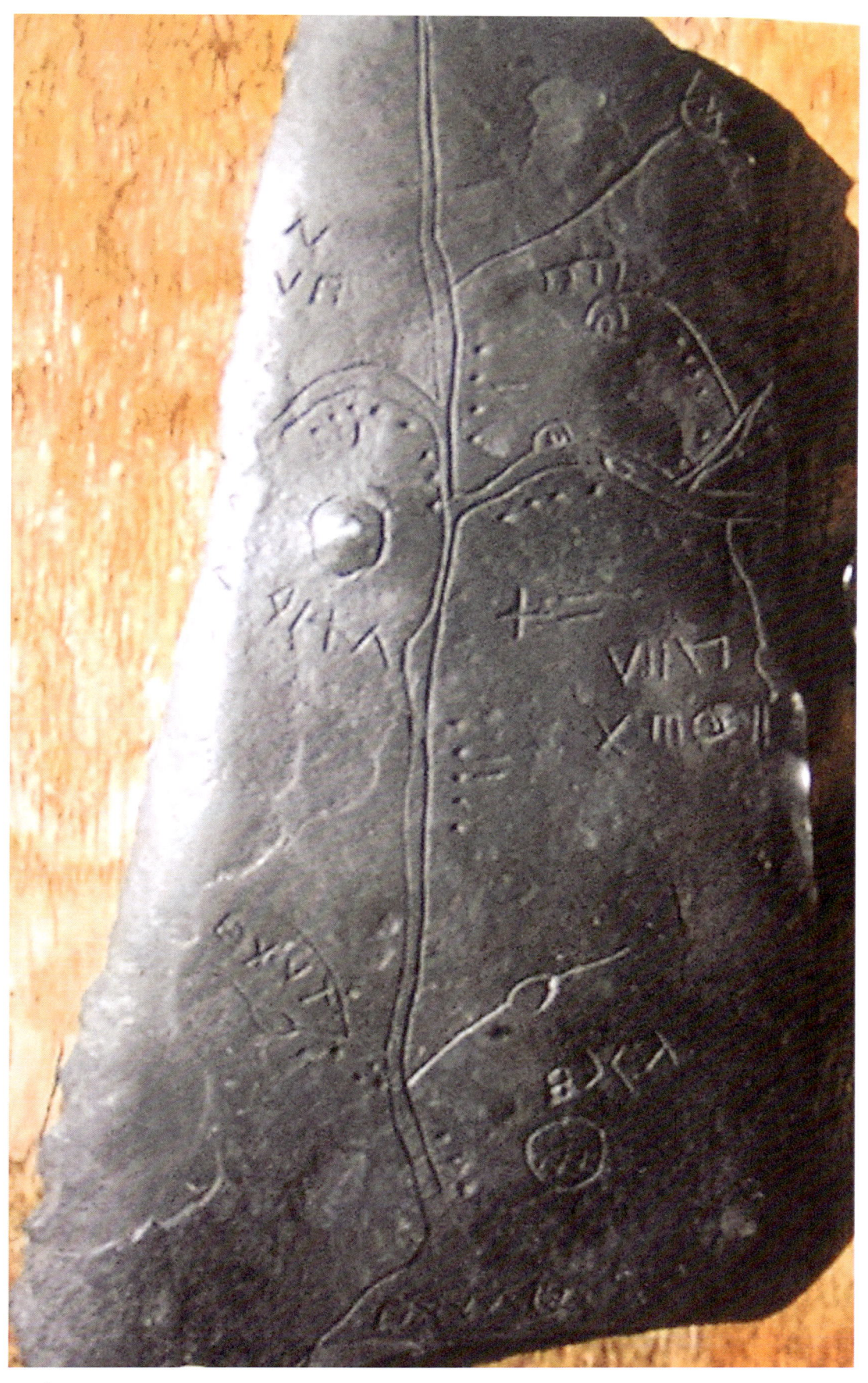

10. Pointed Mound Mississippi Mapstone

11. Round Mound Mississippi Mapstone

12. Allegheny Mountains Mississippi Mapstone

13. Ohio River and East Coast Mississippi Mapstone

14. Great Lakes Mapstone

15. Great Lakes with Ships Mapstone

16. Great Lakes and Routes Mapstone

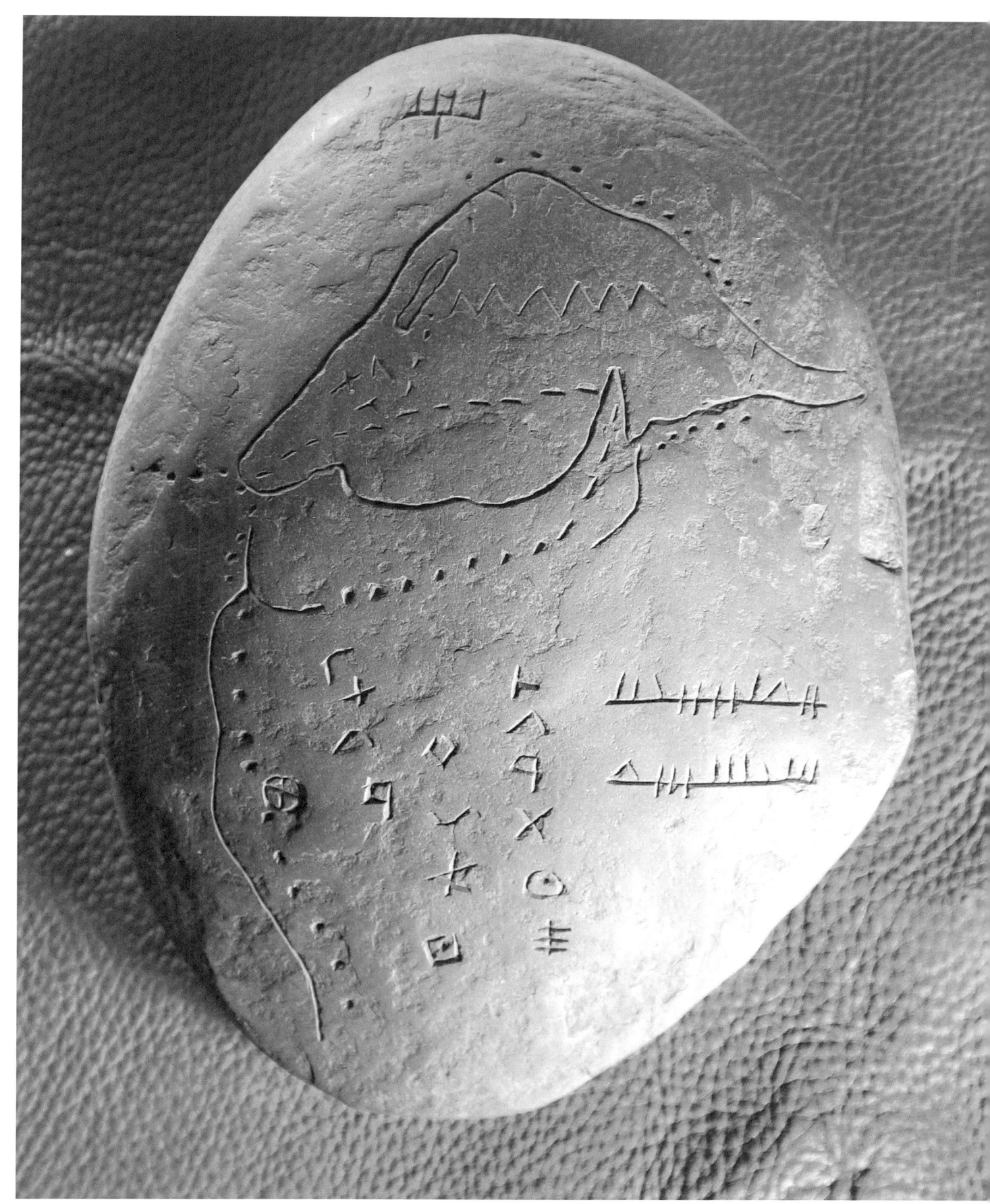

17. Copper Trails Mapstone

149

151

153

www.ingramcontent.com/pod-product-compliance
Lightning Source LLC
Chambersburg PA
CBRC100222100526
44590CB00008B/142